COMPLETE TEACHER'S GUIDE
INCLUDING ALL STUDENT MATERIAL

- Jerome, translating the Vulgate

Latin in the ChristianTrivium

VOLUME I

BY GAIL BUSBY AND MARY HARRINGTON

XL Group

675 Timbermill Lane
Orange Park, FL
32065
www.latintrivium.com

For free tutoring help,
email
mary@latintrivium.com

Latin in the Christian Trivium

curriculum
includes: Textbook
Drill Sheets, Study Sheets, and Tests
Teacher's Guide CD
Map Sheets
Activity Book

Revised and Printed 2016

Cover photo and interior
photos by Stefanie Anderson
Illustrations by Mary Belknap
Printed in the United States of America

Acknowledgements

We are especially thankful to many who have reviewed, corrected, and encouraged us in this undertaking. Most especially we thank Dr. Al DiPippo of Evergreen Valley College in San Jose, California, who, in 1986, reinforced and greatly increased Mrs. Harrington's Latin knowledge, and explained the historical and grammatical concepts in depth. Mrs. Busby's Latin students, and Mrs. Harrington's students Stuart Bottom and Michael Escamilla, who used this book before it was complete, offered many suggestions and corrections. complete, offered many suggestions and corrections. Our primary proofreaders, Tammy Williams, Chris Nagel, Mindy Isaacs and Christine Ku, gave invaluable help in finding typos and refining the course even further.

Pastor Doug Busby assisted by making sure the Biblical concepts were accurately presented, as well as editing and adding pictures. Julie Gentry, Mary's daughter, has spent countless hours working on formatting, the web page, and proofreading etc. Doug Harrington, Mary's son, designed and implemented our web page. Both of our spouses and all of our children have helped in many ways, with phone calls, and other support.

The concept for using the notebook approach for teaching Latin was designed and used by Mrs. Busby in 1989, and is similar to that recommended in *A Guide to American Christian Education* by James B. Rose.

Our editorial consultant was Martha Robinson, of www.homeschoolchristian.com. She reviewed our book, and gave many suggestions for improvements. Karen Koehler-Cesa gave many more ideas for improvement of the Teacher's Guide.

The idea for formatting the text to comprehensively teach Latin in three volumes was originated by Mrs. Harrington.

The structure of the paradigm charts follows the style found in Smith and Thompson's *First Year Latin.*

The use of phonics flash cards follows the style found in *The Writing Road to Reading* by Romalda Spalding, a book we highly recommend.

The idea for the continuing story line found in the book comes from the *Ecce Romani: A Latin Reading Course* by Lawall and Tafe, though ours is of course an original story. The story's main character, Marcus Fidelius Centurio, is based on the Centurion found in Gospels of the New Testament.

Grammatical markings probably originated in Catholic schools long ago. Colored flash cards, an original idea by Mrs. Harrington, were used by our classes in 1989.

We both hope that you will find this book easy to use and understand, and that you will learn to appreciate the English language "from the roots up."

Gail Busby
Mary Harrington
1999, 1989

LATIN IN THE CHRISTIAN TRIVIUM
VOCABULARY CARDS AND NOTEBOOK SHEETS

TYPE	FLASH CARDS (or Notebook Sheet)	INK COLOR
Phonics	White	Black
Verb	White	Blue
Noun:		
Feminine	Pink	Black
Masculine	Blue	Black
Neuter	Yellow	Black
Adjective	Green	Black
Preposition:		
Accusative	White	Red
Ablative	White	Green
Adverb	White	Orange
Pronoun:		
Feminine	Pink	Blue
Masculine	Blue	Red
Neuter	Yellow	Blue
Conjunction	White	Purple
Interjection	White	Brown
Derivatives	Orange	Black
Phrases and Idioms	White	Black

Phrases

Many phrases in Latin have become common in English literature. Write one of these phrases on the board as you begin to study each chapter. Have the students put them into their notebook under "Phrases". You might ask the students to use one in a sentence, or to find one perhaps on a sign or in a book they are reading.

Ad f inem, *to the end*
Ad infinitum, *to infinity, forever*
Ad nauseam, *to the point of nausea*
Alma Mater, *gracious mother, or other mother, used of one's school*
Alter ego, *a second self*
Ante bellum, *before the war, usually referring to the War of Secession*
Bona fide*, with good faith*
Carthago delenda est, *Carthage must be destroyed, often said in the Roman Senate by Cato the Elder*
Cave canem, *beware of the dog*
Corpus Christi, *the body of Christ*
Deo volente, *God willing*
Dum spiro, spero, *While I breathe, I hope*
E pluribus unum, *out of many, one*
Ex post f acto, *having retroactive effect*
Fiat lux, *let there be light!*
Gloria in excelsis Deo, *Glory to God in the highest*
Ipso facto, *by the fact itself*
In toto, *in total*
Ita lex scripta est, *And so the law was written*
Lapsus linguae, *a slip of the tongue*
Laus Deo, *Praise to God*
Mea culpa, *my fault*
Mens sana in corpore sano, *a sound mind in a sound body*

Mirabile dictu, *amazing to say*
Modus operandi, (M.O.), *method of working*
Nolo contendere, *I do not wish to contend*
Non sequitur, *it does not follow; it is not logical*
Omnia ad Dei gloriam, *everything to the glory of God.*
Pater Noster, *Our Father*
Pax vobiscum, *Peace be with you*
Per capita, *per head; per person*
Per diem, *per day*
Per se, *in itself*
Post mortem, *after death*
Prima facie, *on the first appearance*
Pro bono publico, *for the public good usually abbreviated pro bono*
Pro tempore, *for the time*
Q.E.D., quod erat demonstrandum, *which was to be proved*
Rigor mortis, *the stiffness of death*
Semper Fidelis, *always faithful (Marines)*
Semper Paratus, *always ready (Coast Guard)*
Sine qua non, *a necessity*
Te Deum laudamus, *We praise you, God*
Tempus fugit, *time is fleeting*
Terra firma, *solid ground*
Una voce, *with one voice*

LATIN MOTTOES OF THE STATES

State	Latin Motto	English Translation
Arizona	Ditat Deus	God Enriches.
District of Columbia	Iustitia Omnibus	Justice for All
Kansas	Ad astra per Aspera	To the stars through Difficulties
Maryland	Scuto Bonae Voluntatis Tuae Coronasti Nos	With the Shield of Thy Goodwill Thou Hast Covered Us
Mississippi	Virtute et Armis	By Valor and Arms
New York	Excelsior	Higher
Virginia	Sic Semper Tyrannis	Thus Always to Tyrants
West Virginia	Montani Semper Liberi	Mountaineers are Always Free

Forms, Vocabularies, Bibliography, Pater Noster, Pledge of Allegiance, Grammatical and Topical Index at the back of the book

Ruins of the Roman Forum

Directions for playing VINCO.

1. Teacher passes out **VINCO** game and markers to use. *Smarties* candies make good marking pieces.

2. Teacher makes a list of words or places and writes them on the board. Use words YOUR student know.

3. Students copy the list, and place them wherever they wish on their game page.

4. Teacher calls out clues, and if student can find the correct answer, he/she puts a marking piece in that square.

5. When one student has 5 in a row or 4 corners, he or she calls, "**VINCO!**"
   Game is checked and student who wins receives a small prize, or other treat which the teacher provides.

Here are some ideas to get the teacher started. Students will need 24, so you will need at least 30 for them to select from. Be creative!

T eacher writes on board:	Clues given aloud for those words:
auscultamus	**We are listening to…**
agricolis	**to or for farmers**
quibus	**abl. pl., to whom**
infantem	**acc. s., baby**
Quid spectas?	**What are you looking at?**
Quem spectas?	**Whom are you looking at?**

When using history or geography, you might use:

Caesar	**a consul**
Cincinnatus	**a farmer-dictator**
Cicero	**a lawyer-orator**
Circus Maximus	**a racetrack**
Forum	**a marketplace**
Senate	**law-giving body**
Vulgate	**a Bible**
Jerome	**translator of Bible**
Etruscans	**early settlers**
Adriatic	**sea**
Pontifex Maximus	**Jesus**
Rome	**capital of Italy**
Gaul	**first home of Fidelius family as we meet them**
Empire	**form of government that is a dictatorship**
Monarchy	**form of government with a king**
Republic	**form of government ruled by law**
Democracy	**form of government ruled by popular vote**
Tiber	**a river in Rome**
Sardinia	**an island**

V I N C O

<table>
<tr><td></td><td></td><td></td><td></td><td></td></tr>
<tr><td></td><td></td><td></td><td></td><td></td></tr>
<tr><td></td><td></td><td>**Liber**</td><td></td><td></td></tr>
<tr><td></td><td></td><td></td><td></td><td></td></tr>
<tr><td></td><td></td><td></td><td></td><td></td></tr>
</table>

Course Syllabus
Latin I

Course Description
This is the introductory course for the middle school or high school level student of Latin which provides an explanation and practice in beginning Latin. This course focuses on the grammar, vocabulary and structure of the language while introducing some of Roman history and Biblical principles and Scripture.

Course Objectives and Anticipated Results: *At the conclusion of this course, the student will be able to demonstrate*
> 1. Comprehension of the structure of Latin, the forms used, the grammar and syntax of the language.
> 2. Understanding of the similarities and differences between English and Latin.
> 3. Proficiency to allow the student to read simple passages from the Bible.
> 4. Some knowledge of the life of ancient Romans and their culture from a Christian perspective.

Materials of Instruction: Textbook, Study Sheets, and Drill Sheets.
Methods of Instruction: Older students can go through the book themselves; younger students need teacher-led instruction.
Sequence of Instruction: A general sequence is: 1.) Read the grammar, 2.) Learn the vocabulary, 3.) Do Study Sheet to reinforce. 4.) Do Drill Sheet for practice, 5.) Complete the Exercises in the chapter including the Reading Lesson 6.) Quiz orally or use bi-chapter tests to evaluate.
Course Requirements and Assessment Methods: Students are expected to score a minimum score of 75% on each test in order to show comprehension and retention of the materials.

You may give the assessment test on page xii if you are not sure your student is ready.

Chapter One Objectives:

At the end of the lesson students will be able to:

- explain the rationale for learning Latin.
- organize Latin assignments in their notebook.
- identify the parts of speech in English.

Name ____

ASSESSMENT TEST

Example: Tell who or what the sentence is

about. A. My friends came to my house.
          *My friends. (That is the **subject** of the sentence.)*
*What did my friends do? They came. (That is the **predicate**.)*

Here is your work:

1. Joe read four books.

Who or what is the sentence about? _____________________

What did he do? _________________________________

2. Seven tall boys climbed up the mountain.

Who or what is the sentence about? _____________________

What did they do? _________________________________

3. Rocks flew down from the castle walls.

Who or what is the sentence about? _____________________

What did they do? _________________________________

4. We learned about Mark's trip today.

Who or what is the sentence about? _____________________

What did we do? _________________________________

5. Do you like swimming?

Who or what is the sentence about? _____________________

    What do you do? _________________________________

Introduction.

The Teacher's Guide is composed of all the student text, the Study Sheets, the Drill Sheets, and Tests, plus instructions for teaching. Answers are written in **Arial Font** (like this) and the actual text copy is written in **Times New Roman** (like this). Page numbers which correspond with the student text are given at the top of pages, and page numbers for the Teacher's Guide are at the bottom of each page. ***Since there are several editions of this book, the page numbers may just be "close" to your textbook, not always exact.***

The vocabulary lists have diacritical marks and accent marks to help with ecclesiastical pronunciation. You will notice that the rules for this pronunciation are not as strict as they are for the classical pronunciation; some variation occurs.

There are two extra sections of your notebook for which we do not give any information: the "Cultural" and the "Bible" sections. These are places where you can add any historical reports that the students do, music you find that is in Latin, or any extra Bible study which is prompted by the lessons. Material for every other section is included in the text. A textbook is just a "jumping off place" where you get ideas for extra reports, journal activities, etc.

The Lord's Prayer is in the very back of the book.   Please copy the charts in the back of this book, and distribute them to the students or post them on your bulletin board.

Chapter One.
1. Read **I** and **II** together. Discuss.
   In section **I**, you may want to highlight "reasons for studying Latin", and in section **II**, you may highlight "three stages of the Trivium approach to education".
2. Read **III** and set up notebooks and vocabulary card index.
   You will find the definition for the parts of speech in the box on page 3.
3. Read **IV**, and copy the chart. Copy each part of speech on a separate piece of paper with the name of each part of speech as the title. Under that, copy the information in the box for each one, and then put them in the section of your notebook which is titled "Grammar".
4. Have the students title a piece of notebook paper with the word "Phrases". Fold the paper in half lengthwise, making two columns. Title the first column "Latin" and the second column "English". Write the Latin phrase at the beginning of each chapter on this sheet. Discuss the phrase, and have the student put the paper into his or her notebook in the section titled "Phrases". There is a phrase page in the Teacher's Guide. You may also use this to teach the student some commonly used secular phrases.

Student's Written Work:
5. Answer questions 1-4 on the bottom of page 3.
6. Students should memorize the parts of speech and their uses.

Chapter One

Soli Deo Gloria

Glory to God Alone

Introduction; The Trivium Approach; Setting Up the Notebook; Flash Cards; Grammar Review

I. Introduction by Pastor Douglas A. Busby

You are holding **the most comprehensive Latin text book to be produced using the Bible** in Latin as the primary reading source. *Latin in the Christian Trivium* provides a unique opportunity to benefit from learning Latin without having to read the pagan myths and philosophies usually associated with a Latin text book. *Latin in the Christian Trivium* gives moral and spiritual enrichment while studying the foundational disciplines of language and grammar. Instead of having beginning students immerse themselves in stories about pagan gods attacking women and fighting each other, with this book, they can form a Biblical foundation first by reading John 3:16: "sic enim dilexit Deus mundum ut Filium suum unigenitum daret ut omnis qui credit in eum non pereat sed habeat vitam aeternam."

Why study Latin? The inspiration of the Scriptures testifies to the importance of language skills for both comprehending and formulating verbal thought and expression. God has revealed Himself and His plan in words. Words, and the relationship of words, are the basis for ideas, and ideas have consequences in our personal lives and for history. Language skills, therefore, make us more effective in our service to God, and Latin is a powerful and effective vehicle for learning those skills.

Latin has been the most widely used language in all the world's history, and more than any other tongue, it influenced the languages of Europe and the Americas. It has been estimated that between 60 and 70% of our English words are derived from Latin. Some words, such as *area, circus,* and *animal,* are spelled the same in both languages. Others, such as *cause, form,* and *note,* are almost like Latin (**causa, forma, nota**). Still others, like *people, space,* and *peace* (**populus, spatium, pax**), come indirectly from Latin. Indeed, because Latin has been the language of learned men and women, it became the basis for the vocabulary of the sciences, law, technology, music, and medicine. For developing a powerful vocabulary, Latin is a definite plus.

Latin is equally important for learning the structure of language and grammar. The majority of our nation's founders could read both Latin and Greek, and they were able to use the English language the way a surgeon uses his scalpel or an artist his paintbrush. Their ability to write and say what they meant with precision is largely because of the skills they learned in their youth from studying these ancient languages. Furthermore, from Latin, a student can branch out into other languages with ease. Studies have shown that students who study Latin tend to perform better in all academic areas. The study habits and memory development gained in the study of Latin are vital factors for success in college and in getting higher scores on the SAT and ACT entrance exams.

So now the adventure begins. Thousands upon thousands of students in both institutional and home schooling environments have studied Latin on their way to success in every walk of life. With *Latin in the Christian Trivium*, that pathway will have the added guidance and direction provided by studying the Bible in Latin.

"Study to show thyself approved . . ." Sorry, I meant to say, "Sollicite cura te ipsum probabilem exhibere Deo operarium inconfusibilem recte tractantem verbum veritatis" (2Tim 2:15).

II. The Trivium Approach

The trivium approach to learning is a three-step operation. The first stage is called the "grammar stage," not to be confused with English grammar. This is the time when detailed information is learned and memorized. In computer terminology this might be called *"data input."* During this stage of learning, you want to memorize whatever you can. The second stage, the "dialectic stage" (sometimes called the logic stage) is the time for all of this information to be thoughtfully considered in light of Scripture. It is, again in computer terms, *"processing."* You mull things over, and compare each principle and concept you have learned, seeing what things are true and logical (e.g., Scriptural), and what things are fallacies. The final stage is the "rhetoric" stage, the time you display the things you have learned. *"Data output."* At this time you should be able to converse intelligently about the things you have studied.

III. Setting up the Notebook

When you begin studying Latin, you are in the grammar stage of the Trivium. In order to better learn the material you make a notebook and as you learn the subj ect, you enter the information into your notebook under various headings. This way you are re-organizing the material and beginning to process it by cataloguing the information into a different order than is in the textbook. Eventually you will be able to work independently, either writing or reading Latin, understanding for yourself the reasons you studied it. You should know, by that time, what God says about Language, Love, Peace, War and many other things.

To set up your notebook, you will need a 3" wide 3-ring binder with the following index tabs: **Pronunciation, Phrases, Grammar, Cases/Declensions, Conjugations, Vocabulary, (English) Derivatives, Culture, Bible, Study Sheets, Drill Sheets, Exercises, Tests:** 13 altogether. You will put the work you do into one of these sections of your notebook. All the material that you need to copy into your notebook will be enclosed in "boxes" in the textbook.

To store your vocabulary cards you may choose to use a 3 X 5 card file box and 12 - 3X5 tabbed index cards. Label the tabs with the following: **Phonics, Nouns, Pronouns, Verbs, Adjectives, Adverbs, Prepositions, Conjunctions, Prefixes, Suffixes, Interjections,** and **Miscellaneous.** Write the definition of each part of speech on the front of the index tab card which has its name.

IV. Grammar Review

Parts of Speech

Parts of speech in Latin are the same as in English: Nouns, Pronouns, Verbs, Adverbs, Adjectives, Prepositions, Conjunctions, and Interjections. A particular type of adjective is an Article, *a, an* and *the.* There are no words in Latin for these articles, so **agricola** means *a farmer* or *the farmer.* Translate it whichever way sounds best in the sentence.

In the section of your notebook titled "Grammar", title a page for each of the parts of speech: noun, pronoun, verb, adverb, adjective, conjunction, preposition, interjection.

Copy the definitions from the chart below onto each of your title pages for each part of speech.

A **noun** names. It may name a person (*Senator Helms, Patrick Henry, father*), a thing (*chair, book, spaceship*), a quality (*kindness, strength, courage*), a place (*city, Washington, the Red Sea*), or an idea (*reality, peace*). Whatever exists or can be thought to exist has a name. Its name is a noun.

A **verb** expresses an action (*bring, change, carry*), a state of being (*is, will be, seems*), or it declares, asks, or commands (*do, study, see*).

A **pronoun** takes the place of a noun (*I, you, he, she, it, we, they, this, that, everybody, yourself, who, whom, which*).

An **adjective** describes or modifies a noun (*bright, sturdy, lovely*). It can tell how many, such as two men.

An **adverb** modifies verbs, adjectives or other adverbs. It answers the questions how, when, where, or to what extent (*quickly, slowly, wisely, happily*).

A **preposition** is a word that shows how a noun or pronoun is related to some other word in the sentence (*on, in, above*).

A **conjunction** is a word that joins two similar words, phrases or clauses together in a sentence (*and, or, neither, nor*).

An **interjection** is a word standing by itself or inserted in a sentence to exclaim or command attention (*Ouch! Wow!*).

Write the answers to these questions.
1. What are five reasons for studying Latin?
2. What is a reason for studying Latin in a Christian textbook?
3. Name three other examples of each part of speech.
4. What are the three stages of the Trivium approach to education?

<u>Answers:</u>
1. Five reasons for studying Latin are: to understand the Scriptures better, to have better language skills, to improve vocabulary, for memory development, for improved study habits.
2. Studying in a Christian textbook gives moral and spiritual enrichment.
3. Noun: ball, sky, bed. Verb: run, was, says. Pronoun: he, she, it. Adjective: tall, short, quiet. Adverb: hastily, quickly, quietly. Preposition: about, above, across. Conjunction: but, for, moreover. Interjection: Aha! Alas! Mercy!
4. Grammar, Logic, Rhetoric.

Latin in the Christian Trivium – Volume I Teacher's Guide

ROMAN COLOSSEUM A.D. 2001

Name ____Date _________________________

Latin in the Christian Trivium
Study Sheet
Chapter One

Fill in the missing words.
1. A <u>conjunction</u> is a word that joins two similar words, phrases or clauses together in a sentence.
2. A <u>preposition</u> is a word that shows how a noun or pronoun is connected to some other word in the sentence.
3. A <u>verb</u> expresses an action, a state of being, or it declares, asks, or commands.
4. A <u>pronoun</u> takes the place of a noun .
5. An <u>adverb</u> modifies verbs, adjectives or other adverbs.
6. An <u>interjection</u> is a word standing by itself or inserted in a sentence to exclaim or command attention .
7. An <u>adjective</u> describes or modifies nouns and pronouns.

True or False.

8. The Latin word for "the" is "el." <u>False</u>
9. There are three stages to the trivium. <u>True</u>
10. You should study Latin to impress your friends. <u>False</u>
11. The maj ority of English words come from Latin. <u>True</u>
12. *Farmer* is a noun. <u>True</u>
13. *Runs* is an adjective. <u>False</u>
14. *Big* is an adjective. <u>True</u>
15. *Oh!* Is an interjection. <u>True</u>

Chapter Two Objectives:

At the end of the lesson students will be able to:

- pronounce each consonant, vowel, diphthong, and consonant blend sound in Latin.
- distinguish the difference between a structured and an inflected language.
- identify the simple subject and simple predicate of any given sentence.
- name the members of the fictitious Roman family introduced in this lesson.

Chapter Two.

1. Give a quiz on the parts of speech. You can read the definition of each one and have the student write down which part of speech you are describing.
2. Check the student's written work and answer any questions.
3. Do one Latin phrase from Teacher's Guide. See #4 in Chapter One for instructions.
4. Read Section **I** together and discuss.
5. When you reach page 7, the teacher may pronounce the sound and the student echo it, and then have the student pronounce each sound. It is actually very important that they learn the phonics sounds.

For pre-high school students, have the student make flash cards, using white index cards and black ink. Have them put the symbol for the sound on the front of the card and find an English word to go with each sound for the back. Have them put any other information for the sound on the back of the card. Student needs to memorize these, and the teacher needs to test him on the sounds. To test the sounds each time, the teacher calls the sounds out orally and the student writes the symbol for that sound on his paper without looking at the card. Since it will take more than one class period to cover the information in this chapter, the quizzing of the phonic sounds can be broken down into these sections when you drill or test them.

    a. All single letters that have one sound

    b. All single letters that have more that one sound

    c. All two and three lettered sounds

When you give a quiz to the student and after the quiz has been graded, carry over the items missed and give them as part of the next quiz. Drop the missed items from the quizzes when the student is not missing them any more.

6. Have students do the **Study Sheet** for Chapter Two.
7. Read and discuss section **II** in the textbook.
8. You may want to do "**B. Exercise**" with your student, or as a student's self -directed work.
9. Read and discuss **III**. Assign a report on one of the timeline events.
10. You may read and discuss **IV** with your student. Answer the questions at the bottom of the page.
11. Look at the map on **VI**. Have students find Vercellae in the Province of Gallia Transpadana and color the province with a colored map pencil.

Latin in the Christian Trivium Volume I Teacher's Guide

Chapter Two

The Roman Alphabet; Pronunciation; Grammar Review; Timeline; The Roman Family

I. The Roman Alphabet
A. History of the alphabet
The earliest alphabet was not actually an alphabet at all. The Egyptians are credited with the first writing, but their writing was actually picture writing, called *hieroglyphics*. If they wanted to write a word such as *nefer* or *good*, they could either write it with a single sign for the whole word or with three signs, for the sounds *n*, *f*, and *r*. They had no signs for vowels, only consonants. Egyptian writing was picture writing and had some syllabic writing.

The Jews (also called Semites) in about 3000 B.C. developed an alphabetic writing using signs to show the consonants of syllables just like the Egyptians did. They had no symbols or letters to represent vowels either. They developed an alphabet which is not apparently related to the Egyptian one.

Later the Phoenicians (the Canaanites) worked out an alphabet consisting of 22 letters which seems somewhat related to both the Semitic and Egyptian styles. As you know from history, the Phoenicians were famous for sea trading and with their swift ships managed to control the Mediterranean Sea by the year 1000 B.C. The Greeks came in contact with Phoenician traders and learned from them the idea of writing individual sounds of the language. Sometime before 800 B.C., they borrowed Phoenician symbols and modified them to form the Greek alphabet. The Greeks used some of the extra Phoenician consonants to function as vowel sounds. In this way, the Greeks improved over all other alphabets and could write any word they wanted.

When the Etruscans moved to Italy from the Eastern Mediterranean region, they took the Greek alphabet with them. The Romans learned the alphabet from the Etruscans, and developed it into much the same form we use today, except that the Roman alphabet lacked the letters *j* and *w*. Also, the letter *v* originally stood for both the sound of the vowel *u* and the sound of our consonant *w*. Only in recent times have we used the *v* and *u* in Latin texts.

Our own alphabet today therefore is called the Roman alphabet.

B. Pronunciation
There are two methods for the pronunciation of Latin accepted today. The first one is the German pronunciation, which is commonly called the Classical Pronunciation. It is taught in most schools, and is the pronunciation used in many textbooks. The other one is the Italian pronunciation which is also called Church Latin. It is the older of the two, and it relates more to modern Italian, French, Spanish, Portuguese, and Romanian. All Latin music texts use church or ecclesiastical Latin, and this book does as well.

The Latin alphabet contains the same letters as the English except that it had no *w* and no *j* in the time period we are studying. The vowels, as in English, are *a, e, i, o, u, y.* The other letters are consonants. The *i* is used both as a vowel and as a consonant. Before a vowel in the same syllable it is used as a consonant and sounds like *y* in the word *yes*. In the word **Iu-li-us,** the first **i** is a consonant, the second a vowel.

Syllables. There are as many syllables as there are vowels or diphthongs in Latin words.

Accent. **Latin words are NEVER accented on the last syllable**. A word of two syllables is accented on the first. The rules for accents are less consistent with ecclesiastical Latin than with classical Latin, so accents will be marked in your vocabulary.

Remains of an ancient Roman Villa

Copy the following chart onto a piece of paper and put it into your notebook in the section titled, "Pronunciation." If the letter or diphthong is in bold print, it is pronounced the same as it is in English.

Consonants

		Diphthongs	
b		oe	*ay*
c	*k, ch* (when followed by e, i, ae. oe)	ae	*ay*
d		ei	*ay*
f		au	*ow*
g	*g, j* (when followed by e, i)	**eu**	*eu* as in *neutral*, at the beginning of the word: *yoo* as in *Europe*
h		ui	*wee*
k	(K is used chiefly in abbreviations, such as Kal. Kallendae)		
l			
m			
n		**Blends**	
p		ch	*k* as in *character*
q	followed by **u**	ci	*chee*
r		gu	*gu* as in *language*
s	SS (but when between 2 vowels or last, *z*)	**ph**	*ph* as in *phone*
t		su	*sw*
v		th	as the *t* in *take*
x	*ks, gs*	bs	*ps*
z	*dz*	bt	*pt*
		tia	*tsee-ah*

Vowels

ā	as in *father*
ă	as in *abyss* ē
as	in *they*
ĕ	as in *met*
ī	as in *machine*
ĭ	as in *sit*
iū	(when followed by the vowel *u, i* sounds like the consonant *y*) as in *you*
ō	as in *holy*
ŏ	as in *stop*
ū	as in *rude*, or as *oo* in *boot*
ŭ	as in *full*, or *oo* as in *foot*
y	as in *sit*, only in foreign words

Flash Cards. Each chapter beginning with Chapter Three will have vocabulary words. You will need to make flash cards to help you learn them. For *this* lesson you will make flash cards for the phonic sounds and they will be kept in a file box. Make flash cards, one for each letter or phonic shown above, and have someone drill you each day with all of them until you learn the phonics sound. When you have completely learned all these, you may store them in your card file box in the **Phonics** section.

NOTE:

A diphthong is a combination of vowels with a unique sound different from the single vowels themselves.

Latin in the Christian Trivium Volume I Teacher's Guide

II. More Grammar Review
A. Subject and Predicate

Latin, like English, expresses thoughts by means of sentences. In fact, the word **sententia** in Latin means *a complete thought*. A sentence is a combination of words that expresses a thought, and in its simplest form is the statement of a single fact.

Propheta est poeta.   **Puellae ambulant.**
The prophet is a poet.   *The girls are walking.*

In each of these two sentences there are two parts:

	Propheta, *The prophet*		**est poeta.** *is a poet.*
SUBJECT	**Puellae,** *The girls*	PREDICATE	**ambulant.** *are walking.*

NOTA BENE: Both Latin and English have subjects (whomever or whatever the sentence is about plus the words that describe the subject) and predicates (that which is said about the subject and consists of a verb and its modifiers). The simple subject is the noun, nouns, or pronouns that tell what the sentence is about; the simple predicate is the verb (or verbs) that tells the action or existence of the subject.

When you mark a sentence, underline the simple subject with one line, and the simple predicate with two lines.

<u>Susan</u> and <u>Mark</u> <u>played</u> baseball.

The Forum today

B. Exercise
Copy the following sentences onto a piece of paper and underline the subjects with one line and the predicates with a double line.

1. Titus and I played a game.
2. In the early morning Priscilla jumped from her bed.
3. W e bought David three new books.
4. John is our new friend.
5. Did you give me your address?
6. The president is tall.
7. Douglas wrote his grandmother a letter.
8. During vacation I read three historical novels.
9. Traveling from Washington to San Francisco, we saw the Grand Canyon.
10. My husband has given much time to the Lord's work.

C. Structural vs. Inflected Languages

1. English is a structural language. That is, the meaning of a sentence depends on the position of the words in the sentence.

God created man in His own image.

In this sentence we know from the positioning of the words that "God" is the subject of the sentence; what did God do? He "created"; that is the predicate (or verb). What did He create?

He created "man", the direct object of the verb. How did He create him? "In His own image", a prepositional phrase used as an adverb. If we reversed the word order, *"Man created God in his own image,"* the meaning would be totally different.

In English, word position indicates meaning. Copy this chart and put it in your notebook under "Grammar" on a page titled English Syntax.

<table>
<tr><td colspan="2">English Syntax</td></tr>
<tr><td><u>Subject</u> | <u>Predicate</u></td><td>Julie | sang.</td></tr>
<tr><td><u>Subject</u> | <u>Predicate</u> | Direct Object</td><td>Jennifer | wrote a letter.</td></tr>
<tr><td><u>Subject</u> | <u>Predicate</u> | Indirect Object \ Direct Object</td><td>Robert | played me a song.</td></tr>
<tr><td>Adjective <u>Subject</u> | <u>Predicate</u> \Adverb</td><td>The young girl | sang beautifully.</td></tr>
<tr><td><u>Subject</u> | <u>Predicate</u> (linking verb) \ Predicate Nominative</td><td>Denise | is my daughter.</td></tr>
<tr><td><u>Subject</u> | <u>Predicate</u> (linking verb) \ Predicate Adjective</td><td>Susan | seems kind.</td></tr>
</table>

2. Conversely, Latin is an inflected language. That means that the *endings* of words, NOT their position in the sentence, indicate their meanings and functions within the sentence. Thus, the sentence given above, *God created man in his own image,* in Latin could be written, **Deus creavit homines ad imaginem suam,** or **Deus homines ad imaginem suam creavit,** or **Creavit homines Deus ad imaginem suam.** All of these mean exactly the same thing. The words have particular endings, such as **-us,** or **-es,** or others which let us know which word is the subject, verb, direct object, or object of the preposition, and so on.

The basic part of the word remains the same, but different endings to that basic part change the meanings somewhat.

Enter this chart into your notebook in the "Grammar" section on a page titled <u>Latin Syntax.</u>

NOTA BENE: In a Latin sentence the most important word is the *first word;* next in importance is the *last word;* the weakest point is the middle of the sentence. Usually the *subject* is the most important word and is placed *first*; then the *verb* (in the future we will call the predicate the verb.) is placed *last.* The other words of the sentence stand between these two in the order of their importance. However, word order is <u>just a style and</u> <u>not necessarily one way</u> or another. That is why the endings are important to identify the different parts of the sentence.

There is a word order in Latin that is common when no particular emphasis is placed on a particular word and it is below:

This chart is to be put immediately below the last one.

Subject - Modifiers of the Subject - Indirect Object - Direct Object - Adverb - Verb

One reason for this word order is the Romans' fondness for what is called the periodic style; the intent of putting the verb at the end is to keep the reader or hearer in suspense.

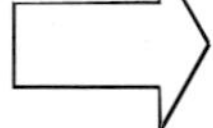

But although this pattern is a good one to follow most of the time, the Romans often changed the order for variety or emphasis.

Roman Amphitheater

III. Timeline

The following is a time line which includes the time period of the story of the Fidelius family. On the left is the legendary date of the founding of Rome. On the right is the date of the ending of the Roman Empire when it was overrun by barbarian tribes: the Huns, the Goths, the Visigoths, and the Vandals.   Some other important events are noted.

753 B.C --A.D.33 -- A.D. 476

Draw a time line of your own and place the following events on the timeline in the appropriate year.

264 – 241 B.C. – *First Punic War*

218 – 202 B.C. – *Second Punic War*

149 – 146 B.C. – *Third Punic War*

58 B.C. – *Caesar conquers Gaul.*

45 B.C. – *Caesar is made dictator of the Roman world.*

44. B.C. – *Death of Julius Caesar*

27 B.C.- *Beginning of the Roman Empire. "The Pax Romana"*

A.D. 29 - ** Resurrection of Jesus Christ*

A.D. 29 – *The Fidelius family is stationed in Gaul.*

A.D. 60 – ** Paul is martyred in Rome*

A.D. 70 – *Titus sacks Jerusalem*

 A.D. 303 – *Diocletian begins his persecution of the Christians.*

A.D. 313 – *Constantine becomes a Christian.*

IV. A Roman Family

The stories in this book are about the Roman family of Romulus Fidelius. When we first meet them, they are living in a Roman villa outside the town of Vercellae in the province of Gaul. They are living there because their father is a centurion in the Roman army and his legion is stationed there. The date is A.D. 26.

In our family there is an older daughter, Fidelia, who is 12, and an older son, Davus, who is 14. The younger son, who is 10, is named Titus, and there is a younger daughter, Priscilla, who is eight. The father's name is Romulus Fidelius Centurio, and the mother's name is Aquila.

The most important thing to Romans was the family. Even though emperors ruled Rome, the father, not the state, had absolute authority over his wife and children. Fidelius is not only responsible for his legion, but he is also responsible for his estate. Legally, he has the power of life and death over his entire household. Aquila manages the home much like mothers do today. She has a sizable group of servants to help her. The children do not go to school outside the home, because they have a Greek tutor named Philippus who teaches them academic subjects. When Fidelius is not off to battle, the boys get a substantial part of their education directly from their father, and the girls get instruction in the domestic arts from their mother.

When he is on duty, Fidelius wears a bright red tunic that is knee-length. Over that he wears armor, and he has a shield, a spear, and a sword, and metal fittings. But when he is at home relaxing with the family, naturally he doesn't wear his armor. There he wears a plain white tunic. Aquila also wears a simple sleeveless white tunic. Over that she wears a **stola** which is a long flounced dress belted at the waist and reaching to the ankles. For outside wear she adds the **palla**, a single piece of material draped around the body. Fidelia and Priscilla dress like their mother.

Davus and Titus, like their father, wear tunics, and in public, togas over that. Both boys and girls wear a **bulla**[*], or good luck charm around their necks, which is given to them at their naming ceremony. Girls continue to wear the bulla until they are married. When boys come of age at sixteen, they dedicate the bulla and the first scrapings of their beards to the household gods.

Romans generally went bareheaded. If they needed protection from the weather, the toga or palla was drawn over their heads. Sometimes the women used parasols and the men used broad-rimmed hats called **petasi** to shield them from the sun. They all wore sandals on their feet.

Our family's villa serves two purposes: it houses the servants who do the agricultural work and it provides accommodation for the owner and his family. The villa has stables, two enclosed courts or farmyards, rooms for pressing grapes or olives, and an adjacent area for threshing. Fidelius has an overseer named John who supervises the other servants.

Questions
1. Who are the members of the Fidelius family?

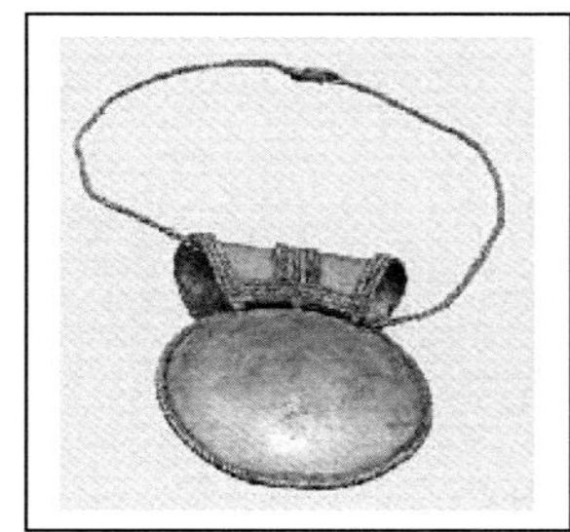

---

[*]World Book Encyclopedia, 1985 , "Clothing", Volume IV, page 548.

2. How does their dress differ from today's American family?
3. How old are boys when they are considered to be men?
4. What is the good luck charm called which is worn around the neck?

Answers
1. Romulus Fidelius Centurio and Aquila are the father and mother. Davus, Titus, Priscilla, and Fidelia are the children.
2. Their clothes were robes, gowns, tunics, and ours are dresses, pants and shirts.
3. Boys are considered to be men at age sixteen.
4. The good luck charm is called the bulla.

Background on ROMULUS FIDELIUS CENTURIO, wife, AQUILA, and family

Romulus Fidelius Centurio was born in 16 B.C. He was the son of Valerius Fidelius Centurio, who served under Augustus, and Claudia, the youngest sister of the Latin historian, Livy. Valerius Fidelius was stationed in Syria, where Romulus and his two younger brothers were born

In 4 B.C. Valerius, who was the **nuncio** for the governor of the province of Judah, was called back to Rome, where he, Claudia, and their three sons returned with one young Judean servant named John. After his term in the Roman army Valerius retired as a tribune, and he and the family moved to Padua, which was the home of Claudia's family.

When Romulus Fidelius was 18, he followed in his father's footsteps and joined the Roman army in A.D. 3, where he served under Tiberius. Tiberius liked Fidelius, and Fidelius soon became a Centurion. He married Aquila in A.D.10. Aquila's father was a Tribune in the Roman army.

When Emperor Augustus died and Tiberius became Emperor, he put Romulus Fidelius in charge of a cohort of soldiers in the Province of Gaul in Northern Italy. This is where the children were born and grew up. Within the household there were eight servants, including John, who was Fidelius' steward and chief assistant, Clara, a Gaul, who was the personal servant to Aquila and the girls, and Philip, the Greek tutor for the children. There were six more servants who all reported to John. The servants were all former servants and orphans, but Fidelius had given them their freedom.

This is where we find them in the year A.D. 26, in a small villa just outside the town of  Vercellae, where all their lives are about to change dramatically.

Latin in the Christian Trivium Volume I Teacher's Guide

V. The Centurion Romulus Fidelius and his family

V. Map of Italy

Find Vercellae in the Province of Gallia Transpadana and color the entire province of Gallia Transpadana to the "Boundary before Augustus. "

*A better map for students is in the Teacher's Resource disc.

A Mosaic in the Vatican today
Jesus and Peter

Latin in the Christian Trivium Volume I Teacher's Guide

Latin in the Christian Trivium
Study Sheet
Chapter Two

Grammar

1. What does the word **sententia** mean?
The word **sententia** means "a complete thought."
2. What do we mean by the term "structural language"?
Structural language means that the meaning of a sentence depends on the *position of the words in the sentence.*
3. What do we mean by the term "inflected language"?
The *endings of words*, **not** their position in the sentence, indicate the meanings and functions within the sentence in an inflected language.
4. In a Latin sentence which word is usually first in the sentence?
The most important word is first in a Latin sentence. (often the subject)
5. In Latin, which syllable is never accented?
The last syllable is never accented.
6. How do you tell how many syllables there are in a Latin word?
There are as many syllables as there are vowels or diphthongs.

The Alphabet

7. What is the name for the Egyptian style of writing?
he Egyptian style of writing is called hieroglyphics.
8. Which people added vowels to their alphabet?
Greeks added vowels to their alphabet.
9. What is the name of our alphabet today?
Our alphabet is called the Roman alphabet.
10. What are the two methods of pronunciation used in Latin texts?
Two methods of pronunciation are classical (German) and church (Italian).

Sentence Practice

Underline the simple subjects with one line and the simple predicates with two lines in the following sentences.

11. The dead leaves blew into the swimming pool.
12. I talked to the teacher after class for half an hour.
13. The refrigerator contains nothing.
14. Long sideburns have been popular in the South at least since the War of Secession.
15. Two reams of paper were missing from the storage cabinet.
16. Tourists flock to the County Fair each September.
17. Bill drink s fruit juice every day.
18. The star center won the game for us.
19. Frederick had lived near the river all his life.
20. All my friends bring me their most difficult problems.
21. The prosecutor promised her immunity.
22. Jogging can damage your knees and your feet.

23. <u>Traffic jams</u> <u>upset</u> Angela.
24. <u>Jonathan</u> <u>kept</u> the dog in the backyard every day.

Culture
25. Where does the Fidelius family reside at the time of our story?
<u>The Fidelius family lives outside the town of Vercellae in the province of Gaul.</u>
26. In what ways was the Roman system of family government similar to the Biblical pattern and in what way was it different?
<u>Both the Roman family and the Biblical pattern are patriarchies, that is, the father is the head of the family. But the Roman father had the power of life and death over all in his family, and in the Biblical pattern, the father is the head of the family, but he is under God's Law.</u>
27. Tell the names of two of the items of clothing worn by a soldier.
<u>A soldier wore a red tunic. Over that he wore armor, and he had a shield, a spear, a sword, and metal fittings.</u>
28. What were the clothes called that were worn by a woman?
<u>A woman wore a sleeveless white tunic, and over that she wore a stola, and for a warm covering she wore a palla.</u>

<hr>

NOTE TO TEACHER REGARDING TEST SCORING: The easiest way to grade the tests is to count the number of possible correct answers, then subtract any mistakes from that total, and divide again by the number possible.

Example: In this test, there are 23 possible answers. If a student misses 3, then his score is 22/25, which is equal to 92%. We normally give 5 possible points for each sentence they have to translate.

<hr>

Test One to be taken after the completion of Chapter Two
Parts of Speech Review   *Write the name of the Part of Speech of the underlined words.*

1. a <u>big</u> hat	<u>adjective</u>	6. Jim walks <u>fast</u>.	<u>adverb</u>
2. <u>in</u> the box	<u>preposition</u>	7. Michael is <u>smart</u>.	<u>adjective</u>
3. <u>he</u> and I were running	<u>pronouns</u>	8. Stuart is a good <u>writer</u>.	<u>noun</u>
4. a big <u>hat</u>	<u>noun</u>	9. Keith and Michael <u>study</u>.	<u>verb</u>
5. <u>Wow</u>!	<u>interjection</u>	10. <u>Denise</u> is a scientist.	<u>noun</u>

Grammar
11. Give two reasons for studying Latin. <u>Any of these: To understand Scriptures better, to have better language skills, to improve vocabulary, for memory development, for improved study habits</u>
12. Which syllable is NEVER accented in Latin words?   <u>the last syllable</u>
13. Is English a structural or inflected language?   <u>structural</u>
14. Is Latin a structural or inflected language?   <u>inflected</u>
15. Which word is usually, but not always, last in a Latin sentence? <u>verb</u>
16. What part of speech names a person, place, or thing?   <u>A noun</u>

History
17. Which people used hieroglyphics or picture words? <u>Egyptians</u>
18. What is our alphabet called?   <u>the Roman alphabet</u>

Roman Family

19. What are **petasi**? <u>hats</u>
20. What kind of shoes do they wear? <u>sandals</u>
21. What is the father's name in our story? <u>Romulus Fidelius Centurio</u>
22. What is the mother's name in our story? <u>Aquila</u>
23. How many children does the Fidelius family have? <u>four</u>

Chapter Three Objectives:

At the end of the lesson students will be able to:

- define the person and number of a verb.
- recite the four principal parts and English meaning of each verb in the chapter vocabulary.
- conjugate orally and on paper each verb.
- use each English derivative in a sentence.
- identify the location of various tribes who settled Italy, and the seas surrounding Italy.

Chapter Three

1. Give a quiz on Latin phonics sounds.
2. Check student's written work and discuss.
3. You might want to check the student's notebooks at this point to see if he or she is having any problems with it. Make any corrections needed.
4. Read and discuss **I** and **II** in the chapter. As you enter conjugations (and then cases) into the notebook, keep them together, i.e., all cases together, all conjugations together.
5. You may either have the student copy as you go over the material together, or assign it for him or her to do later.
6. Student(s) may now do the **Study Sheet**.
7. Read and discuss **III** in the textbook. The teacher pronounces the word and the student echoes. (Use CD of Latin pronunciations if necessary.)
8. Follow the directions for "Vocabulary". Do this with your student at first.
  a. Write the Latin words on the front of the card and the meanings on the back with the derivatives in parentheses.
  b. EXTRA FOR THOSE NEEDING MORE PRACTICE. This is also done on notebook paper and placed in the vocabulary section of the notebook.
9. The student must memorize the vocabulary and the chart on conjugating verbs. As this will probably take more that one day to cover all this material, the student must be tested often (give a short quiz once or twice a week if needed) to help him or her memorize and understand the concepts and vocabulary in this chapter.
Drill the student using each vocabulary word by reciting all four principal parts and then taking the first two principal parts and conjugating them using the chart under **II B.**
Drill vocabulary cards every day. Give the student a vocabulary quiz frequently. (Remember to retain the material missed on the quizzes, and drop the items when they are not missed anymore.)
10. Do the **Drill Sheet** for Chapter Three.
11. Supplementary exercise:
  Enter English derivatives on orange index cards with black ink. Find definitions f or each one.

12. Read and discuss **IV** and **V**. Follow the directions in **V** to do the
"Map Work." This may be done with your student or done as a student assignment.
13. Explain the directions for **VI**. Exercise A. The teacher reads the Latin words.
Student echoes the teacher, or you may use the CD. In exercises **B** and **C**, the student
should copy the verb, and then mark 1, 2, or 3 over the verb to tell which person it is,
and he should write an **s.** or a **pl.** to show if it is singular or plural. In the English to Latin
work, if the second person ("you") is singular, it will not be labeled. If it is plural, it will say
"pl."

3/ s.   1 /pl.

Ex. ambula**t = he** walks or ama**mus = we** love

2/s   2/pl.

you relate = narras   **you (pl.)** ask = rogatis

The First Conjugation Verb; Four Principal Parts;
A Brief History of Italy

A verb is the part of speech that expresses action, motion, being, suffering, or a request or command to do anything. The verb affirms, declares, asks, or commands (Webster's 1828 Dictionary).

The verb is the most important word in a sentence. In fact, a verb by itself can BE an entire sentence. For example: *Listen!* This verb is a complete thought and is therefore a complete sentence.

I. Grammar

Enter the following information on the page titled <u>Verbs</u> in the "Grammar" section of your notebook.

A verb can be identified according to its…	
Person	(I, you, he, she, it, we, you, they)
Number	(Singular or Plural)
Voice	(Active or Passive)
Tense	(Present, Past, or Future)
Mood	(Indicative, Imperative, or Subjunctive)

Write this chart and put it on the <u>English Syntax</u> page of the "Grammar" section.

		Singular	Plural
Number refers to Singular or Plural.			
Person refers to the person who is the subject of the verb:			
First person: the speaker or speakers		I	we
Second person: the person(s) spoken to		you	you (all)
Third person: whomever or whatever is spoken about		he, she, it	they

Person and Number

In English the **person** and **number** of a verb are shown by a pronoun subj ect shown above. In Latin they are shown by **personal endings** of the verb. Thus, we look at the ending of the Latin verb first, then look at the stem.

Below are the personal endings of verbs in Latin for the active voice:

	SINGULAR	PLURAL
1ST PERSON	**-o** or **-m,** *I*	**- mus,** *we*
2ND PERSON	**-s,** *you*	**-tis,** *you (all)*
3RD PERSON	**-t,** *he, she, or it*	**-nt,** *they*

NOTA BENE: Memorize these endings now. In each subsequent lesson there are new ones to learn, so it is important that you take the time to memorize as you go along.

Agreement

A verb agrees with its subject in person and number. Number means, "Is the subject of the sentence singular or plural?" If the subject of a verb is singular, then the verb must also be singular. Person means, "Are we speaking about 'me', 'you', or 'someone else'?"

II. The First Conjugation

A. Four Principal Parts

Verbs are learned in four forms, which are called the four principal parts.

1	2	3	4
a′mo	**ama′re**	**ama′vi**	**ama′tus**
I love	*to love*	*I have loved*	*having been loved*

Enter this information in the "Grammar" section of your notebook on the page titled <u>Verbs</u>.

The first two of the principal parts are named as follows:
Present Indicative: present active first person singular   **amo**, I love
Present Infinitive: used to form the present stem   **amare**, to love

Romans played various dice games. Originally the dice were made from knucklebones.

B. Paradigm

A chart or pattern is called a *paradigm*. This paradigm is the pattern used to conjugate a verb. This particular verb is being conjugated in the present tense, indicative mood, active voice. The present stem of the verb is found by removing the **-re** from the second principal part. Take the **–re** off **amare** and you have **ama-** left. To this we will add the endings as shown below in the box. For the first person singular, you do not write the "a" of the stem before the "o."

Copy the following paradigm and put it into your notebook in the section titled, "Conjugations." Title the Page <u>First Conjugation</u>:

<table>
<tr><td colspan="3">Present Tense, Indicative Mood, Active Voice</td></tr>
<tr><td></td><td>SINGULAR</td><td>PLURAL</td></tr>
<tr><td>1ST PERSON</td><td>ā′mō, I love, I do love, I am loving</td><td>āmā′mus, we love, we do love, we are loving</td></tr>
<tr><td>2ND PERSON</td><td>ā′mās, you love, you do love, you are loving</td><td>āmā′tĭs, you (all) love, you (all) do love, you are loving</td></tr>
<tr><td>3RD PERSON</td><td>ā′māt, he, she, or it loves, he, she, or it does love, he, she, or it is loving</td><td>ā′mānt, they love, they do love, they are loving</td></tr>
</table>

You mentally read Latin verbs from right to left. Look at the endings **first**.
For example, **amamus** = mus, *we* + ama = *love,* = *we love.*

III. Vocabulary   **English Derivatives**

Write each of these verbs onto a white index card using blue ink to use for flash card drills. You will need 33 white cards. Long vowels are marked and short vowels are left unmarked.

ām′būlō, āmbūlā′rē, āmbūla′vī, āmbūlā′tūs, *walk, stroll*   (ambulatory, ambulance)
ā′mō, āmā′rē, āmā′vī, āmā′tūs, *love, like*   (amiable, amicable, amatory)
āppel′lō, āppellā′rē, āppellā′vī, āppellā′tūs, *address, name, call*   (appellation)
auscūl′tō, auscūltā′rē, auscūltā′vī, auscūltā′tūs, *listen to, overhear*
cān′tō, cāntā′rē, cāntā′vī, cāntā′tūs, *sing*   (cantata, cantor)
clā′mō, clāmā′rē, clāmā′vī, clāmā′tūs, *shout*
confīr′mō, confīrmā′rē, confīrmā′vī, confīrmā′tūs, *strengthen, declare* (confirmation)
consē′crō, consēcrā′re, consēcrā′vī, consēcrā′tūs, *bless*   (consecrate)
cū′rō, cūrā′rē, cūrā′vī, cūrā′tūs, *care for, take care of*   (curator)
dō, dā′rē, ded′ī, dā′tūs, *give*   (donation)
hā′bītō, hābītā′rē, hābītā′vī, hābītā′tūs, *live, dwell*   (inhabit)
hon′ō rō, honōrā′rē, honōrā′vī, honōrā′tūs, *honor*
lābō′rō, lābōrā′rē, lābōrā′vī, lābōrā′tūs, *work, suffer, am hard pressed*   (laboratory)
lā′crīmō, lācrīmā′rē, lācrīmā′vī, lācrīmā′tūs, *cry, weep*
lau′dō, laudā′rē, laudā′vī, laudā′tūs, *praise*   (laudable)
lī′berō, līberā′rē, līberā′vī, līberā′tūs, *set free, free*   (liberate)

nār′rō, nārrā′rē, nārrā′vi, nārrā′tūs, *tell, relate*   (narration)
nā′vīgō, nāvīgā′rē, nāvīgā′vī, nāvīgā′tūs, *sail, steer a ship*   (navigate)
nūn′tīō, nūntīā′rē, nūntīā′vī, nūntīā′tūs, *announce, report*   (enunciate, nuncio)
oppū′gnō, oppūgnā′rē, oppūgnā′vī, oppūgnā′tūs, *attack, assault, besiege*
pā′rō, parā′rē, parā′vī, parā′tūs, *prepare*   (pare, prepare for)
pōr′tō, pōrtā′rē, pōrtā′vī, pōrtā′tūs, *carry*   (portable)
pū′gnō, pūgnā′rē, pūgnā′vī, pūgnā′tūs, *fight*   (pugnacious)
pū′tō, pūtā′rē, pūtā′vī, pūtā′tūs, *think*   (impute, compute)
rō′gō, rōgā′rē, rōgā′vī, rōgā′tūs, *ask, ask for**   (interrogate)
sālū′tō, sālūtā′rē, sālūtā′vī, sālūtā′tūs, *greet*   (salutation)
sānctī′fīcō, sānctīfīcā′rē, sānctīfīcā′vī, sānctīfīcā′tūs, *set apart for God' s purpose,*
       *bless***   (sanctification)
sā′nō, sānā′rē, sānā′vī, sānā′tūs, *cure, heal*   (sanitize)
ser′vō, servā′rē, servā′vī, servā′tūs, *save, guard, protect*   (preserve, conserve)
spec′tō, spectā′rē, spectā′vī, spectā′tūs, *look at, watch*   (spectacle, inspect)
sū′perō, sūperā′rē, sūperā′vī, sūperā′tūs, *defeat, overcome, surpass*   (supreme)
temp′tō, temptā′rē, temptā′vī, temptā′tūs, *try, attempt, test*   (temptation)
vō′cō, vōcā′rē, vōcā′vī, vōcā′tūs, *call, summon*   (vocation, vocal)

***rogo** takes two accusatives, the thing asked for, and the person asked.

****sanctifico** can mean a negative "setting apart" or a positive one.

Agricola in agro arat.

IV. A Brief History of Italy

The Etruscans were people who lived in what is now called central Italy. Most scholars today believe that the Etruscans came to Etruria (a part of Italy which extended from the Arno River in the north to the Tiber River in the south, and from the Apennine Mountains in the east to the Tyrrhenian Sea in the west) about 800 B.C. from the east, probably by sea. The Etruscans conquered the people who were already living in Italy. They spread throughout Italy and the Etruscan kings controlled much of what is now Italy and developed 12 cities. The Etruscans had an urban civilization which brought their culture to the farming communities of Latium, the early name for Italy. Under the Etruscan kings the little village of Rome developed into a powerful and prosperous city.

Eventually Etruscan control of the Po Valley was broken by European barbarian tribes called Gauls in the 400′s B.C. The land called Gaul encompassed primarily what is now F rance, but also extended to north of the Alps. The city of Rome took control of central Italy from the Gauls by the 200′s B.C.

The area now called Italy was inhabited by different tribes who were primarily agrarian: the Latins, the Hernicans, the Aequians, and the Volscian tribes to name a few. According to legend, Rome was founded as a city in 753 B.C. by two brothers Romulus and Remus who were descendants of the mythical Aeneas. They had wanted to establish a city, and fought over its location. Romulus killed Remus, and then chose the spot, calling it Rome after himself. This is a myth, but it is a colorful story.

THE FIRST

SETTLERS

You are now going to hear about the building of Rome, the capital of Italy, in Europe. By looking at your maps, you will soon find in Europe a peninsula, shaped somewhat like a boot, and surrounded on three sides by the Mediterranean and Adriatic seas. This peninsula is Italy. To the north are the snow-topped Alps, a chain of high mountains which separate this country from the rest of Europe; and through the peninsula run the Apennines, a less lofty mountain range.

As Italy is in the southern part of Europe, it has a very mild and delightful climate. The tall mountains in the north prevent the cold winds from sweeping down upon it, and many plants which you see here in hothouses grow there in the open ground.

Orange and almond trees, camellias and pomegranates, are all covered with fruit or flowers, and the vine and olive both yield rich harvests in this beautiful land. The soil is so rich that people do not need to work very hard in order to have fine crops, and, as the weather is generally clear, they can live out of doors almost all the year round.

As the climate is so pleasant, the land so fertile, the skies so blue, and the views so beautiful, travelers have always liked to visit Italy, and have spoken about its charms to all they met. It is no wonder, therefore, that many people have gone to settle there, and you will easily understand that the whole country was occupied long, long ago.

So many years ago that no one can really tell when it was, Italy was already inhabited by a people who, judging from what we have heard of them, must once have lived in Central Asia. These people were probably crowded at home, and left their native land in search of good pasture for their cattle, and a fertile country where they might dwell.

They traveled on and on, day after day, and coming finally to the great mountains, some of them climbed up to see what was on the other side. When they beheld the

green valleys of Italy, and saw how beautiful the country was, they told
their companions, and all made haste to cross the mountains.

These people traveled on foot, with their families, cattle, and all their household
goods; and they were very rude and uncivilized. Little by little, however, they
learned to build houses, to cook their food, to make rude pottery from the clay they
found in the valleys, to spin and weave the wool from their sheep, and to fashion this
homemade stuff into garments.

Although each family at first lived by itself, they soon discovered that if several families
joined together, they could cultivate the ground better, could hunt more successfully, and
that in time of danger they could more easily defend themselves.

Thus several families would form a tribe under the strongest and cleverest man among
them, whom they chose as their leader. These leaders selected the best place for them
to settle in, told them what to do in time of war, and thus became chiefs or kings over
their own tribes.

There were a number of such little kingdoms scattered throughout Italy, and as the
people grew richer, wiser, and more numerous, they occupied more and more land.

Now it was from some of these tribes that the Romans were mostly descended. Their
city became in time the greatest in the world, and many histories have been written
about it; but none of them were begun until several centuries after Rome was founded.
Hardly any records had been kept of the distant past, and the best that could be done
was to write down some stories that had been told by parents to their children, and thus
had been preserved from generation to generation. These had become much changed
by being told so many times, and they were connected and rounded out by pure
guesswork; but the whole was soon accepted as true, and was believed in by ever y one
for ages.

You will now read the story from the beginning, as the Romans themselves told it. Many
of the events in the first part of it never really happened; but no one can tell exactly
where the mere stories leave off, and the true history begins. And every well -educated
person is expected to know the whole story.

V. Map Work   (Use the map on page 15.)

Identify on a map the location of the Volsci, the Aequi, Etruria, the Samnium, Gallia Cispadana, (near the Alps Mts.), Gallia Transpadana, Sicilia, Corsica, Sardinia, Roma, Carthago, the Tyrrhenian Sea, and the Adriatic Sea.

Teacher, there is a large blank map to copy for the students in the CD, titled Chapter 3_V.Blank Map Italy.

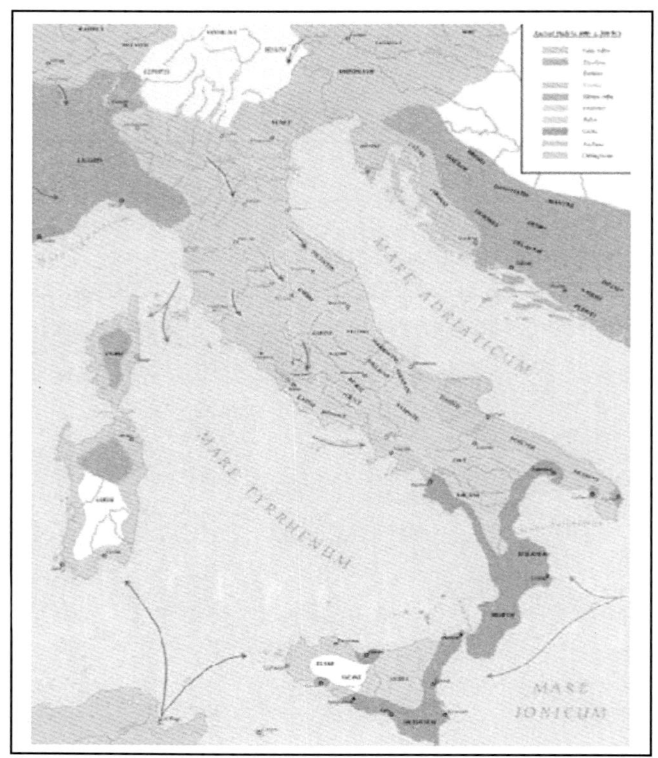

Latin in the Christian Trivium Volume I Teacher's Guide

VI. Exercises

A. Identify the stem and *conjugate seven of the verbs from the vocabulary.
One example:
<u>stem</u> = para
<u>conjugation</u>:
paro, paras, parat
paramus, paratis, parant

B. Translate the following verbs. Look at the ending and notice if the ending shows you that the subject is first, second, or third person, and if it is singular or plural.

1. ambulas = you walk	2/s
cantatis = you sing	2/pl
do = I give	1/sg
2. curamus = we care for	1/pl
salutas = you greet	2/sg
auscultatis = you listen to	2/pl
3. puto = I am thinking	1/sg
putamus = we think	1/pl
spectas = you look at	2/s
4. lacrimatis = you cry	2/pl
sanctificamus = we set apart for God's purpose	1/pl
das = you do give	2/sg
5. amatis = you love	2/pl
laudamus = we are praising	1/pl
spectant = they watch	3/pl
6. portat = he carries	3/sg
cantat = she sings	3/sg
lacrimamus = we cry	1/pl
7. nuntiant = they report	3/pl
nuntiat = he reports	3/sg

---

*To *conjugate* a verb means to give it in all six forms, such as **amo, amas, amat, amamus, amatis, amant.**

laboratis = you work	2/pl
8. honoramus = we honor	1/pl
lacrimo = I cry	1/sg
cantas = you sing	2/sg
9. oppugnatis = you attack	2/pl
pugnatis = you are fighting	2/pl
confirmat = she strengthens	3/sg
10. sanat = he does heal	3/sg
habitamus = we live	1/pl
narrat = she relates	3/sg
11. voco = I am calling	1/sg
paras = you do prepare	2/sg
sanatis = you heal	2/pl
12. rogant = they are asking for	3/pl
superatis = you overcome	2/pl
liberant = they set free	3/pl
13. appellamus = we are naming	1/pl
servatis = you guard	2/pl
sanctificat = he sets apart for God's purpose	3/sg
14. narramus = we relate	1/pl
dat = he gives	3/sg
cantant = they sing	3/pl
15. auscultas = you overhear	2/sg
auscultamus = we overhear	1/pl
damus = we do give	1/pl
16. putant = they are thinking	3/pl
pugnant = they fight	3/pl
spectant = they do watch	3/pl

C. Translate from English to Latin. "You" is singular, unless it says "(pl.)", in which case it is plural.

1. we love = amamus	1/pl
we take care of = curamus	1/pl
you are asking = rogas	2/sg
2. you are looking at = spectatis	2/pl
we set apart for God's purpose = sanctificamus	1/pl

he is carrying = portat	3/sg		they are thinking = putant	3/pl
3. they are relating = narrant	3/pl		5. she is preparing = parat	3/sg
we are crying = lacrimamus	1/pl		they give = dant	3/pl
we do sing = cantamus	1/pl		it cures = sanat	3/sg
4. you attack = oppugnatis	2/pl			
we ask = rogamus	1/pl			
6. we cure = sanam us	1/pl		you are dwelling = habitas	2/sg
you are crying = lacrimas	2/s		he is giving = dat	3/sg
we attack = oppugnamus	1/pl		12. you (sing.) are relating = narras	2/sg
7. it attacks = oppugnat	3/sg		we work = laboramus	1/pl
she strengthens = confirmat	3/sg		we suffer = laboramus	1/pl
she sings = cantat	3/sg		13. she is hard pressed = laborat	3/sg
8. he guards = servat	3/sg		they are giving = dant	3/pl
she is looking at = spectat	3/sg		you do praise = laudas	2/sg
we do weep = lacrimamus	1/pl		14. we heal = sanamus	1/pl
9. you do prepare = paratis	2/pl		we watch = spectamus	1/pl
we are listening to = auscultamus	1/pl		we guard = servamus	1/pl
he likes = amat	3/sg		15. you overhear = auscultatis	2/pl
10. he loves = amat	3/sg		he carries = portat	3/sg
she is loving = amat	3/sg		I set apart for God's purpose	
they love = amant	3/pl		sanctif ico	1/sg
11. I look at = specto	1/sg			

D. Translate sentences into English.
1. Amo ambulare. 2. Amas laborare. 3. Temptamus cantare. 4. Amatis rogare.

D. 1. I like to walk. 2. You like to work. 3. We are trying to sing. 4. You like to ask.

Latin in the Christian Trivium Volume I - Teacher's Guide

Name ____Date ___________________

Latin in the Christian Trivium
Study Sheet
Chapter Three

Grammar

1. How are the person and number of a verb shown in English grammar? <u>They are shown by the pronoun subject.</u>

2. How are the person and number of a Latin verb shown? <u>They are shown by the personal endings of the verbs.</u>

3. Which person is "they"? <u>"They" is 3rd person, plural.</u>

4. In what two ways do Latin verbs agree with their subj ects? <u>Latin verbs agree with their subjects in person and number.</u>

5. Out of the nine things a verb can do, name four. <u>Verbs express action, motion, being, suffering, requests, commands, or affirms, declares, and asks.</u>

6. How do you find the stem of a first conjugation verb? <u>You find the stem of a first conjugation verb by removing the **-re** from the second principal part of the verb.</u>

7. What is another word that means *pattern* or *chart?* <u>A *paradigm* is a pattern or chart.</u>

Verb Work

8. Write the personal endings for the active voice of Latin verbs, and give the English pronoun equivalents.

SINGULAR PERSONAL ENDING	ENGLISH PRONOUN(S)	PLURAL PERSONAL ENDING	ENGLISH PRONOUN
1. o or m	I	1. mus	we
2. s	you	2. tis	you
3. t	he, she, it	3. nt	they

9. Write the conjugation of **ausculto** in the present tense, indicative mood, active voice.

SINGULAR	PLURAL
ausculto	auscultamus
auscultas	auscultatis
auscultat	auscultant

10. Give two of the nine possible translations of **cantat**. <u>(any two of these) he sings, he is singing, he does sing, she sings, she is singing, she does sing, it sings, it does sing, it is singing.</u>

11. After each of the English expressions below write the equivalent Latin word.

I cure	<u>sano</u>	I set apart for God's purpose	<u>sanctifico</u>
I carry	<u>porto</u>	I cry	<u>lacrimo</u>
I praise	<u>laudo</u>	I attack	<u>oppugno</u>

12. Write the number, person, and translation for the following verbs:

	PERSON	NUMBER	TRANSLATION
EX. **nuntiant**	3rd	plural	they announce
a. liberas	2nd	sing.	you set free, you free
b. liberatis	2nd	plural	you set free, you free
c. rogo	1st	sing.	I ask, I ask for
d. damus	1st	plural	we give, we are giving, we do give
e. ambulat	3rd	sing.	he, she, or it walks
f. confirmant	3rd	plural	they strengthen or declare
g. amas	2nd	sing.	you love or you like
h. appellamus	1st	plural	we are naming or calling
i. putatis	2nd	plural	you are thinking
j. nuntiamus	1st	plural	we are reporting or announcing

History

13. Who were four of the tribes who originally settled in what is now called Italy?
<u>Original tribes in Italy include Latins, Hernicans, Aequians, and Volscians.</u>

14. What changes occurred in the area as the Etruscans took control over the land?
<u>The Etruscan kings organized the village of Rome into a powerful and prosperous city.</u>

15. What do we mean by the terms *urban* and *agrarian*?
<u>Urban refers to the city, and agrarian refers to farmland.</u>

Write the four principal parts:

Ex. praise--   laudo, laudare, laudavi, laudatus

1. work, suffer, am hard pressed -- laboro, laborare, laboravi, laboratus
2. honor -- honoro, honorare, honoravi, honoratus
3. walk -- ambulo, ambulare, ambulavi, ambulatus
4. cry, weep -- lacrimo, lacrimare, lacrimavi, lacrimatus
5. call, summon -- voco, vocare, vocavi, vocatus
6. live, dwell -- habito, habitare, habitavi, habitatus
7. love, like -- amo, amare, amavi, amatus
8. look at, watch -- specto, spectare, spectavi, spectatus
9. set free, free -- libero, liberare, liberavi, liberatus
10. give -- do, dare, dedi, datus
11. address, name, call -- appello, appellare, appellavi, appellatus
12. save, guard, protect -- servo, servare, servavi, servatus
13. tell, relate -- narro, narrare, narravi, narratus
14. care for, take care of -- curo, curare, curavi, curatus

WRITE PERSON AND NUMBER, AND TRANSLATE INTO LATIN:

15. we are looking at --	spectamus	1/pl
16. you (pl.) announce ---	nuntiatis	2/pl
17. they do prepare --	parant	3/pl
18. we are listening to --	auscultamus	1/pl
19. I am setting apart for God's purpose --	sanctifico	1/s
20. he thinks --	putat	3/s
21. you think --	putas	2/s
22. we set free --	liberamus	1/pl
23. she is crying --	lacrimat	3/s
24. they are giving --	dant	3/pl
25. we greet --	salutamus	1/pl
26. they attack --	oppugnant	3/pl
27. you (pl.) do sing --	cantatis	2/pl
28. they are calling --	vocant	3/pl
29. we heal --	sanamus	1/pl
30. he saves --	servat	3/s
31. she is guarding --	servat	3/s
32. we praise --	laudamus	1/pl
33. you are declaring --	confirmas	2/s
34. I like --	amo	1/s
35. they cure --	sanant	3/pl
36. we are suffering --	laboramus	1/pl

CAPITOLIUM

Chapter Four Objectives:

At the end of the lesson students will be able to:

- label the case required for each noun in a given sentence.
- recite the endings for each case, singular and plural, for first declension nouns.
- say the meanings for each vocabulary word in the lesson.

<u>**Chapter Four**</u>

1. Enter the phrase at the top of the chapter's first page into the notebook.
2. Read and discuss **I** and **II** in Chapter Four.
3. Copy the boxes in section **IB** following the directions. Merely understanding the material in **IB** is sufficient, but the information in the box, **II Paradigm** has to be memorized.
4. Do **Drill Sheet Four**. Try to do the Drill Sheets orally from now on.
5. Pronounce and discuss section **Vocabulary III**. All of the words labeled "f." should be put on the pink cards. "Poeta" is the only one that you need to put on a blue card. "Propheta" can be either masculine or feminine. It is **very** important to **emphasize** that when the word <u>in</u> is followed by a noun in the accusative case, its meaning is different than when it is followed by a noun in the ablative case.

   (<u>For pre-high schoolers:</u>) Use pink (for feminine) and blue (for masculine) pieces of notebook paper, folded in half the long way up to the holes. Leave the papers folded. The vocabulary words are then written down the columns with the Latin words on the outside. Unfold and then write the English meanings and derivatives on the two inside columns. The vocabulary words are written in black ink.

6. Student must memorize vocabulary by drilling vocabulary cards every day, and drilling each noun in the vocabulary list, until they are all learned.
7. Do the **Study Sheet**.
8. Read and discuss section **IV** of the text. Follow the directions and copy the information in the boxes on page 26 and have the student(s) enter it into his or her notebook.
9. Written work- **V. Exercises**. Teacher reads the Latin; the student echoes. (or uses the CD) to begin Exercise A.
   a. <u>To easily conjugate the verbs</u>, fold a paper in half to make two columns; title the first column "singular" and the second column "plural." Copy the paradigm given in the box on page 25, using different verbs.
   b. Do **Exercises B** and **C**, following the directions in the chapter.
   c. For **Exercise D**, thestudent needs to copy the sentences, leaving a blank line between sentences as he copies them. Then, follow the directions given.
12. Read and discuss **VI**. Teacher may read a sentence aloud; student reads the same sentence after the teacher. Have the student read the sentence in Latin first aloud, then translate it into English orally. Do the same with the questions at the end of the story. Then have the student do the **Reading Lesson** as a written work assignment.
13. Look at the maps in section **VII**. On the top map have the student find the city of Roma and mark it with a red pencil.
On the bottom map have the student find the city of Vercellae and mark it with a red pencil. On the top map, find the approximate location of the city of Vercellae, and mark it with a red map pencil.
14. Review all the material, and then the following day give student **Test Two**.

Chapter Four

Dominus pastor meus; nihil mihi deerit.
The Lord is my shepherd; I shall not want.

First Declension Nouns; Uses of the Nominative Case; Ablative of Place Where; <u>Life in Gaul (pt. I)</u>

A noun is a word that names a person, place or thing. A declension is a family of nouns. In Latin there are five declensions that have different endings which identify them as being part of a particular family of nouns. We identify the declension by noticing the endings of the genitive singular: **-ae, -i, -is, -us,** and **-ei.**

I. Grammar

In Latin, every noun has four properties or qualities: **Number, Gender, Case and Declension.**

Number refers to **Singular** (one) or **Plural** (more than one).

Gender means the sex of the person, place, or thing. There are in Latin, as in English, three genders: **Masculine, Feminine,** and **Neuter.** In English, there is only natural gender; that means male beings are masculine, female beings are feminine, and all others are neuter. In Latin, the gender of a term may be either natural or grammatical. For example: *earth, forest,* and *wisdom* are feminine, *book, field* and *cart* are masculine, *war, heaven,* and *town* are neuter simply because this is the gender assigned to them. Most first declension nouns are feminine, except **agricola,** *farmer,* **nauta,** *sailor,* and **poeta,** *poet.*

A. English Cases

In each of the declensions the various endings show in what "case" the word is. A case means the job (or *function*) of the word is in a particular sentence. You may already know that in English, there are three cases: <u>Nominative</u>, <u>Possessive</u>, and <u>Objective</u>. Notice that in the following sentences we are speaking about a masculine person, a feminine person, and a neuter object. We can use nouns or pronouns, but when we use pronouns we can more easily see that the function in the sentence changes the form of the word.

Marcus drew a *picture* for *Flavia.*	*He* drew *it* for *her.*
Publius saved the *picture* for *Gaius.*	*He* saved *it* for *him.*
Marcus' artwork was similar to *Flavia's* drawing.	*His* artwork was similar to *her* drawing.
The *picture's* similarity to mine was amazing.	*Its* similarity to mine was amazing.

The words *Marcus, Flavia, Publius, Gaius,* and *picture* keep nearly the same form no matter what their function in the sentence. The only change is the addition of *'s* to show possession. But when we use pronouns, the form changes completely. This is an illustration of the way Latin words also change according to their use in a sentence.

B. Latin Cases

Copy this information and put it on the first page in your "Cases/Declensions" section of your notebook.

Cases

Latin has seven cases: **Nominative, Genitive, Dative, Accusative, Ablative, Locative, and Vocative.**
The most commonly used cases and their most <u>common</u> uses in a sentence are:

English Case	Latin Case	Usual Function in a sentence
Nominative	**Nominative**	**Subject, Predicate Nominative**
Possessive	**Genitive**	**Shows possession (of, -'s, or s')**
Objective	**Dative**	**Indirect Object**
Objective	**Accusative**	**Direct Object; Object of some prepositions**
Objective	**Ablative**	**Object of some prepositions**

Each declension is distinguished from the other by the ending of the genitive singular. Each case will have a different ending in Latin, and we will add the ending to the stem of the word. The stem for nouns is found by taking off the genitive singular ending. That is why you learn both the nominative singular and the genitive singular when you learn a vocabulary word.

    rae′da, rae′dae, *carriage.* The genitive form is **raedae**. Remo ve the **-ae** ending and your stem is **raed-**. That is the stem to which we add all the endings.

Raeda

II. Paradigm

    In your notebook in the section "Cases/Declensions", title a page for each of the declensions and cases: First Declension, Second Declension, Third Declension, Fourth Declension, Fifth Declension, Nominative Case, Genitive Case, Dative Case, Accusative Case, and Ablative Case. Vocative Case, and Locative Case may both go on one page. You will have 11 pages titled in all.

The following is a chart of forms for first declension nouns. When you write each word with its different endings it is called *declining* the noun. Again, the stem of a noun is found by removing the genitive singular ending (**-ae** for the first declension). You add the endings to that stem.

Copy this chart onto the page that is titled <u>First Declension</u>. Memorize each ending.

Cases	Singular		Endings	Usual Function
Nom.	patri**a**	*a (the) country*	**-a**	subject
Gen.	patri**ae**	*of a (the) country, the*	**-ae**	possessive
Dat.	patri**ae**	*country's to, for a (the) country*	**-ae**	indirect object
Acc.	patri**am**	*a (the) country*	**-am**	direct object
Abl.	patri**ā**	*by or with a (the) country*	**-a**	obj. of prep.
	Plural			
Nom.	patri**ae**	*the countries*	**-ae**	
Gen.	patri**arum**	*of the countries, the countries'*	**-arum**	
Dat.	patri**is**	*to, for the countries*	**-is**	
Acc.	patri**as**	*the countries*	**-as**	
Abl.	patri**is**	*by or with the countries*	**-is**	

III. Vocabulary   English Derivatives

Write each of these nouns onto a colored index card to use for flash card drills. Use pink cards with black ink for feminine nouns, and blue cards with black ink for masculine nouns. Use white cards with purple ink for the conjunctions, and white cards with blue ink for the verbs, a white card with orange ink for the adverb. You need 21 pink cards, 2 blue cards and 6 white cards.

ān′cīlla, ān′cīllae, f., *handmaiden, maidservant*   (ancillary)
ā′qua, ā′quae, f., *water*   (aquatic, aquamarine)
bālae′na, bālae′nae, f., *whale*
Eurō′pa, Eurō′pae, f., *Europe*
fāmī′līa, fāmī′līae, f., *family*   (familial)
Gāl′līa, Gāl′līae, f., *Gaul*
Ītāl′īa, Ītāl′īae, f., *Italy*
iustī′tīa, iustī′tīae, f., *justice, righteousness*
pā′trīa, pā′trīae, f., *homeland, home, country, fatherland*   (patriotic, expatriate)
pōē′ta, pōē′tae, m., *poet*
prōphē′ta, prōphē′tae, m. or f., *prophet*
prōvin′cīa, prōvin′cīae, f., *province*   (provincial)
puel′la, puel′lae, f., *girl*
rae′da, rae′dae, f., *carriage, coach*
Rō′ma, Rō′mae, f., *Rome*
sāpīen′tīa, sāpīen′tīae, f., *wisdom*
sil′va, sil′vae, f., *forest, woods*   (sylvan, Pennsylvania)
stel′la, stel′lae, f., *star*   (stellar, interstellar)
ter′ra, ter′rae, f., *earth, land, ground*   (terrain)
tū′nīca, tū′nīcae, f., *tunic*
tūr′ba, tūr′bae, f., *common crowd, turmoil, crowd*   (turbulent, disturb)
vī′a, vī′ae, f., *way, road, street*
vīl′la, vīl′lae, f., *house, country home, farmhouse, villa*

et, conj unction, *and*   **est**, irregular verb, *there is, he, she or it is*
sed, conjunction, *but*   **sūnt**, irregular verb, *there are, they are*
-quē, enclitic[*] *and*; <u>may</u> be used when connecting words of like syntax

Use a white card with green ink for the ablative and red ink for the accusative.

in, prep. When followed by a noun in the ablative case, translate as *in* or *on*.
    When followed by a noun in the accusative case, translate as *into* or *against*.

IV. Latin syntax

In the "Cases" section of your notebook page titled <u>Nominative Case</u> copy the following information:

> **Subject.** The subject of a verb is in the Nominative Case.
> **Predicate Nominative.** A noun after a linking verb to define or make a statement about the subject is in the nominative; such a noun is called a *predicate nominative.*
>
> **Italia est patria.** *Italy is (my) homeland.*
> **Feminae sunt ancillae.** *The women are maidservants.*

On the page titled <u>Ablative Cases</u> in the section "Cases/Declensions" copy the following:

> **Ablative of Place Where.** The Ablative case is used after **in** to show the position **in** or **on** something. This construction is called the Ablative of Place Where.
> **In silva cantant.** *They are singing in the forest.*

V. Exercises. There are always several possible answers; you can usually use common sense and figure out alternatives. The most common answers are given.

A. Decline seven of the nouns in the vocabulary like the paradigm shown in Section II.

> **One of the nouns from the vocabulary lesson.**
> villa, *farmhouse*   villae, *farmhouses*
> villae, *of the farmhouse*   villarum, *of farmhouses*
> villae, *to/for a farmhouse*   villis, *to/for farmhouses*
> villam, *the farmhouse*   villas, *farmhouses*
> villa, *by/with a farmhouse*   villis, *by/with farmhouses*

---

[*]An enclitic is a syllable that is attached to a word and gives additional meaning, such as *and*. **-Que** may be used instead of **et** in many cases. Either will be correct even when the answer key only has **–que** given.

B . Give case and number of each noun and then translate into English.

1. provinciis (two ways)	9. vias
2. villam	10. terram
3. familias	11. poetarum
4. Gallia (two ways)	12. puellis (ablative)
5. patriae (three ways)	13. Est silva.
6. stellas	14. Gallia est provincia.
7. balaenis (dative)	15. Puellae sunt in villa.
8. ancillarum	

	CASE	NUMBER	TRANSLATION
1.	dat.	pl.	to/for the provinces
	abl.	pl.	by/with the provinces
2.	acc.	sg.	the farmhouse
3.	acc.	pl.	the families
4.	nom.	sg.	Gaul
	abl.	sg.	by/with Gaul
5.	nom.	pl.	the countries
	gen.	sg.	country's, of a country
	dat.	sg.	to/for a country
6.	acc.	pl.	stars
7.	dat.	pl.	to/for whales
8.	gen.	pl.	of the handmaidens, the handmaidens'
9.	acc.	pl.	roads, ways
10.	acc.	sg.	land, earth
11.	gen.	pl.	of the poets, the poets'
12.	abl.	pl.	by/ with girls
13.	nom.	sg.	There is a forest.
14.	nom.	sg.	Gaul is a province.
15.	nom.	pl.	girls
	abl.	sg.	in the farmhouse; the girls are in the farmhouse.

C. Give case and number of each noun and then translate into Latin.

1. to the handmaidens	7. for Italy
2. the girl (accusative)	8. (with) the families
3. of the carriage	9. of a province
4. forest (nominative)	10. There is Gaul.
5. (with) the way	11. They are girls.
6. a farmhouse (nominative)	12. The province is Gaul.

	CASE	NUMBER	TRANSLATION
1.	dat.	pl.	ancillis
2.	acc.	sg.	puellam
3.	gen.	sg.	raedae
4.	nom.	sg.	silva
5.	abl.	sg.	via
6.	nom.	sg.	villa
7.	dat.	sg.	Italiae
8.	abl.	pl.	familiis
9.	gen.	sg.	provinciae
10.	nom.	sg.	Est Gallia.
11.	nom.	pl.	Sunt puellae.
12.	nom.	sg.	Provincia est Gallia.

D. Translate these phrases, being careful to notice which cases follow each preposition so you will translate them correctly. Teacher, they may use any of the meanings given in the vocabulary, not only the one given in the answer key. (Example: **in** or **against** and **in** or **on**.)

1. in raedā. <u>in the carriage</u>
2. in raedam <u>into the carriage</u>
3. in Galliā <u>in Gaul</u>
4. in Galliam <u>into Gaul</u>
5. in aquā <u>in the water</u>
6. in aquas <u>into the waters</u>
7. in aquis <u>in the waters</u>
8. in aquam <u>into the water</u>
9. in familiā <u>in a family</u>
10. in familiam <u>into the family</u>
11. in provinciā <u>in the province</u>
12. in provinciam <u>against the province</u>
13. in silvā <u>in the forest/ woods</u>
14. in silvam <u>into the forest</u>
15. in silvas <u>into the forests</u>
16. in silvis <u>in the forests</u>
17. in terrā <u>on land</u>
18. in terram <u>into the ground/earth</u>
19. in viā <u>on the road/street</u>
20. in vias <u>into the roads</u>
21. in viis <u>on the roads</u>
22. in viam <u>into the road</u>
23. Balaena in aquā est. <u>A whale is in the water.</u>
24. Balaenae in aquis sunt. <u>Whales are in the waters.</u>
25. Puella in silvā est. <u>The girl is in the forest.</u>
26. Puella in silvam ambulat. <u>The girl is walking into the forest.</u>
27. Familia in viā est. <u>The family is on the street. (or road)</u>
28. Familiae in viam ambulant. <u>The families are walking into the street.</u>
29. Turba in viā est. <u>The common crowd is in the street.</u>
30. Turbae in viis sunt. <u>Common crowds are in the streets.</u>

For the Teacher:
Helps for Translation from Latin to English

1. Underline all endings of words so you can see what case they are in.
2. Notice any prepositional phrases. Circle them; now they are out of the way of the main sentence structure.
3. Look for verb(s). Underline the endings. Notice the tense, person, and number.
4. Look for words which may be in the nominative case, and may function as the subject of the verb.
5. Note any words in the accusative case which have no prepositions preceding them. They might be the direct objects of verbs.
6. Translate the sentence literally at first, and then say the same thought in good English. The goal of translating is to translate the thought, not necessarily the exact words.

For the Teacher:
Review of Translation from English to Latin

1. Circle or put parentheses around all prepositional phrases if there are an y. Write above each circle the preposition needed plus the case which follows it. Example: **cum + abl.**
2. Find the subject next. About *whom* or *what* is the sentence (or clause)? Underline it once and write "nom." (for nominative) above it. Be sure to underline once the adjective which modifies it also.
3. Next, what does the subject *do*? Or what word *links* the subject to a predicate nominative? That will help you identify the verb. Underline the verb with two lines. Notice what person, number and tense it is, and abbreviate that above the word also.
4. For any nouns which show possession or which should be in the genitive case, write "gen." above them.
5. If there is a direct object, the subject does something to someone or something. If there is one, underline it with a wavy line, and write "acc." above it.
6. If the subject "equals" something, then there is a predicate nominative after the linking verb. Write "nom." above any predicate nominatives.
7. Notice any nouns of direct address, adverbs, or conjunctions.
8. Go back through and mark "s." or "pl." for singular or plural; "m., f.," or "n." for masculine, feminine or neuter nouns, pronouns, or adjectives.

E. Mark these sentences by putting prepositional phrases in parentheses (if any), underlining the subject with one line, the verb with two lines and the direct object (if any) with a wavy or dotted line, then translate into Latin.

       nom.s.   3/s.   in + abl. s.   3/s.   acc.s.
1. The family is singing (on the street) and greeting the poet.
      Familia in via cantat et poetam salutat.

       1/pl.   acc.s.   infinitive   1/pl.
2. We are preparing **to sing,** but we do not (**non**) shout.
      Cantare paramus sed non clamamus.

       nom.s. 3/s. acc.s.   dat. pl.
3. The poet gives water (to the handmaidens and girls).
      Poeta aquam ancillis et puellis dat.

       nom.s. 3/s. acc.s.   3/s.   acc.s.
4. The whale likes water and he hears the common crowd.
      Balaena aquam amat et auscultat turbam.

      nom. pl. 3/pl.   in + abl. pl.   3/pl.   dat. pl. acc.s.
5. Prophets live (in the provinces), and they give the poets wisdom.
      Prophetae in provinciis habitant, et poetis sapientiam dant.

      nom. s.   3/s.   in + abl. s.   3/s.   acc.s.
6. The common crowd is (in the street), and *they are asking for land.
      Turba est in via, et terram rogat. (Use "it is asking for" because it is a crowd.)

      nom. pl. 3/pl.   in + acc.s.   3/pl.   acc.s.
7. The girls are walking (into the water), and they like the water.
      Puellae in aquam ambulant, et aquam amant.

      nom.s.   3/s.   acc.s.   nom.s.   3/s.   acc.s.
8. The family is greeting the prophet and the prophet blesses the family.
      Familia prophetam salutat et propheta familiam consecrat (or *sanctificat*).

      3/s.   acc.s.   3/s. adv.
9. She is preparing the coach but she is not watching.
      Parat raedam sed non spectat.

      3/s.   nom.s.   in + abl. s. conj. adv.   in + abl. s.
10. There is wisdom (in Europe) but not (in the common crowd).
      Est sapientia in Europa sed non in turba.

---

*Some use "they", considering that a crowd is a group; either singular or plural is correct.

VI. Reading Lesson

Read aloud and translate. Remember, the second principal part of a verb is translated like curare, *to care for.* **(-re** = *to*)

Vita (Life) in Galliā (part one)

Est familia in Vercellis (**Vercellis** = the city of *Vercellae*) in Galliā. Roma est patria familiae sed habitant in Galliā. Gallia est provincia in Europā. Roma est in Italiā, et Italia est in Europā. Fidelia et Priscilla sunt puellae in familiā. Puellae amant ambulare et cantare in silvā et in villā et in viā. Clara est ancilla. Curat puellas. In villā Clara puellis aquam dat. Puellae Claram amant.

<u>Reading Lesson</u>

Life in Gaul (Part one)

There is a family in Vercellae in Gaul. Rome is the homeland of the family, but they live in Gaul. Gaul is a province in Europe. Rome is in Italy, and Italy is in Europe. Fidelia and Priscilla are the girls in the family. The girls like to walk and sing in the forest, and in the farmhouse, and on the road. Clara is a handmaiden. She takes care of the girls. In the farmhouse Clara gives the girls water. The girls love Clara.

Responde Latine. Answer in a complete sentence.

1. Qui *(who)* sunt puellae?
2. Ubi *(where)* habitant?
3. Ubi est Gallia?
4. Ubi est Italia?
5. Ubi puellae cantant?
6. Quis *(who)* est ancilla?

1. Who are the girls? Puella sunt Fidelia et Priscilla.
2. Where do they live? Habitant in Vercellis.
3. Where is Gaul? Gallia est in Europa.
4. Where is Italy? Italia est in Europa.
5. Where do the girls sing? Cantant in silva, in villa, et in via.
5. Who is the handmaiden? Clara est ancilla.

VII. Map of the Province of Gaul

This is the <u>Province</u> of Gallia where our Roman family lives, just north of Roma on the southern side of the Alps, but there is also a country Gallia. It has three provinces occupied by the Belgae, Celtae, and Aquitani. Color these three provinces on the map, yellow, pink, and light blue and circle Vercellae on the bottom map.

Teacher: *there is a larger map on the CD, titled* Chapter 4 - VII. Map of the Province of Gaul.

TEACHER: If you want to include the mythological stories about the founding of Rome, we are continuing on with *The Story of the Romans* by H. A. Guerber.

ESCAPE FROM THE BURNING CITY

In the days when the Greeks were fighting against Troy,—that great city in Asia Minor which the y besieged for ten years,—the people in Italy were divided into several small kingdoms, among which were those of the Etruscans and the Latins.

The Etruscans occupied the northern part of Italy, or the top of the boot, and called their country Etruria, while the Latins dwelt farther south, in a province named Latium. Each of these kingdoms had its own leader or king, whom all the people obeyed.

Now the King of Latium in those days was Latinus. He had a beautiful daughter called Lavinia, and as soon as she was old enough to marry, he thought of getting her a good husband. One night King Latinus dreamed that the gods of his country came and spoke to him, telling him to be sure and give his daughter in marriage to a stranger whom they would send to Latium.

When Latinus awoke, he was very much troubled, because his wife was anxious that Lavinia should marry Turnus, a neighboring king. The queen soon persuaded Latinus to allow this engagement to take place, but he insisted that the marriage should be postponed for some time longer. In the meanwhile the city of Troy had at last fallen into the hands of the Greeks. The brave Trojans were attacked by night, and only a few among them managed to escape death.

Among these few, however, there was a prince named Æneas. His father was Anchises, the cousin of the King of Troy, and his mother was Venus, the goddess of beauty. As Venus did not want her son to die with the rest of the Trojans, she appeared to him during the fatal night when the Greeks had secretly entered Troy, and were plundering and burning the houses. She showed him that resistance would be useless, and bade him flee from the city, with all his family. Æneas had been taught to obey every word the gods said; so he at once stopped fighting, and hurried back to his house. Then he lifted his poor old father up on his back, took his little son Iulus by the hand, and called to his wife and servants to follow him. This strange group of fugitives quickly passed out of the city, where the flames were now rising on all sides, and, under cover of the darkness, made their way to a temple near by.

Here they paused to rest, and Æneas counted his followers to make sure that they were all there. Imagine his sorrow when he found that his beloved wife was missing! He rushed back into the burning city, and searched everywhere for her, calling her name aloud, in spite of the danger. At last he met someone who told him that his wife had been killed, and that she wished him to escape to a better country, where he should found a new kingdom, and where a new wife should take her place, and make him happy once more. Æneas sorrowfully turned back, and at the temple found that his followers had been joined by others who had managed to escape unseen amid the smoke and darkness. He led the way to a place of safety, and not long afterwards set sail with his little band of faithful Trojans, who all promised to obey and follow him wherever he went.

The ships drifted aimlessly for a long time, because Æneas had no idea where he was to found his new kingdom. Twice he tried to settle down, but each time something happened to drive him away. Finally he asked the advice of his father, Anchises, a wise and pious old man, who had snatched up his gods when he left his house, and had brought them with him on the ship. The old man now said that he would consult these images, and he offered them a sacrifice. The next night Æneas dreamed that the gods spoke to him and told him that he should go to Italy, a land whence one of his ancestors had come to Troy.

The little band therefore sailed for the west, although it was foretold that they would have to suffer many hardships before they could reach Italy, and that they would not be able to settle until they had eaten the very boards upon which their food was served. As Æneas was a brave man, the prospect of a terrible famine did not fill his heart with despair, and he calmly sailed on in search of a home. There are almost countless islands in that part of the Mediterranean, and thus the boats were seldom out of sight of land. They stopped from time to time, but Æneas did notdare to settle anywhere, because he thought the gods opposed it; and he always urged his people to embark again and sail on. The Trojans were by this time very tired of sailing, but they loved Æneas so well that they gladly followed him, although they would have liked to make their homes in the islands they visited.

A ROMAN FAMILY

Latin in the Christian Trivium
Study Sheet
Chapter Four

Grammar

1. What is a definition of a declension? A declension is a family of nouns.
2. How is a noun determined to be in a particular declension? It is found to be in a particular declension by noticing the ending of the genitive singular form.
3. What are the three cases of nouns and pronouns in English? The cases of nouns in English are nominative, possessive, and objective.
4. What are the four ways we identify a Latin noun? The four properties of a Latin noun are number, gender, case, and declension.
5. Of what gender are most first declension nouns? Most first declension nouns are feminine.
6. What are the exceptions? Exceptions are **agricola**, **nauta**, and **poeta**.
7. With what letter do first declension nouns end in the nominative singular? a
   With what letters in the genitive singular? ae
8. How is the stem of a Latin noun determined? The stem is determined by dropping the genitive singular ending.
9. What is the stem of **patria** to which the different endings are added? The stem of patria is **patri-**.

Noun Work

10. Complete the declension of **turba.**

CASE	LATIN WORD	ENGLISH MEANING	ENDING
Singular			
Nom.	turba	*crowd*	-a
Gen.	turbae	*of a crowd*	-ae
Dat.	turbae	*to/for a crowd*	-ae
Acc.	turbam	*crowd*	-am
Abl.	turba	*by/with a crowd*	-a
Plural			
Nom.	turbae	*crowds*	-ae
Gen.	turbarum	*crowds'*	-arum
Dat.	turbis	*to/for crowds*	-is
Acc.	turbas	*crowds*	-as
Abl.	turbis	*by/with crowds*	-is

11. After each of the Latin words fill in the blanks with the correct information.

	GENITIVE	GENDER	ENGLISH MEANING
puella	puellae	f.	girl
sapientia	sapientiae	f.	wisdom
stella	stellae	f.	star
balaena	balaenae	f.	whale
Europa	Europae	f.	Europe
turba	turbae	f.	crowd
villa	villae	f.	farmhouse
provincia	provinciae	f.	province

12. Fill in the blanks with the case, number, and a translation of each word listed.

	CASE	NUMBER	TRANSLATION
EXAMPLE: **turbarum**	genitive	plural	of the crowds
a. **familiarum**	gen.	pl.	families', of the families
b. **sapientiam**	acc.	sg.	wisdom
c. **silvis**	dat.	pl.	to/for forests
	abl.	pl.	by/with forests
d. **ancillae**	gen.	sg.	of the handmaiden, handmaiden's
(three ways)	dat.	sg.	to/for the handmaiden
	nom.	pl.	the handmaidens
e. **viā**	abl.	sg.	by/with the way
f. **provinciis**	dat.	pl.	to/for the provinces
	abl.	pl.	by/with the provinces
g. **tunicas**	acc.	pl.	the tunics
h. **terrae**	gen.	sg.	the earth's, of the earth
(three ways)	dat.	sg.	to/for the earth
	nom.	pl.	the earths
i. **familiis**	dat.	pl.	to/for families
	abl.	pl.	by/with families
j. **silvam**	acc.	sg.	a forest

13. Underline the English word groups which correctly translate the Latin verbs.

a. **portamus**	<u>we are carrying</u>	you carry	I carry
b. **amant**	they are loved	we love	<u>they love</u>
c. **spectat**	<u>he is looking at</u>	she looked at	they looked
d. **oppugnatis**	we attack	<u>you are attacking</u>	he prepares
e. **laudas**	he praises	we praise	<u>you praise</u>
f. **parant**	he prepares	<u>they are preparing</u>	we prepare
g. **cantat**	we sing	I am singing	<u>he is singing</u>
h. **ambulo**	I walked	<u>I walk</u>	he walks

Mark and Translate.   (One line under the subject and two under the verb)

nom. sg. 3/sg.
14. Puella amat. The girl loves.

nom. pl.   3/pl.
15. Prophetae oppugnant. Prophets attack.

nom. pl. 3/pl.
16. Ancillae laudant. Handmaidens praise.

nom. pl. 3/pl.
17. Puellae vocant. Girls call.

nom. pl.   3/pl.
18. Poetae laudant. The poets praise.

nom. pl.   3/pl.
19. The handmaidens are calling. Ancillae vocant.

nom. pl. 3/pl.
20. The girls are praising. Puellae laudant.

nom. sg.   3/sg.
21. The poet is calling. Poeta vocat.

nom. sg.   3/sg.
22. The handmaiden prepares. Ancilla parat.

nom. s g. 3/sg.
23. The poet loves. Poeta amat.

DRILL SHEET AFTER CHAPTER FOUR

TRANSLATE INTO LATIN:

1.   tunics - accusative plural - tunicas
2.   of whales - genitive plural - balaenarum
3.   fatherlands - nominative plural - patriae
4.   wisdom - dative singular - sapientiae
5.   forest - accusative singular - silvam
6.   stars - ablative plural - stellis
7.   common crowds - accusative plural - turbas
8.   prophets - nominative plural - prophetae
9.   water - dative singular - aquae
10. earth - ablative singular - terra
11. maidservant - dative singular - ancillae
12. Gaul - nominative singular - Gallia
13. families - genitive plural- familiarum

14. whales - dative plural - <u>balaenis</u>
15. roads - accusative plural- <u>vias</u>
16. star - accusative singular- <u>stellam</u>
17. forests - nominative plural- <u>silvae</u>
18. family - accusative singular- <u>familiam</u>
19. prophets - genitive plural- <u>prophetarum</u>
20. provinces - dative plural- <u>provinciis</u>
21. water - accusative singular - <u>aquam</u>

TRANSLATE INTO ENGLISH. TRY TO FIGURE OUT THE MEANINGS OF WORDS THAT ARE SIMILAR TO ENGLISH WORDS. IF YOU CANNOT FIGURE THEM OUT, LOOK IN THE VOCABULARY AT THE BACK OF THE TEXTBOOK.

GALLIA

Gallia est in Europā. Gallia est provincia. Italia est in Europā. Germania est in Europā. Roma est in Italiā, et Genava in Helvetiā. Poetae in Italiā sunt. Feminae et puellae in Italiā et in Germaniā sunt. Propheta in provinciā est. Poeta naturam amat.

Translation

<table><tr><td> Gaul Gaul is in Europe. Gaul is a province. Italy is in Europe. Germany is in Europe. Rome is in Italy, and Geneva is in Switzerland. The poets are in Italy. The women and girls are in Italy and in Germany. The prophet is in the province. The poet loves nature.</td></tr></table>

Test Two to be taken after the completion of Chapter Four
Grammar Section

1. What are the names of the five most commonly used cases in Latin? <u>Nominative, Genitive, Dative, Accusative, Ablative</u>

2. In what case is the subject of a verb? <u>The subject of a verb is in the Nominative case.</u>

3. In what case is the direct object of a verb? <u>The direct object of a verb is in the Accusative case.</u>

4. In what two cases are the objects of most Latin prepositions?
   <u>Objects of most prepositions are usually in the Accusative or Ablative cases.</u>

5. In what case is the indirect object of a verb? <u>Indirect object of a verb is in the Dative case.</u>

6. Is English a structured or an inflected language? <u>English is a structured language.</u>

7. Is Latin a structured or an inflected language? <u>Latin is an inflected language.</u>

8. A chart or pattern is called <u>a paradigm</u>.

9. How do you find the stem of a Latin noun? <u>To find the stem of a Latin noun, remove the genitive singular ending.</u>

10. How do you find the stem of a first conjugation Latin verb? <u>To find the stem of a first conjugation Latin verb, remove the **–re** ending of the second principal part.</u>

11. When we want to express Place Where, in what case is the noun following the preposition?
    <u>The Ablative case is used to express Place Where.</u>

12. A noun after a linking verb is called a Predicate Nominative and is in the <u>Nominative</u> case.

History and Culture Section

13. What is the name of the Egyptian style of writing? <u>Egyptian writing is called *hieroglyphics.*</u>

Latin in the Christian Trivium – Volume I Teacher's Guide

14. What is another name for Semites?   <u>Semites are also called Jews.</u>
15. Which nation added vowel sounds to their alphabet? <u>The Greeks added vowel sounds to the alphabet.</u>
16. What is a bulla?   <u>A bulla is a good luck charm worn by boys and girls.</u>
17. Name two items of clothing that the Romans wore. <u>Items of clothing include: tunics, stolas, pallas, and togas.</u>
18. What is the name of the group of people who came to Italy from the Mediterranean region and settled there? <u>Etruscans settled in Italy, probably coming from the region near Troy.</u>
19. Who were the Latins, the Hernicans, the Aequians, and the Volscians? <u>Latins, Hernicans, Aequians, and Volscians were the names of tribes living in Italy.</u>

Translation Section

20. Decline in Latin one of these two nouns in all five commonly used cases: **crowd** or **star**.

SINGULAR	PLURAL	SINGULAR	PLURAL
turba	turbae	stella	stellae
turbae	turbarum	stellae	stellarum
turbae	turbis	stellae	stellis
turbam	turbas	stellam	stellas
turba	turbis	stella	stellis

21. Conjugate one of these two verbs in Latin: **look at** or **honor**.

specto	spectamus	honoro	honoramus
spectas	spectatis	honoras	honoratis
spectat	spectant	honorat	honorant

Translate these sentences, writing the case and number above the word. If there are several possibilities, consider each until you look at the rest of the sentence and determine the context.

    nom.pl. 3/pl. acc.s.
22. Balaenae amant aquam.   Whales like water.

    nom.s. 3/s. in + abl.s.
23. Familia est in Galliā.   The family is in Gaul.

    acc.s.   1/s.
24. Turbam saluto.   I greet the crowd.   (or I am greeting the crowd.)

Vocabulary Work

Looking at the following words, and you will notice that the word in capital letters has part of a Latin word in it. Circle that root word and then figure out what the word probably means. Then circle the closest meaning of the possible definitions given:

25. AQUATIC a). relating to horses b). study of fish <u>c). dealing with water</u> d). upside down
26. PATRIOT <u>a). one who displays love of country</u> b). father of a large family
    c). Revolutionary War soldier d). a buyer
27. TERRAIN <u>a). a landscape</u> b). a type of car c). flat, plateau-like d). belonging to Teresa
28. LAUDATORY a). notable <u>b). praiseworthy</u> c). high volume, loud d). a washroom
29. AMICABLE a). ignorant b). dealing with guns c). able to tolerate <u>d). loving</u>

Chapter Five Objectives:

At the end of the lesson students will be able to:

- define a conjunction.
- recite from memory the conjugation of **sum** in the present tense.
- identify direct objects in a sentence.
- say the meanings for each vocabulary word in the lesson.
- compose a sentence using a Complementary Infinitive.
- state the rule of Agreement of subject and predicate (verb).
- point out Roma, Jerusalem, Caesarea, the island of Crete, the Mediterranean Sea, the Atlantic Ocean and the Black Sea on a map.

<u>Chapter Five</u>

1. Copy the Latin phrase from the box at the beginning of Chapter Five.
2. Read and explain section **I**.
3. Copy information in the boxes following the instructions.
4. Memorize chart on the conjugation of "sum" in section **I D**.
5. Read and discuss **I A - E.**
6. Put Vocabulary (**II**) words on cards.
    For those needing the extra practice, add feminine nouns to the pink vocabulary sheet; add the one masculine noun to the blue sheet. Add the one verb to the white verb sheet, in blue ink, and put the one adverb on a white sheet of paper with orange ink. Put the two conjunctions on white paper with purple ink.

7. Do the **Drill Sheet.**
8. Do the **Study Sheet.** The teacher will need to help the student by giving an example sentence. Examples are given here.

    a. <u>Puella</u> cantat. b. Propheta est <u>poeta</u>. c. Ancilla <u>raedam</u> parat.
    d. Ambulamus <u>in via</u>. e. <u>Sunt</u> stellae.

9. Discuss the map in **III**. Circle Rome, Jerusalem, Caesarea, the island of Crete. Color the Mediterranean Sea, the Atlantic Ocean, the Black Sea blue.

10.   Do **Exercises A** and **B** in the chapter text.

11. **Exercise C**. At this point, you really need to stress marking
the Latin and English sentences. This becomes even more important as
the sentences become more difficult.

To mark a Latin sentence:

        nom .pl. acc. s. gen. pl.   3/pl.
        Puellae   gloriam feminarum honorant.

To mark an English sentence:

    nom.s.   gen. s.   3/s   acc. s.
    The poet (of Italy) is praising the fatherland.

12. Reading **Lesson V**. Have the student say each Latin sentence, and then
translate it into good English. When you are finished with the Reading Lesson,
ask the student to summarize what you have just read.

13. Continue to drill and quiz. Be sure your student understands and has done all
the work before going on.

Chapter Five

Conjugation of Sum; Conjunctions;
Direct Object; <u>Life in Gaul (pt. II)</u>

I. Grammar

A. Conjunctions are words that connect words, phrases, clauses, or sentences. Some conjunctions also have the double purpose of introducing a clause and connecting it with the rest of the sentence. A clause is a complete thought; therefore, a sentence is a clause.

This chart is to be copied and put in the "Grammar" section on a page titled <u>Conjunctions</u>.

Conjunctions

There are three kinds of conjunctions:

1. Coordinating, those that connect words, phrases, or clauses which are equal, such as *and, but, for, nor, or, so, yet;*

2. Correlative, which are coordinating conjunctions that are used in pairs such as *both…and, either…or, neither…nor, not only…but also, whether…or;*

3. Subordinating, those that introduce and connect subordinate clauses to main clauses, such as *after, although, as, because, before, if, since, when, where, while,* and so on. Some subordinating conjunctions can be used as prepositions but when they are used to connect a clause to another clause, they are considered conjunctions in that sentence.

B. Direct Objects

In your notebook, on a page titled, <u>Accusative Case</u> in the section "Cases/Declensions", write the following:

Direct Objects.   A direct object is a noun or pronoun that is immediately affected by the action of a verb. In English, the direct object of a verb is in the Objective case. In Latin it is in the Accusative Case.

> **Amamus patriam.** *We love the homeland.*
> **Puellas feminasque curat.** *He cares for girls and women.*

C. Linking verbs

A linking verb is one which means that the subject of the sentence "equals" something else. The most common linking verb is "is", which is "est" in Latin. The first principal part of "est" is "sum." It is an irregular verb, but it has the regular personal endings.

Copy this chart and put it in the "Conjugation" section of your notebook on a page that you title <u>Irregular Verbs</u>.

The four principal parts of sum are **sum**, *I am*, **esse**, *to be*, **fui**, *I have been* or *I was*, **futurus**, *about to be.*

Present Tense

sūm	*I am*	sū′mus	*we are*
es	*you are*	es′tis	*you are*
est	*he, she, it is*	sūnt	*they are,*
	there is		*there are*

D. Agreement of verb and subject

Write the following information and put it in the "Grammar" section on the page titled <u>Verbs</u>.

Agreement. A verb agrees with its subject in person and number:
Femin**ae** ambula**nt**. *The women are walking.* (both 3rd person plural)
Poet**a** ancillam saluta**t**. *The poet greets the maidservant.* (both 3rd person singular)

E. Complementary Infinitives

Copy this chart and put it on the page titled <u>Verbs</u> in the "Grammar" section.

Complementary Infinitives. Some verbs do not take a direct object, but they are completed by the infinitive *(to do, to love, to study, to run)* of another verb, such as the following examples. *I want to go. I like to study. You ought to learn.*
The infinitive form of a Latin verb is its second principal part.
Puellae amant ambulare et cantare in silvā et in villā et in viā.
The girls like to walk and to sing in the forest, farmhouse, and on the road.

II. Vocabulary – more first declension nouns -   English Derivatives

Put the feminine nouns on pink cards with black ink (14) and the masculine nouns on blue with black ink. (2) Put conjunctions on white cards with purple ink (2) and adverbs on white cards with orange ink (1) and verbs on white with blue ink (1).

agri′cōla, agri′cōlae, m., *farmer*   (agriculture)
āmicī′tīa, āmicī′tīae, f., *friendship*
ēpis′tūla, ēpis′tūlae f., *letter*   (epistle)
fa′būla, fa′būlae, f., *story, fable*
fē′mīna, fē′mīnae, f., *woman, wife*   (feminine)
fī′līa, fī′līae, f., *daughter*   (filial)
        (**filia** is irregular in two forms; the dative and ablative plural are **fīlīā′būs**.)
fōrtū′na, fōrtū′nae, f., *fortune, luck, chance*
glō′rīa, glō′rīae, f., *glory*
in′sūla, in′sūlae, f., *island, apartment*   (insulate, peninsula)
lin′gua, lin′guae, f., *language, tongue*   (linguist)
lit′tera, lit′terae, f., *letter* (of the alphabet); pl., *epistle or letters* (literature)
mēmō′rīa, mēmō′rīae, f., *memory*
nātū′ra, nātū′rae, f., *nature*
nau′ta, nau′tae, m., *sailor*

tū′ba, tū′bae, f., *trumpet*

vī′ta, vī′tae, f., *life, mode of life*   (vital, vitality, vitamin)

et′iām, conj unction, *also, and also, even*

[6]**ne′quē…ne′quē,** conjunction, *neither…nor*

nōn, adverb, *not*

sūm, es′sē, fū′ī, fūtū′rūs, *be, am, are, is*

III.   Map of the Roman Empire

Be able to locate Judea, the Adriatic Sea, Jerusalem, Corsica, Sicily, Britain, the Mediterranean Sea, and the Black Sea.

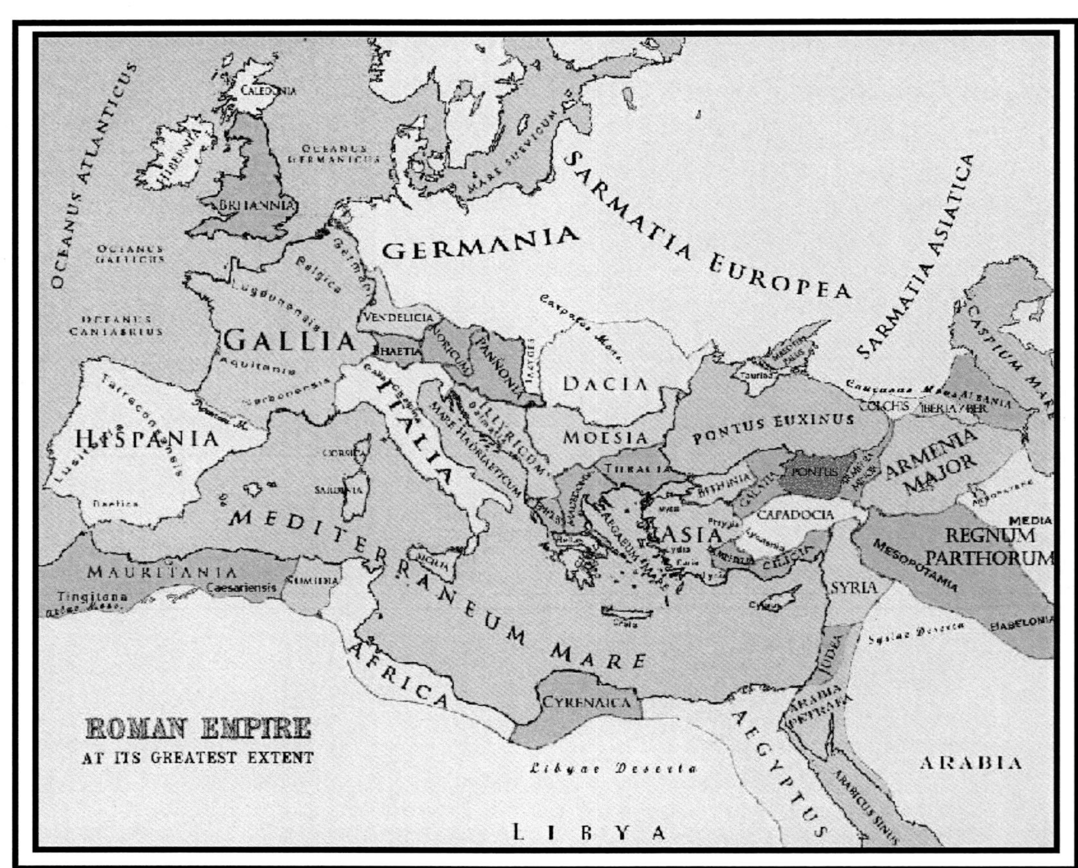

---

[6]When used two times in a sentence.

IV. Exercises

A. Decline all the new nouns in the vocabulary lesson.

	SINGULAR	PLURAL
Nom.	littera	litterae
Gen.	litterae	litterarum
Dat.	litterae	litteris
Acc.	litteram	litteras
Abl.	littera	litteris

B. Give the case and number of each noun, person and number of each verb and translate.

1.   nom. pl. in + abl.s. 1st/pl.
   Poetae in Italiā sumus.   We are poets in Italy.

2.   nom.s. abl. s. in + abl.s. 3/s.
   Puella in villā in Romā est.   The girl is in the farmhouse in Rome.

3.   nom. pl. acc. pl. acc. s. 3/pl.
   Poetae agricolas amicitiam rogant.   The poets are asking the farmers for friendship.

4.   nom. pl. 3/pl. dat. pl. acc.pl.
   Feminae parant poetis tubas.   The women prepare the trumpets for the poets.

5.   acc. s. in + abl.s. 2/s
   Vitam in terrā sanctificas.   You set apart (your) life on earth for God's purpose.

6.   nom. pl. acc. s. gen. pl. 3/pl.
   Puellae gloriam feminarum honorant. The girls honor the glory of women.

7.   nom.s. 1/s. adv. nom. s.
   Puella sum non femina.   I am a girl not a woman.

8.   nom.s. 3/s abl. sg. conj. nom.s. adv.
   Poeta laborat in villā, sed agricola non.
   The poet works in the farmhouse but the farmer does not.

9.   nom. pl acc. pl. in + abl.s. 3/pl.
   Agricolae familias in Galliā liberant.   The farmers set the families in Gaul free.

10.   nom. s. acc. s. 3/s.
    Amicitia patriam confirmat.   Friendship strengthens the homeland.

11.   3/s. nom. s.
    Putat poeta.   The poet is thinking.

12.	Femina familias in villā in Galliā curat.
	The woman cares for the families in the house in Gaul.

C. Translate from English to Latin.

First, put parentheses around prepositional phrases, if any; underline the subject with one line, the verb with two, and the direct object with a wavy line. Then note the case of each word above it.

> **REMINDER**: Remember that the subject and verb must agree in person and number. If the subject is plural, you know that the verb is plural. Mark it as soon as you determine that. Then notice if the subject is "I, you," or "someone else," *first, second*, or *third* person. Mark it accordingly.

The farmer   (in Rome)   is carrying   water.

Agricola (in) Romā* aquam portat.

> First, circle or put parentheses around prepositional phrases; then underline verb with 2 lines; then underline subject with one line; last underline direct object of each verb (if any) with either a dotted line or a wavy line.

1. I am strengthening the memory (of the girl).
	Memoriam puellae confirmo.

2. The handmaidens are carrying water (into the house).
	Ancillae aquam in villam portant.

3. Girls and women love friendship.
	Puellae et feminae amicitiam amant.

4. The poet is praising the fatherland.
	Poeta patriam laudat.

5. The farmhouse is (in Rome) and we live in Rome.
	Villa est in Roma et habitamus in Roma.

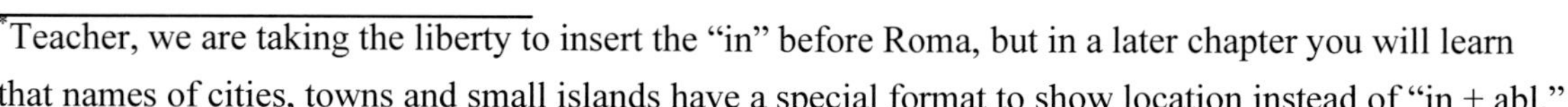

---

*Teacher, we are taking the liberty to insert the "in" before Roma, but in a later chapter you will learn that names of cities, towns and small islands have a special format to show location instead of "in + abl."

Also, the students do not have to put the line above the **a** (**ā**). It is done in Latin to help them identify the ablative case, but may have been inadvertently omitted now and then. It is not necessary, only a help.

    1/pl.   conj.   nom.pl.   nom .pl. 1/pl. nom .pl

6. <u>We are</u> neither <u>farmers</u> nor <u>poets</u>; <u>we are women</u>.
    Sumus neque agricolae neque poetae; sumus feminae.

> To be perfectly proper, you do not have to repeat the "sumus" in the second part of sentence #6. It is understood to be there. Either way is acceptable.

    nom. s. 3/s   acc. pl.

7. The <u>family is asking</u> the <u>prophets</u> for
acc.s.
<u>wisdom</u>.
  Familia prophetas sapientiam
  rogat.

     3/s   nom.s.   abl.s.

8. <u>There is</u> a <u>forest</u> (on the island.)
    Est silva in insula.

> The subject of this sentence is "forest."

   nom.pl. 3/pl.   3/s.   acc. s.

9. The <u>girls honor</u> and <u>love</u> the <u>family</u>.
    Puellae familiam honorant et
    amant.

     3/s   acc.s.   (in + abl.s.)

10. <u>He is guarding</u> the <u>girl</u> (in the common
crowd).
    Puellam in turba servat.

    3/pl.   conj.   3/pl.

11. <u>They are suffering</u> and <u>they are crying</u>.
    Laborant et lacrimant.

  nom. pl. 3/pl. infinitive   acc.s.

12. The <u>poets</u> <u>like</u> **to praise** <u>righteousness</u>.
    Poetae iustitiam laudare amant.

> "**To praise**" is in bold print. It is a complementary inf initive, completing the verb, "like." Have students put a <u>box</u> around infinitive phrases when they are marking a sentence.
>
> In English, the entire phrase, "to praise righteousness" functions as the direct object of the verb, "like." However, that concept may be confusing to beginning students.

V. Reading Lesson   Read aloud and translate.

Vita in Galliā (part two)

Clara puellas curat, sed etiam Fidelia Priscillam curat. Fidelia Priscillam amat et Priscilla Fideliam amat. Familia puellarum in villā habitat. Fidelia et Priscilla agricolas spectant. Agricolae in terrā familiae puellarum laborant. Fidelia et Priscilla in silvā ambulare et naturam spectare amant. Aquam portant. Poetas in silvā auscultant. Poetae sapientiam et iustitiam laudant. Femina villae est Aquila. Clara filias in villam vocat. Amant vitam in provinciā Galliā.

<u>Reading Lesson</u>

Life in Gaul (part two)

Clara takes care of the girls, but Fidelia also takes care of Priscilla. Fidelia loves Priscilla, and Priscilla loves Fidelia. The family of the girls live in the country in a farmhouse. Fidelia and Priscilla look at the farmers. The farmers work on the land of the family of the girls.
Fidelia and Priscilla like to walk in the forest and look at nature. They are carrying water. They listen to the poets in the forest. The poets praise wisdom and justice. The woman (or, *lady*) of the farmhouse is Aquila. Clara calls the daughters into the farmhouse. They like life in the province of Gaul.

Responde Latine. Answer in a complete sentence.

1. Quem *(whom)* Fidelia et Priscilla spectant?
2. Ubi Priscilla et Fidelia ambulare amant?
3. Quos *(whom)* auscultant in silvā?
4. Quid *(what)* poetae laudant?
5. Quis *(who)* filias vocat?
6. Ubi est Aquila?

Signa Romana

<u>Questions</u>
1. Whom do Fidelia and Priscilla watch? Fidelia et Priscilla agricolas spectant.
2. Where do Priscilla and Fidelia like to walk? Priscilla et Fidelia in silva ambulare amant.
3. Whom do they listen to in the forest? Poetas auscultant.
4. What do the poets praise? Poetae sapientiam et iustitiam laudant.
5. Who calls the daughters? Aquila filias vocat.
6. Where is Aquila? Aquila est in villa.

Inside the
Vatican
Museum

Name ____Date __________________

Latin in the Christian Trivium
Study Sheet
Chapter Five

Grammar
1. What are the regular personal endings of verbs in the active voice?
   Sing. (1) <u>-o or -m</u> (2) <u>-s</u> (3) <u>-t</u>
   Plural (1) <u>-mus</u> (2) <u>-tis</u> (3) <u>-nt</u>

2. Write the conjugation of the verb **sum**, *to be,* in Latin in the present tense and opposite each word write its English equivalent.

LATIN	ENGLISH		LATIN	ENGLISH
SINGULAR			PLURAL	
sum	I am		sumus	we are
es	you are		estis	you are
est	he, she it is		sunt	they are
	there is			there are

3. Write an original Latin sentence illustrating each of the following constructions:
<u>Answers vary.</u>

    a. The nominative as the subject of a verb: ____________________________
    b. A predicate nominative: ____________________________________
    c. The direct object of a verb: __________________________________
    d. The ablative of place where: __________________________________
    e. The predicate use (*there is, there are*) of **sum**: ____________________

Practice
To help you master the different forms of **sum**, underline the correct translation of each sentence.

4. **Puellae estis**.   We are girls. <u>You are girls.</u> The girls are. They are girls.
5. **In Italiā sum**.   We are in Italy. Italy is near. <u>I am in Italy.</u>
6. **Es poeta**.   The poet is. <u>You are a poet.</u> Is he a poet?
7. **Sunt litterae**.   <u>There are letters.</u> We are littering. Here is a letter.

Sentences Write and mark the translation of the following. (Mark these sentences with your student and then let him or her translate them for credit.)

8. Ancilla poetam curat. <u>The handmaiden cares for (or takes care of) the poet.</u>
9. Tunicam portamus. <u>We are carrying the tunic.</u>
10. Spectat stellas. <u>He is looking at the stars. (or *she is…*)</u>

11. Filia feminam et ancillam vocat. <u>The daughter is calling the woman and the handmaiden.</u>
12. Poetae putant. <u>Poets are thinking.</u>
13. Puellae balaenas spectant. <u>The girls are looking at the whales.</u>
14. Feminae ambulant in silvā. <u>Women walk in the forest.</u>
15. Honoramus sapientiam et iustitiam. <u>We honor wisdom and righteousness.</u>
16. Puella poetam auscultat. <u>The girl is listening to the poet.</u>
17. Non ausculto turbam, sed prophetam. <u>I do not listen to the common crowd, but to the prophet.</u>
18. Patriam servant. <u>They save the country.</u>
19. Amat amicitiam. <u>She likes friendship.</u>
20. Damus aquam agricolis. <u>We are giving water to the farmers.</u>

Understanding the Cases
21. In sentence 8, **poetam** is in the <u>accusative</u> case because<u> it is the direct object of the </u>
<u>verb, "curat."</u>

22. In sentence 9, **tunicam** is in the <u>accusative</u> case because <u>it is the direct object of </u>
<u>the verb,"portamus."</u>

23. In sentence 12, **poetae** is in the <u>nominative</u> case because <u>it is the subject of the verb.</u>

24. In sentence 13, **balaenas** is in the <u>accusative</u> case because <u>it is the direct object of "spectant."</u>

25. In sentence 14, **silvā** is in the <u>ablative</u> case because <u>it is the object of the preposition "in", </u>
<u>and it is the Ablative of Place Where.</u>

26. In sentence 16, **puella** is in the <u>nominative</u> case because <u>it is the subject of the </u>
<u>verb, "auscultat."</u>

27. In sentence 17, **turbam** and **prophetam** are in the <u>accusative</u> case because they are
<u>direct objects of the verb, "ausculto."</u>

Mark and Translate. (One line under the subject, two lines under verb, and wavy line under
direct object.) (Only line markings are done. It is up to you as the teacher to decide if you
want more markings than these.)

28. <u>Puellae</u> aquam (in villam) non <u>portant</u>. <u>The girls do not carry water into the house.</u>

29. <u>Provinciam</u> (in Galliā) <u>oppugnas</u>. <u>You are attacking the province in Gaul.</u>

30. <u>Poeta</u> patriam <u>laudat</u>. <u>The poet praises the country.</u>

31. <u>Puellae</u> non <u>oppugnant</u>. <u>The girls are not attacking.</u>

32. <u>Femina</u> insulam <u>spectat</u>. <u>The woman looks at the island.</u>

33. The <u>poet</u> <u>loves</u> the <u>country</u>. <u>Poeta patriam amat.</u>

34. <u>We</u> <u>are</u> not <u>carrying</u> <u>letters</u>. <u>Litteras non portamus (or *epistulas*).</u>

35. The <u>girls</u> <u>praise</u> the <u>friendship</u> (of the women).   <u>Puellae amicitiam feminarum laudart.</u>

Latin in the Christian Trivium – Volume I Teacher's Guide

36. The <u>women</u> <u>love</u> the <u>forest</u> (in Gaul). <u>Feminae silvam in Gallia amant.</u>

37. <u>They</u> <u>praise</u> <u>Gaul</u>. <u>Galliam laudant.</u>

38. <u>We</u> <u>love</u> <u>Italy</u>. <u>Italiam amamus.</u>

39. <u>You</u> (all) <u>attack</u> the <u>province</u>. <u>Provinciam oppugnatis.</u>

40. <u>You</u> (all) <u>prepare</u> <u>letters</u>. <u>Epistulas (or *litteras*) paratis.</u>

41. The <u>handmaiden</u> <u>carries</u> <u>water</u> (into the apartment). <u>Ancilla aquam in insulam portat.</u>

42. <u>You</u> <u>look at</u> the <u>forest</u>. <u>Silvam spectas.</u>

43. There <u>is</u> not <u>luck</u>. <u>Non est fortuna.</u>

44. There are <u>daughters</u> (in the family). <u>Sunt filiae in familia.</u>

45. The <u>women</u> <u>are singing</u> (to the daughters). <u>Feminae filiabus cantant.</u>

DRILL SHEET AFTER CHAPTER FIVE
TRANSLATE INTO LATIN:

1. of the farmer-- <u>agricolae</u>
2. the fatherlands-- <u>patriae</u>
3. to the poets-- <u>poetis</u>
4. even the nature-- <u>etiam natura</u>
5. for the daughter-- <u>filiae</u>
6. in the water-- <u>in aqua</u>
7. lives (as direct object)-- <u>vitas</u>
8. trumpet (as direct object)-- <u>tubam</u>
9. neither friendship nor memories-- <u>neque amicitia neque memoriae</u>
10. (by, with) daughters-- <u>filiabus</u>
11. of lives-- <u>vitarum</u>
12. of glory-- <u>gloriae</u>
13. (by, with) friendships-- <u>amicitiis</u>
14. you are (plural)-- <u>estis</u>
15. they are-- <u>sunt</u>
16. there is-- <u>est</u>
17. we are-- <u>sumus</u>
18. I am-- <u>sum</u>
19. she is-- <u>est</u>
20. it is-- <u>est</u>

Translate into English. Try to figure out the meanings of words that are similar to English words. If you cannot figure them out, look in the vocabulary at the back of the textbook.

PROVINCIA GALLIA

Gallia est provincia magna *(large)* in Europā. Italia etiam in Europā est. Gallia est patria agricolarum. Agricolae et poetae provinciam amant. Poetae Deum *(God)* laudant. Multae *(many)* silvae in provinciā sunt. Puellae silvas Galliae amant.

<u>**Translation:**</u>

Gaul The Province

      Gaul is a large province in Europe. Italy is also in Europe. Gaul is the country of farmers. The farmers and the poets like the province. The poets praise God. Many forests are in the province. The girls like the forests of Gaul.

Chapter Six Objectives:

At the end of the lesson students will be able to:

- recite the endings for second declension masculine nouns.
- tell the usual function of the genitive case.
- explain the meaning of the word "appositive."

<u>Chapter Six</u>

NOTE TO TEACHER: At different time periods in the history of the Latin language, sometimes the genitive singular of the second declension ended in **–i** and in other time periods the ending was **–ii**. Example: <u>filius, filii</u> changed to <u>filius, fili</u>. In this text, use the single "i" f or genitive singular, and the stem still includes the one **–i**.

1. Enter the Latin phrase on the first page of Chapter Six into the notebook, and another from Teacher's Guide.
2. Read aloud and discuss **I Grammar.**
3. Copy the boxes **I A, B** and **C**, following the directions in the textbook.
4. Memorize the noun endings in the chart on second declensions.
5. Do the **Study Sheet**.
6. Turn to **II Vocabulary** work. Be sure to go over the different types of masculine nouns.
7. Do the **Drill Sheet**.
8. It is **not** important to always identify each type of second declension nouns; just know that there <u>are</u> different types. It **IS** important to learn the nominative and genitive singular form, and to read the notes in the bottom of the box in **II A**.

    1st type - most of the nouns in the list are this type. Have the student identify them.
    2nd type - fil**ius**, glad**ius**, nunt**ius**, Pharisae**ius** and Fidel**ius**. Again have the student find them and mark them with a 2.
    3rd and 4th types - 3 pu**er**, 4 vir
    5th type – 5 ag**er**, 5 lib**er**, 5 magist**er**

8. Do **Exercise A**.
9. Complete the **Drill Sheet**. Write the abbreviations for <u>cases</u> (Nom., Gen., Dat., Acc., Abl.), and <u>number</u> (sg., pl.) for nouns, and for verbs write <u>person</u> (1st, 2nd, 3rd) and <u>number</u> above the Latin words.

10.   **Exercise B.**
11.   **Exercise C.**
12.   **Reading Lesson** and questions. It is a good idea to do them orally, and then have your student(s) write them out as homework.
13.   Review for the test.
14.   Take Test Three when they are ready, and correct the test.

NOTE TO TEACHER: When talking about persons who live in Gaul (or Rome, etc.) you use the masculine gender, **Galli** or **Romani**. When talking about a country, it is in the feminine gender, **Gallia** or **Roma**. When you have a word with which which you are familiar, like **servus**, and it has feminine endings, **-a** or **-ae**, you can rightly assume that it has the same meaning, only is speaking about a feminine person. **Servus** is a male servant, and **serva** is a female servant.

A model of a century led by a standard bearer and a centurion.

Monday	Tuesday	Wednesday	Thursday	Friday

Chapter Six

Deo volente
God Willing

Second Declension Nouns - Masculine; Genitive of Possession; Appositives; <u>Roman Family in Gaul</u>

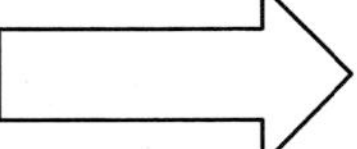

Second declension nouns are recognized by the ending **-i** in the genitive singular. Second declension nouns are either masculine or neuter, with the following exceptions: names of cities and towns ending in **-us, names of plants and gems, and a few other words; all of these are feminine.**

I. Grammar
A. Second Declension paradigm

Enter the following information on the page titled <u>Second Declension</u> in the "Cases/Declensions" section of your notebook.

Second declension nouns are usually *masculine* **if** they end in **-us -er** or **-ir*** in the nominative singular.

	ānʹgēlūs	fīʹlīūs	pūʹer	vīr	liʹber
	angel, messenger from God	*son*	*boy*	*man*	*book*

Singular

Cases	1	2	3	4	5		Endings
Nom.	angel**us**	fili**us**	puer	vir		liber	-us, -er, -ir
Gen.	angel**i**	fil**i***	puer**i****	vir**i*****		libr**i**	-i
Dat.	angel**o**	fili**o**	puer**o**	vir**o**		libr**o**	-o
Acc.	angel**um**	fili**um**	puer**um**	vir**um**		libr**um**	-um
Abl.	angel**o**	fili**o**	puer**o**	vir**o**		libr**o**	-o

Plural

Cases	1	2	3	4		Endings
Nom.	angel**i**	fili**i**	puer**i**	vir**i**	libr**i**	-i
Gen.	angel**orum**	fili**orum**	puer**orum**	vir**orum**	libr**orum**	-orum
Dat.	angel**is**	fili**is**	puer**is**	vir**is**	libr**is**	-is
Acc.	angel**os**	fili**os**	puer**os**	vir**os**	libr**os**	-os
Abl.	angel**is**	fili**is**	puer**is**	vir**is**	libr**is**	-is

* In the second declension nouns ending in **-ius** the **-i** of the stem is dropped before the ending of the genitive singular. This was not true in the earliest classical times however.

** Notice that the **e** is kept as part of the stem in **puer** and omitted in **liber**. This is another reason it is important to learn both the nominative and genitive forms of each noun.

*** Only **vir** ends in **-ir** of the second declension nouns.

B. Genitive Case

Enter the following information on the page titled <u>Genitive Case</u> in the "Cases/Declensions" section of your notebook.

The first use of the genitive case can be to show possession. In English, there are two ways to show possession:
1. Using the preposition **of:** the home **of** a friend (the home belongs to the friend).
2. Using **'s and s'.**
   You add **'s:** to a singular noun: girl**'s** dress   Bob**'s** bicycle
   a plural noun **not** ending in **s:** men**'s** work
   You add the apostrophe (**'**) to:
   a plural noun ending in **s:** horses**'** hooves
   a proper name ending in **s:** Jesus**'** life

In Latin, the genitive case is translated *of, 's or s':*
villa puellae   *the home of the girl or the girl's home*
villae puellarum   *the homes of the girls or the girls' homes*

Note: The genitive should be placed next to the noun of which it shows possession. If you place a genitive between two nouns the sentence is not clear.
Puer legati gladium portat can mean either *the boy carries the lieutenant's sword* or *the lieutenant's boy carries the sword.*

To avoid this problem write:
Legati puer gladium portat. *The lieutenant's boy carries the sword.*
Puer gladium legati portat. *The boy carries the lieutenant's sword.*

C. Appositives

Put this chart in your notebook under the section "Grammar," on the page <u>Latin Syntax.</u>

A noun used to describe another noun or a pronoun is said to be an appositive, or to be in apposition with it. An appositive must refer to the same person or thing as the noun or pronoun to which it applies; it agrees with its noun or pronoun in case. The appositive usually follows its noun or pronoun.

Puella Petrum apostolum amat. *The girl loves Peter, the apostle.*

A noun may be in apposition with an understood subject.
Femina Deum laudo.   *I, the woman, am praising God.*
                          I, as a woman, praise God.
                          I, being a woman, praise God.

II. Vocabulary   English Derivatives

When making flash cards for masculine nouns, make them on blue cards with black ink (34).

ā′gēr, ā′grī, m., *field, land*   (agriculture)
āmī′cūs, āmī′cī, m., *friend*
ān′gēlūs, ān′gē lī, m., *angel, messenger from God*
ā′nīmūs, ā′nīmī, m., *soul, mind, spirit,*   (animated)
       heart (not physical, but spiritual) in plural, courage
ān′nūs, ān′nī, m., *year*   (annual, biennial)
apos′tōlūs, apos′tōlī, m., *apostle*
cām′pūs, cām′pī, m., *field, plain*
cār′rūs, cār′rī, m., *cart, wagon*   (carriage)
discī′pūlūs, discī′pūlī, m., *disciple*   (discipline)
dō′mīnūs, dō′mīnī, m., *lord, master, ruler*   (dominate, dominion)
equ′ūs, e′quī, m., *horse*   (equestrian)
fī′līūs, fī′lī, m., *son*   (filial)
glā′dīūs, glā′dī, m., *sword*   (gladiator)
lēgā′tūs, lēgā′tī, m., *lieutenant, ambassador, envoy*   (legate, legation)
lī′ber, lī′brī, m., *book*   (library)
lū′dūs, lūd′ī, m., *game, school, sport*   (prelude, interlude)
magis′ter, magis′trī, m., *master, teacher*   (magistrate)
mūn′dūs, mūnd′ī, m., *world*   (mundane)
nū′merūs, nū′merī, m., *number, group*   (enumerate)
nūn′tīūs, nūn′tī, m., *message[8], messenger*   (announcer)
o′cūlūs, o′cūlī, m., *eye*   (oculist)
po′pūlūs, pop′ūlī, m., *nation, people* (*not* **persons**)   (population)
pū′er, pū′erī, m., *boy,* plural, *boys, children*   (puerile)
ser′vūs, ser′vī, m., *servant, servant*   (servant)
vīr, vī′rī, m., *man, husband*   (virile)

Chrīs′tūs, Chrīs′tī, m. *Christ*
Dā′vūs, Dā′vī, m., *Davus or David*
Dē′ūs, Dē′ī, m., *God*   (deify)
Iā′cōbūs, Iā′cōbī, m., *Jacob* or *James*
Iōā′nnēs, Iōā′nnis, (3rd declension), m., *John*
Pet′rūs, Pet′rī, m., *Peter*
Philip′pūs, Philip′pī, m., *Philip*
Phārisae′iūs, Phārisae′ī, m., *Pharisee*
Ro′mūlūs Fīdē′līūs Centū′riō, m., *Romulus Fidelius the Centurion*
Tī′tūs, Tī′tī, m., *Titus*

This vocabulary contains some interesting words. List ten derivatives, in addition to those given.

---

[8]When doing additional research for this revision, we discovered that most textbooks use **nuntius** as *messenger* or *message*, but the actual Latin dictionary gives the only neuter **nuntium** as *message*.

Dominie, from the word **dominus**, is a word often used of ministers.

The suffix **-ter (tor)** means *doer*, so a **minister** is a *doer of the lesser things* (**minus** means *less*), while a **magister** is a *doer of the greater things* (**magis** means *greater*).

NOTE: Some words that are masculine may become feminine with a change of ending. Examples: **magister, magistra; discipulus, discipula; amicus, amica**

III. Exercises

A. Decline the following nouns in all five cases, singular and plural:
equus, magister, liber, ager, puer, vir, filius, animus, nuntius.

equus	equi	magister	magistri
equi	equorum	magistri	magistrorum
equo	equis	magistro	magistris
equum	equos	magistrum	magistros
equo	equis	magistro	magistris

animus	animi	ager	agri
animi	animorum	agri	agrorum
animo	animis	agro	agris
animum	animos	agrum	agros
animo	animis	agro	agris

nuntius	nuntii
nunti	nuntiorum
nuntio	nuntiis
nuntium	nuntios
nuntio	nuntiis

Others are given at the beginning of the chapter.

B. Translate, giving the case and number of each noun, and the person and number of each verb.

Note that when the subject is singular, the verb is also singular, and when the subject is plural, the verb is also plural.

     acc. s. gen.s. 1/pl.
1. Angelum Domini spectamus.
       We are looking at an angel of the Lord.

     2/pl. abl.s.   2/pl. acc.s.
2. Ambulatis in viā et portatis gladium.
       You are walking on the road, and you are carrying a sword.

    nom.pl. nom.pl.   acc.s. 3/pl.
3. Puellae puerique Deum honorant.
       Girls and boys honor God.

   1/pl.   acc.s. acc.s.
4. Amamus Dominum Deum.
       We love the Lord God.

5. Feminae Deo cantant.
    The women are singing to God.

nom.s. 3/s. gen.s.
6. Terra est Domini.
    The earth is the Lord's.

nom.s.   nom.s.   3/s.
7. Dominus Deus est.
    The Lord is God. (or, *He is the Lord God*.)

1/s.   nom.s.   nom.s.
8. "Sum Dominus Deus."
    "I am the Lord God."

nom.s.   acc.s.   3/s.
9. Angelus nuntium portat.
    The angel is carrying a message.

nom.pl. nom.pl.   nom.pl nom.pl.   acc.s.   3/pl.
10. Viri et feminae et pueri et puellae Dominum vocant.
    The men, women, boys, and girls are calling the Lord.

C. Translate from English to Latin, marking every sentence as you have been taught.

gen.s.   nom.s.   3/s.   acc.pl.
1. The Lord 's <u>righteousness</u> <u>frees</u> <u>nations</u>.
    Domini iustitia populos liberat.

nom.pl.   3/pl.   acc.s.
2. The <u>Pharisees</u> <u>overhear</u> <u>Christ</u>.
    Pharisaeii Christum auscultant.

nom.s. 3/s.   nom.s.   gen.s.
3. <u>John</u> <u>is</u> an <u>apostle</u> (of Christ.)
    Ioannes est apostolus Christi.

nom.pl.   3/pl. adv.   acc.pl.
4. <u>Good</u> (**Boni**) <u>boys</u> <u>do</u> not <u>tempt</u> (their) <u>friends</u>.
    Boni pueri amicos non temptant.

1/pl.   acc.pl.   acc.sg.
5. <u>We</u> <u>are guarding</u> the <u>eyes</u> and the <u>tongue</u>*.
    Oculos et linguam servamus.

———————————————

*meaning, *our eyes and our tongue*. What does this mean?

6. The <u>disciples</u> <u>are setting</u> the <u>nations</u> (of the world) <u>free</u>.
   Discipuli populos mundi liberant.

7. <u>Christ</u> <u>takes care of</u> <u>groups</u> (of people).
   Christus numeros populi curat.

8. The <u>lieutenant</u> <u>is asking</u> the <u>Lord</u> for <u>wisdom</u>.
   Legatus Dominum sapientiam rogat.

9. The <u>man</u> <u>gives</u> the <u>book</u> (to the son).
   Vir librum filio dat.

10. <u>We do</u> not <u>praise</u> <u>nature</u> and <u>men</u> but <u>God</u>.
   Naturam et viros non laudamus sed Deum.

NOTE: In this Reading Lesson, observe that **serva** is used in this context: **Clara est serva.** "Serva" is the feminine form of **servus**, and means *servant*.

IV. Reading Lesson

Romana Familia in Galliā

In villā in Galliā habitat vir. Est Romulus Fidelius Centurio, qui est centurio *(centurion)* Romae et pater *(father)* Davi et Titi et Priscillae et Fideliae. Est etiam vir Aquilae. Fidelius in villā est quod *(because)* villam curat. Ioannes servus est qui curat terras Fideli. Fidelius et Ioannes in villā laborant etiam. Aquila, quae *(who)* est femina Fideli et mater *(mother)* filiorum et filiarum Fideli, et laborat cum *(with)* servis qui *(who)* villam curant.

Fidelia et Priscilla in campis *(fields)* ambulant. Priscilla cantat. Fidelia auscultat Priscillam. Clara ambulat in campis. Clara est serva. Fideliam et Priscillam curat.

Davus et Titus in ludo sunt. Philippus est magister Davi et Titi. Philippum auscultant. Pueri litteras (in)* libris (in) linguis Romae et Galliae scribunt *(write)*. Laborant sed animi puerorum in agris sunt, et equos vocant.

<u>Reading Lesson</u>

The Roman Family in Gaul

In the farmhouse in Gaul lives a man. He is Romulus Fidelius Centurio, who is a centurion of Rome and the father of David, Titus, Priscilla, and Fidelia. He is also the husband of Aquila. Fidelius is in the house because he is taking care of the house. John is a servant who takes care of the lands of Fidelius. Fidelius and John work in the house also. Aquila, who is the wife *(woman)* of Fidelius and the mother of the sons and daughters of Fidelius, works with the servants who take care of the house.

Fidelia and Priscilla are walking in the fields. Priscilla is singing. Fidelia is listening to Priscilla. Clara is walking in the fields. Clara is a servant. She takes care of Fidelia and Priscilla.

David and Titus are in school. They are listening to Philip. Philip is the teacher of David and Titus. The boys write *(their)* letters in *(their)* books in the languages of Rome and Gaul. They work but the hearts of the boys are in the fields, and they call the horses.

TEACHER, add "their" wherever it sounds best in translating.

Questions   Responde Latine.

1. Ubi est Fidelius? 2. Quis est Fidelius? 3. Quis est Aquila? 4. Quis Ioannes est?   5. Quam *(What)* Ioannes curat? 6. Ubi Aquila laborat? 7. Ubi puellae ambulant? 8. Quis Clara est? 9. Ubi Davus et Titus sunt? 10. Quis Philippus est?

Questions

1. Where is Fidelius? Fidelius in villa est. 2. Who is Fidelius? Fidelius est centurio Romae et pater Davi et Titi et Priscillae et Fideliae. 3. Who is Aquila? Est femina and mater filiorum et filiarum Fidelii. 4. Who is John? Ioannes est servus. 5. What does John take care of? Ioannes curat terras Fideli. 6. Where does Aquila work? Aquila laborat in villa. 7. Where do the girls walk? Puellae in agris ambulant. 8. Who is Clara? Clara est serva. 9. Where are David and Titus? Davus et Titus in ludo sunt. 10. Who is Philip? Philippus est magister Davi et Titi.

---

*"In" is not needed here in Latin, but it is added to help you in translation.

Latin in the Christian Trivium
Study Sheet
Chapter Six

Grammar

1. What is the genitive singular ending for nouns of the second declension? <u>Genitive singular ending is **-i**.</u>
2. Of what gender are most nouns of the second declension if they end in **-er** or **-us**?
   <u>Masculine</u>
3. What are the usual English translations of the genitive case? <u>of, 's, or s'</u>
4. In what way do appositives agree with their noun or pronoun? <u>In case. (but sometimes in gender and number)</u>
5. What is the stem of the following nouns?

populus	<u>popul-</u>	**vir**	<u>vir-</u>	**magister**	<u>magistr-</u>
liber	<u>libr-</u>	**Petrus**	<u>Petr-</u>	**nuntius**	<u>nunti-</u>

6. What kinds of nouns of the second declension are feminine? <u>names of cities and towns ending in **-us**, names of plants and gems, and a few others.</u>

Practice
Write the case, number, and translation of each word below.

WORD	CASE	NUMBER	TRANSLATION
EX. **populorum**	genitive	plural	of the nations
7. **apostoli**	gen.	sing.	the apostle's , of the apostle
	nom.	plural	the apostles, apostles
8. **angelos**	acc.	plural	angels
9. **mundis**	dat.	plural	to/for the worlds
	abl.	plural	by/ with the worlds
10. **agrum**	acc.	sing.	the field

Sentence Work
This will help you "think through" how endings show you the use of nouns and the number of the nouns. All words have not been analyzed, but do them all mentally yourself. Complete each statement.

11. **Puer Deum amat.** The ending **-er** shows that **puer** is used as the   <u>subject</u>
of the verb <u>amat</u> and it is in the <u>nominative</u> case. It is <u>singular</u> in number, and is translated <u>the boy.</u>

The verb **amat** is   singular in number and therefore agrees with its subject. The ending **-um** shows that **Deum** is in the accusative case, and is used as the direct object of the verb and is singular in number. Translation: The boy loves God.

12. **Davus et Philippus aquam portant.** The ending **-us** shows that both **Davus** and **Philippus** are in the nominative case and used as the subjects of the verb portant. Because there are two of them, the verb must be plural in number. Translation: David and Philip are carrying the water.

13. **Romulus Fidelius discipulum Petrum appellat.** The ending **–us** shows that **Romulus Fidelius** is in the nominative case and is the subject of the verb. The ending **-um** shows that **discipulum** is used as the direct object of the verb appellat and is singular in number. The ending **-um** shows that **Petrum** is also in the same case and it is functioning as an   appositive with **discipulum.** Translation: Romulus Fidelius calls the disciple Peter.

14. **Filius libros magistrorum portat.** The ending **-us** shows us that **filius** is used as the subject of the verb portat and is singular in number. The ending **-orum** shows that **magistrorum** is in the genitive case and is plural in number. The ending **-os** shows that **libros** is used as the direct object of the verb portat and is in the accusative case and plural in number. Translation: The son carries the teachers' books. (or *The son carries the books of the teachers.*)

Translate these sentences into Latin, marking each word.

      nom.pl   in + abl.s.   3/pl.   acc.pl.
15. The lieutenants (in the farmhouse) are calling the farmers.
      Legati in villa agricolas vocant.

    1/pl.   adv.   acc.s. (objective * gen.pl.
16. We do not praise a number (of men).
      Numerum virorum non laudamus.

      nom.pl.   gen.pl   3/pl.   acc.pl. in + abl.s.
17. The teachers (of the boys and girls) are looking at the servants (in the field).
      Magistri puerorum puellarumque servos in agro spectant.

    nom.pl. 3/pl.   acc.pl.   acc.pl.
18. The boys do honor the teachers and apostles.
      Pueri magistros et apostolos honorant.

   1/pl.   acc.s.
19. We praise God.
      Laudamus Deum.

    2/sg.   gen.s. acc.s.
20. You are carrying the farmer's tunic.
      Agricolae tunicam portas.

   3/pl.   nom.pl.   gen.s.   gen.s.
21. They are the daughters (of Titus and the woman).
      Sunt filiae Titi et feminae.

---

*Teacher: They cannot translate this as a possessive; later on, they will learn about Objective Genitives.

     1/pl.   acc.pl.   dat.s.
22. We give *the lives (to God).
      Vitas Deo damus.

     nom.pl.   gen.s.   3/pl. nom.pl.
23. The letters (of Peter) are books.
      Epistulae (or, *litterae*) Petri sunt libri.

     3/pl.   acc.pl.   acc.pl.
24. They are looking at the angels and the trumpets.
      Angelos et tubas spectant.

     gen.s. nom.s.   3/s.   acc.s.
25. Peter's servant is carrying a tunic.
      Petri servus tunicam portat.

     1/pl.   in + abl.s.
26. We live (in Europe).
      Habitamus in Europa.

     nom.s.   gen.s.   3/s.   acc.s.   gen.s.
27. The family (of Peter) loves the righteousness (of God).
      Familia Petri iustitiam Dei amat.

     nom.pl. adv. 3/pl.   nom.pl. nom.pl.   3/pl.
28. The angels are not singing, but the men and women sing.
      Angeli non cantant, sed viri feminaeque. (or *viri et feminae*)

(NOTE: **Cantant** may be omitted in the second clause, because it appears earlier in the sentence.)

     nom.s. nom.s.   3/s.   acc.pl. gen.pl.   gen.pl.
29. The Lord God **strengthens the spirits (of boys and girls). (this means *encourages*)
      Dominus Deus animos puerorum puellarumque confirmat. (or *puerorum et puellarum*)

     nom.s. 3/s. acc.s. dat. s.   (in + abl.s.) conj.
30. God gives life (to the people) (in Europe) also.
      Deus vitam populo in Europa etiam dat.

     nom.s. 3/s. (in + abl.s.)   1/pl.   acc.pl. in + abl.s.
31. The school is (in a field); we praise the schools (in Italy).
      Ludus in campo est; ludos in Italia laudamus.

     nom.s. 3/s. acc.s.   dative pl.
32. God gives wisdom (to the disciples and apostles and to men and women).
      Deus sapientiam discipulis apostolis et viris et feminis dat. (or, *viris feminisque*)

     nom.pl.   3/pl.   acc.s.   gen.s.
33. The Pharisees do not love the wisdom (of God).
      Pharisaeii sapientiam Dei non amant.

---

*meaning, *our* lives
**Strengthen the heart* is often translated *encourages*.

TRANSLATE INTO LATIN: Practice these phrases from Latin to English, noticing case endings and number.

1. Domini - gen.s.; angelus- nom.s. = the angel of the Lord
2. magistri - gen.s.; equum- acc. s. = the teacher's horse
3. Christo Domino- both dative s. = to or for Christ the Lord
4. nunti - gen.s.; oculi- nom.pl. = the messenger's eyes
5. numerus - nom.s.; virorum et feminarum- gen. pl. = a number of men and women
6. Titus et Petrus- nom.s. = Titus and Peter
7. ludus- nom.s.; Domini- gen.s. = the school of the Lord
8. patria - nom.s.; apostolorum - gen. pl. = the homeland of the apostles
9. legati - gen. s.; servus - nom.s. = the lieutenant's servant
10. animus - nom. s.; feminae - gen. s. = the heart (*mind, soul*) of a woman
11. Vir Petrus est apostolus. = The man Peter is an apostle.
12. Appellat filium Petrum. He names the (*his*) son Peter.
13. Appellamus Filium Dei Christum. We call the Son of God Christ.
14. Aquila filiam Priscillam amat. Aquila loves the daughter Priscilla.
15. Petrus narrat nuntium Christi Dei Fili viris (dative case). Peter tells the message of Christ, the Son of God, to the men.

Write two sentences of your own in Latin using an appositive in each.

16. Varies.
17. Varies.
18. oculi mundi- the eyes of the world
19. numerus virorum- a number of men (Objective Genitive, not possessive)
20. animi apostolorum- the spirits of the apostles
21. viri et feminae- men and women (or *of the man* and *of the woman*)
22. Dominus virorum feminarumque- the Lord of men and women
23. Discipuli Christi- disciples of Christ
24. feminae oculi- the woman's eyes
25. Stellas spectamus. We are looking at the stars.
26. Stellas spectatis. You are looking at the stars.
27. Dei sapientia populos mundi sanat. God's wisdom heals the nations of the world.
28. Rogamus puellam librum. We are asking the girl for a book.
29. Christus est Filius Dei. Christ is the Son of God.
30. Ancilla tunicam portat. The handmaiden carries a tunic.
31. Tunicam portamus. We are carrying a tunic.
32. Ancilla tunicam puero dat. The handmaiden gives a tunic to the boy.
33. Pueri ancillae tunicam dant. The boys give a tunic to the handmaiden.
34. Petrus est servus Domini. Peter is a servant of the Lord.
35. Philippus Petrusque servi Domini sunt. Philip and Peter are servants of the Lord.
36. Animum puero puellaeque Dominus dat. The Lord gives a soul to the boy and girl.
37. Apostolus servus Domini librum portat. The apostle, a servant of the Lord, is carrying a book.
38. Apostolum servum Domini amatis. You love the apostle, a servant of the Lord.
39. Filius apostolo servo Domini equum dat. The son gives a horse to the apostle, a servant of the Lord.

40. Dominus animos virorum confirmat. <u>The Lord strengthens the hearts of the men.</u>
(or, *The Lord encourages men. The master encourages his men.*)
41. Angeli non cantant. <u>Angels do not sing.</u>
42. Deo cantamus. <u>We sing to God.</u>
43. Puellae lacrimant. <u>Girls cry (or *the girls are crying*).</u>
44. Puella lacrimat. <u>The girl cries. (or *the girl is crying*).</u>
45. Feminae non lacrimant. <u>Women do not cry. (Or *the women are not crying*.)</u>
46. Prophetae et familia viros salutant. <u>Prophets and the family greet the men.</u>
47. Temptas servare magistros. <u>You are trying to guard the teachers.</u>

Test Three to be taken after the completion of Chapter Six (75 possible points)

Grammar Section

1. What is a word called that connects words, phrases, or clauses? <u>Conjunction</u>
2. In Latin, in what case is the direct object of a verb? <u>It is in the Accusative case.</u>
3. In what two ways do a subject and verb agree? <u>In person and number.</u>
4. Second declension nouns are recognized by what ending of the genitive singular? <u>**-i**</u>
5. What case in Latin shows possession? <u>Genitive case</u>
6. What is the noun called that describes another noun or pronoun? <u>an appositive</u>

Noun and Verb Work

7. Decline one of these two second declension nouns: **messenger** or **book.**

NOM.	nuntius	nuntii	liber	libri
GEN.	nunti	nuntiorum	libri	librorum
DAT.	nuntio	nuntiis	libro	libris
ACC.	nuntium	nuntios	librum	libros
ABL.	nuntio	nuntiis	libro	libris

8. Decline one of these two first declension nouns: **island** or **memory.**

NOM.	insula	insulae	memoria	memoriae
GEN.	insulae	insularum	memoriae	memoriarum
DAT.	insulae	insulis	memoriae	memoriis
ACC.	insulam	insulas	memoriam	memorias
ABL.	insula	insulis	memoria	memoriis

9. Give the four principal parts for the verb **to be.**
   sum esse fui futurus

10. Conjugate the verb **to be** in all three persons, singular and plural, with meanings.

sum, *I am*	sumus, *we are*
es, *you are*	estis, *you are*
est, *he/she/it is are there is*	sunt, *they are, there are*

Translate the following sentences. First, underline the subject of the verb with one line, then the verb (or predicate) with a double line, and put either a wavy or dotted line under the direct objects if there are any. Note any other cases, and THEN translate.

      1/pl.   acc.s.   1/pl.
11. We are praising God and singing.
      Deum laudamus et cantamus.

    nom.pl. conj. nom.pl. 3/pl. acc.s.
12. Women and girls love friendship.
      Feminae et puellae amicitiam amant.

   (adv.) 3/s. nom.s.   gen.pl.   in + abl.s.
13. There is a *number (of teachers) (in the school).
    Est numerus magistrorum in ludo.

Word Work

Write the Latin word from which the underlined word is derived and write a brief meaning
or synonym of the underlined word.

14. Several trained linguists work for Wycliffe Bible Translators. lingua, a person who
      studies different languages.
15. Hillarie rides in many equestrian events for 4-H. equus, horse events
16. We are to take dominion over all areas of life for the Lord. dominus, lordship
17. Your behavior in that difficult situation is very laudable. laudo, praiseworthy
18. If we insulate our homes they stay warm in winter and cool in summer. insula, isolate from
      surroundings
19. Your report confirmed my findings as well. confirmo, strengthened

Translation Work

20-30.

      Familia in Italiā habitat. Sunt filii et filiae in familiā. Pueri sunt in ludo. Puellarum vitae
sunt beatae (*happy*). Amant spectare naturam et cantare. Neque pueri neque puellae lacrimant,
sed (*but*) temptant esse beati (*happy*).

A family lives in Italy. There are sons and daughters in the family. The boys are in school. The girls' lives are happy. They like to look at nature and to sing. Neither boys nor girls are crying, but they try to be happy.

---

*Although this is technically correct since in some cases, number means "group", languages change over time. Many grammarians consider "number" as a plural noun in some cases, saying "there are a number of teachers…"

- recite from memory the commonly used prepositions in English listed on page 44.
- give the rules for Accusative of Place to Which and Ablative of Place from which.
- tell which case follows each preposition in the Vocabulary Lesson.

Chapter Seven

1. Enter the phrase on the first page of Chapter Seven into the notebook, and also one from Teacher's Guide.
2. Read and discuss section **I**. Emphasize the last paragraph.
3. Copy the boxes **I A** and **B**
4. Memorize English prepositions in **I A**. This may be done in sections, one column at a time. The student should be able to recite by memory the English prepositions in alphabetical order. Test the student on this.
5. Do the **Study Sheet.**
6. **Vocabulary II**. Make cards, following the directions in the text. If you are making notebook sheets, put the accusative prepositions on a white sheet of paper with red ink, and put the ablative prepositions on a white sheet of paper with green ink.
7. Notice that "motion" indicates accusative case; if indicating position, use the ablative case.
8. Do **Exercises A** and **B**. Have the student tell whether the phrase is Accusative of Place to Which, or Ablative of Place from Which if either one applies.

Δ **A good thing to remember is that if you are "moving" something from one place to another, you would use Accusative of Place to Which. If you are "giving, saying, showing," or "telling," something to or for someone, you would use the Dative Case, which is the case for the indirect object. Sometimes students are confused about the differences.**

9. Next, do the **Supplementary Study Sheet**.
10. Do the **Drill Sheet** orally. Notice if it is Ablative of Place from Which, or Accusative of Place to Which. Do page two orally with your student.
11. Read and discuss **III**. Tell them that **exit** means, literally, "it goes out."
12. Copy the box titled "Prefixes". Write **ad** in red ink. Write the verbs in blue ink, with the bold print (prefixes) in green (abl.) or red ink (acc.). This will help your student retain the information.
13. **Exercises C** and **D**.
14. **V. Reading Lesson**.

Chapter Seven

Prepositions; Prefixes; Accusative of Place to Which; Ablative of Place from Which; <u>A Messenger from Rome</u>

A preposition is a word that shows how a noun or a pronoun is related to another word in the sentence.

I. Grammar
A. Prepositions and Adverbs
This chart should be put under <u>Prepositions</u> in the section titled "Grammar."

> The word "preposition" comes from the Latin word **praepositus** which means *placed in front*. Originally the case endings alone were enough to show the meaning of nouns in a sentence. But the accusative and ablative cases came to be used in so many ways that certain adverbs began to be used to make the relationship of the words clearer. These adverbs came to be called prepositions because they were placed in front of the nouns and formed prepositional phrases.

Add the following to the page titled <u>Prepositions</u> in your notebook.

> The bird sat *on* the house.
> The bird was *above* the house.
> The bird flew *under* the house.
> The bird stepped *off* the perch.
> The bird stood *between* the trees.

The prepositions *on, above, under, off,* and *between* show how *the bird* is related to the nouns *house, perch, trees.* Each preposition has an object that makes up a **prepositional phrase:** *on the house, above the house,* etc. A preposition which has no object in English is an adverb. Thus, in the sentence, "The sky is above," *above* has no object, so in that instance it is an adverb.

Write this list of commonly used English prepositions in your notebook on the page titled <u>Prepositions</u> in the Grammar section of your notebook. Memorize them all.

aboard	at	concerning	into	past	until
about	atop	despite	like	regarding	unto
above	before	down	near	round	up
across	behind	during	of	since	upon
after	below	except	off	through	with
against	beneath	excepting	on	throughout	within
along	beside	for	onto	to	without
amid	between	from	out	toward	
among	beyond	in	outside	under	
around	by	inside	over	underneath	

B. Accusative of Place to Which and Ablative of Place from Which

This chart should be copied and placed on the page titled <u>Accusative Case</u> in the "Cases/Declensions" section of your notebook.

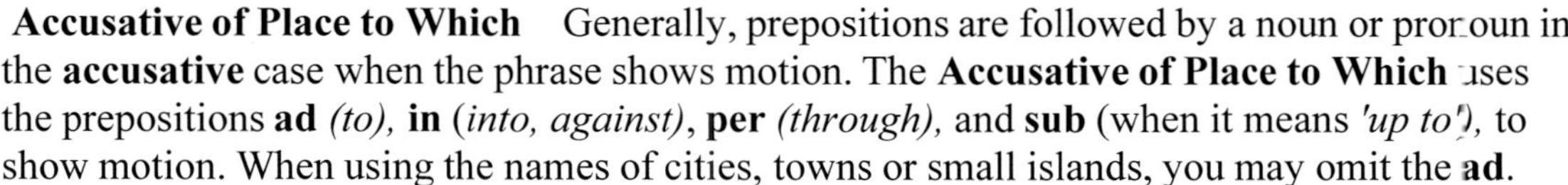

Accusative of Place to Which   Generally, prepositions are followed by a noun or pronoun in the **accusative** case when the phrase shows motion. The **Accusative of Place to Which** uses the prepositions **ad** *(to)*, **in** (*into, against*), **per** *(through)*, and **sub** (when it means *'up to'*), to show motion. When using the names of cities, towns or small islands, you may omit the **ad**.

Pueri in silvam ambulant.
The boys are walking into the forest.
Aquam Romam portamus. (Or, Aquam ad Romam portamus.)
We carry water to Rome.

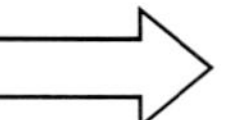

NOTE: Prepositions **in** (*in, on*), and **sub** (*under, below, beneath*) are followed by a noun or pronoun in the **ablative** case to show *location* or *position*.

The following information belongs on the page titled <u>Ablative Case.</u>

Ablative of Place From Which uses the prepositions **a,** or **ab*** (away from), **de** (down from), **e** or **ex*** (from, out of), to show the position from which motion begins. While all three prepositions (ab, de, ex) <u>can</u> mean *from*, **ab** means "away from the outside;" **de** means "down from the inside;" **ex** means "out from the inside." <u>All can mean *from* when it is not important to distinguish.</u> Again, you *may* omit the preposition with names of cities, etc.

LOCATION: **Puella est in silvā.** *The girl is in the forest.*
                       Gladius est sub equo. *The sword is beneath the horse.*

PLACE FROM WHICH: **Ambulat ex ludo.** *He is walking from school.*
                       Ambulat ab ludo. *He is walking away from school.*
                       Ambulat de ludo. *He is walking down from school*

A (or **ab)** denotes *from near* a place; **ē** or **ex**, *out from* it; and **dē**, *down from* it. This may be represented graphically as follows:

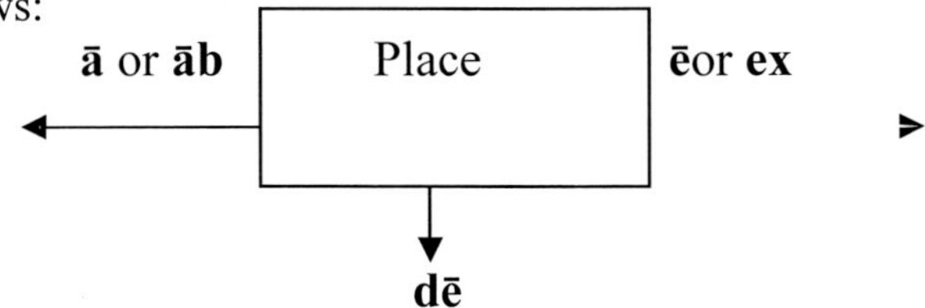

When you memorize the Latin prepositions, be sure to remember which case follows each one. Prepositions are followed by a noun or pronoun in the **ablative** case to show location or position. The prepositions **in** (in, on), and **sub** (under, below, beneath) show location.

II. Vocabulary   English Derivatives

Write the prepositions on white cards with red ink for accusative, and write ablative prepositions on white cards with green ink (22).

ād + accusative	*to, toward, near, beside, at*	(advent)
ān′tē + accusative	*before, in front of*	(antecedent)
cīr′cūm + accusative	*around, about* (location)	(circle)
con′tra + accusative	*against*	(contradict)
in + accusative	*into, against*	
in′ter + accusative	*between, among*	(intercept)
ob + accusative	*because of, on account of*	
per + accusative	*through, along, by* (location)	(perspire)
pōst + accusative	*after, behind*	(postpone)
prō′pē + accusative	*near, nearby*	(propinquity)
prop′ter + accusative	*because of, on account of*	
sŭb + accusative, after verbs of motion,	*up to, up to the foot of, close to, under*	
sū′per + accusative	*above*	
trāns + accusative	*across, over*	(transport)
ā, āb* + ablative	*from, away from, by*	(absent)
cūm + ablative	*with*	
dē + ablative	*concerning, about, from, down from*	(deport)
ē, ēx* + ablative	*from, out of*	(export)
in + ablative	*in, on*	(invoke)
prō + ablative	*in front of, on behalf of, for*	(professor)
sī′nē + ablative	*without*	(sinecure)
sŭb + ablative	*at the foot of, under, beneath*	(subway)

> *Before vowels or 'h', **ab** or **ex** must be used in order to speak more smoothly. Before consonants usually just the **e** or **a** are used. This is like the rule in English regarding *a* or *an*.
> Only use *by* when you are speaking of a person, like *The letter was written by a man.*

> **NOTE:** Keep in mind that a translation of a preposition which is followed by the accusative case indicates *motion*, and one followed by the ablative case usually indicates *position* or *location*.

III. Word Study: Prefixes

Many of the prepositions in Latin are used as *prefixes* j oined to root words. Some of the adverbs which later became prepositions were used before verbs, and eventually became part of the verb itself. They are called prefixes from the Latin words, **prae + fixus**, *attached in front*. When you read a Latin sentence sometimes the prefix is attached to the verb, and is repeated in the other part of the sentence as a preposition with an object.

    Puellas a pueris avocat. *She calls the girls away from the boys.*

Normally prefixes have the same meanings as their corresponding prepositions, but sometimes they have additional meanings.

Prefixes

a-, ab-, abs-: *away, off*
e-, ex-: *out, throughout*
ad-: *to, towards, near*   **in-, im-:** *in, on, against, not*
de-: *down, upon*   **sub-, sup-:** *under, up from under, secretly, somewhat*

When these prefixes are added to some of the verbs you have learned, you can see the meanings change a little:

abs-: **as**porto, *I carry **away**, I carry **off*** (abl.)
    absum, *I am **away**, I am **absent*** (abl.)
    avoco, *I call **away*** (abl.)
ad-: **a**specto, *I look **towards*** (acc.)
    adsum, *I am **here*** (acc.)
de-: **de**porto, *I carry **down**, I carry **away*** (abl.)
    despecto, *I look **down upon*** (abl.)
e-, ex-: **ex**porto, *I carry **out*** (abl.)
    expugno, *I conquer, I take by assault* (abl.)
    exspecto, *I look **out for**, I await* (abl.)
    evoco, *I call **out*** (abl.)
in-: **im**porto, *I carry **in**, I bring **in*** (acc.)
    invoco, *I call **upon**, I invoke* (abl.)
sub-: **sup**porto, *I carry **up**, I support* (acc.)
    subsum, *I am **under**, I am **concealed***

Sometimes the prefixes may change or leave off a letter before combining with the verb to make it easier to pronounce.

IV. Exercises

A. Pronounce and translate.

1. cum feminis
2. a villis
3. a pueris
4. e familiā
5. in Galliā
6. sine amicis
7. pro silvis Italiae
8. ab insulā
9. de ludis poetarum
10. ad aquam

Latin in the Christian Trivium – Volume I Teacher's Guide

1.   with women
2. from the farmhouses (Abl. Place from Which)
3. away from the boys (Abl. Place from Which)
4. from the family (Abl. Place f rom Which)
5. in Gaul (Abl. Place Where)
6.   without friends
7. in front of the forests of Italy
8. away from the island (Abl. Place from Which)
9. concerning the schools (or *games*) of the poets
10. near the water (Acc. Place to Which)

B. Remember to use the correct case following each preposition.

1. with the messenger
2. through the forests of Italy
3. before the game
4. across the provinces
5. among friends
6. concerning the letter
7. through the fields
8. toward the horses
9. against Rome
10. because of the teacher

1. cum nuntio
2. per silvas Italiae
3. ante ludum
4. trans provincias
5. inter amicos

6. de littera (or *de litteris* or *de epistula*)
7. per agros
8. ad equos (Acc. Place to Which)
9. contra Romam
10. propter (or *ob*) magistrum

C. Sentences   Note the case and number before you translate.

nom.s.   dat.s.   acc.s.   3/s.
1. Propheta populo amicitiam dat.
> The prophet gives friendship to the people. (or *nation*)

nom.s. acc.s.   acc. s.   3/s.
2. Deus iustitiam et vitam amat.
> God loves righteousness and life.

3/s. nom.s. gen.s.   gen.s.
3. Est magister ludi etiam villae.
> He is the master of the school and also of the house.

nom.s. 3/s. nom.s. gen.s.
4. Petrus est servus Dei.
> Peter is a servant of God.

2/pl.   acc.s.   3/s. nom. s.
5. Salutatis Petrum et est vestra (*your*) amicus.
> You are greeting Peter and he is your friend.

nom.pl. 3/pl. nom.pl. gen.s.   acc.s.   dat.s. 3/pl.
6. Angeli sunt nuntii Domini et gloriam Deo dant.
        Angels are messengers of the Lord and they give glory to God.

nom.pl.   dat.pl.   gen.s. acc.s.   3/pl.
7. Discipuli familiis Italiae amicitiam dant.
        The disciples give friendship to the families of Italy.

> REMINDER TO TEACHER: **Rogo** takes two accusatives: the thing asked for, and the person(s) of whom it is asked.

3/pl.   acc.pl.   acc.pl. acc.pl.   acc.pl. (ad + acc.s.) 3/pl.
8. Rogant feminas et filias libros et libros ad villam portant.
        They are asking the women and daughters for books and they carry the books to the farmhouse.

nom.pl.   nom.pl. acc.pl. (ad + acc.) 3/pl.   nom.pl.
9. Neque magistri neque feminae libros ad villam portant, sed servi.
        Neither the teachers (or masters) nor the women carry the books to the farmhouse, but the servants do.

nom.s.   acc.pl.   gen. pl. 3/s.   3/s.(cum + abl. pl)
10. Christus animos virorum sanat et est cum viris.
        Christ heals the hearts of men and He is with men.

D. Mark every word as you have been taught.
When you mark an English sentence for translation, put parentheses around any prepositional phrases before you mark the rest of the sentence.

1/pl.   acc.pl.   (a + abl.pl.)
1. We are calling the men (from the provinces).
        Viros a provinciis vocamus.

3/pl.   acc.pl. (in + abl.s.)
2. They do attack the men (in Italy).
        Viros in Italia oppugnant.

2/sg.   acc.s.
3. God blesses the nations.
        Deus consecrat populos. (o r *sanctificat*)

nom.pl. 3/pl. acc.pl.   3/pl.   3/pl.   (ab or ex or a or e + abl. pl.)
4. The men set the servants free and they walk (away from the fields).
        Viri servos liberant et ab agris ambulant. (or, *e campis*)

1/s.   infinitive   acc.pl.
5. I try to honor the prophets.
        Prophetas honorare tempto.

nom.s.   3/s.   3/s. acc.s.
6. The common crowd is singing and also praising God.
        Turba cantat et Deum etiam laudat.

nom.s.   3/s.   acc.pl.
7. James does greet the apostles.
        Iacobus apostolos salutat.

nom.s.   gen.s.   3/s.   (in + abl.) (Abl. Place from Which- pl.)

8. The <u>family</u> (of Peter) <u>lives</u> (in Gaul) (away from the towns).
    Familia Petri in Gallia habitat ab oppidis.

nom.pl.   nom.pl.   nom.pl.   3/pl.   infinitive

9. The <u>women</u> and <u>girls</u> and <u>handmaidens</u> <u>are preparing</u> **to sing**.
    Feminae et puellae et ancillae cantare parant. (or, *feminae puellaeque et ancillae*)

1/pl.   (pro + abl.s.)   1/pl.   acc.s.

10. <u>We</u> <u>cry</u> (on behalf of the world), but <u>we</u> <u>praise</u> God.
    Lacrimamus pro mundo sed laudamus Deum.

V. Reading Lesson

Nuntius e Romā[*]

    Pueri ante villam ambulant. Viros in agris spectant. Subito *(suddenly)* est nuntius in equo. Nuntius pueros salutat.

    "Quis *(Who)* es?" Davus rogat.

    "Nuntius e Romā sum," vocat. Nuntium spectant. "Porto nuntium *(message)* ad Romulum Fidelium."

    "Filii Romuli Fideli sumus. In villā est," vocat Davus.

    Titus vocat Fidelium, "Nuntius hic *(here)* e Romā est." Fidelius salutat nuntium. Nuntius epistulam Fidelio dat. Epistula a [**]Tiberio, domino Romae est, qui *(who)* Fidelium et familiam (ad) Romam revocat *(calls back)*. Fidelius familiae de epistulā narrat.

<u>Reading Lesson</u>

Messenger from Rome

    The boys are walking in front of the farmhouse. They are looking at the men in the fields. Suddenly there is a messenger on a horse. The messenger greets the boys.

    "Who are you?" David asks.

    "I am a messenger from Rome," he calls. They look at the messenger.

    "I am carrying a message to Romulus Fidelius."

    "We are the sons of Romulus Fidelius. He is in the house," calls David.

    Titus calls Fidelius, "A messenger is here from Rome."

    Fidelius greets the messenger. The messenger gives Fidelius a letter. The letter is from Tiberius, the ruler of Rome, who is calling Fidelius and the family back to Rome.

    Fidelius tells the (his) family about the letter.

Responde Latine. Answer in a complete sentence.

1. Quem *(Whom)* pueri spectant?

---

[*]Teacher, we are using the "e", or in some cases "ex", before cities such as Roma to help with translation, but it is not necessary to use it. It is used in the Latin Bible, but not by some textbooks.

[**]Tiberius, the emperor of Rome, reigned from AD 14 until AD 37.

2. Ubi nuntius habitat?
3. Quem *(What)* nuntius Fidelio dat?

Questions.
1. At whom are the boys looking? Spectant nuntium. 2. Where does the messenger live? In Roma habitat. 3. What does the mess enger give Fidelius? Epistulam Fidelio dat.

Name ____Date _______________________

Latin in the Christian Trivium
Study Sheet A
Chapter Seven

Grammar
1. What do we call a preposition and its object? <u>a prepositional phrase</u>
2. What are the two cases used after Latin prepositions? <u>accusative and ablative</u>
3. When motion is expressed, what is the case used with a preposition? <u>accusative case</u>
4. If we want to show location or position, what is the case used after prepositions? <u>ablative case</u>

Practice
Write the meanings of the following prepositions and also the case of the noun or pronoun which is its object.

	CASE	MEANING
5. per	acc.	through, along
6. contra	acc.	against
7. in (acc.)	acc.	into, against
8. in (abl.)	abl.	in, on
9. trans	acc.	across, over
10. e, ex	abl.	from, out of
11. de	abl.	from, down from, about, concerning
12. sine	abl.	without

Sentence Work

       1/pl.   acc.pl. gen.s.
13. <u>We</u> <u>are defeating</u> the <u>men</u> (of Gaul).
      Viros Galliae superamus.

     (ob + acc.s.)   gen.pl.   1/pl.   acc.pl.
14. (Because of the <u>wisdom</u>) (of the men), <u>we are freeing</u> the <u>women</u>.
        Ob sapientiam virorum feminas liberamus. (or, *propter sapientiam...*)

     (ante + acc.s.)   nom.s.   3/s.   acc.pl.
15. (In front of the farmhouse) the <u>messenger</u> <u>greets</u> the <u>men</u>.
        Ante villam nuntius viros salutat.
        (Alternate may be *Pro villa*....)

     nom.pl.   3/pl.   (in + abl.s.)   nom.pl. 3/pl. (in + abl.s.)
16. The <u>angels</u> <u>do</u> not <u>dwell</u> (on earth), but <u>men</u> <u>dwell</u> (on the earth).
        Angeli in terra non habitant, sed viri [habitant in terra]. (May or may not be repeated.)

Latin in the Christian Trivium – Volume I Teacher's Guide

nom.pl. 3/pl. acc.pl. (ad + acc.s.)
17. <u>Boys</u> <u>carry</u> <u>books</u> (to school).
     Pueri libros ad ludum portant.

nom.s. 3/s. acc.pl. acc.pl.
18. The <u>teacher</u> <u>likes</u> <u>boys</u> and <u>girls</u>.
     Magister pueros puellasque amat.

3/s. acc.s. (de + abl.s.)
19. <u>He</u> <u>calls</u> the <u>book</u>, *Concerning Nature*.
     Librum <u>De Natura</u> appellat.

(trans + acc.s.) 2/s. acc.pl.
20. (Across the <u>road</u>) <u>you</u> <u>are looking at</u> the <u>common crowds</u>.
     Trans viam turbas spectas.

nom.s. 3/s. (de + abl.s.)
21. <u>Peter</u> <u>is thinking</u> (about Christ the Lord).
     Petrus de Christo Domino putat.

nom.s. nom.s. 3/s. nom.s. nom.s. gen.s.
22. The <u>man John is</u> not a <u>slave</u>, but an <u>apostle</u> (of Christ).
     Vir Ioannes non est servus sed apostolus Christi.

3/s. (in + abl.s.) (gen.s.)
23. <u>He is</u> (in the world), but not (of the world).
     Est in mundo sed non mundi.

> **NOTA BENE:**
> Student will underline titles, but in a published work, they are italicized. Cicero wrote *Concerning Nature*.

Name _______________________________________ Date _______________________

Latin in the Christian Trivium
Supplementary Study Sheet B
Chapter Seven

Tell which Latin preposition you would use for each of the underlined words in these sentences. Sometimes there are two that are both correct. Then tell which case would follow that use of the preposition.

1. He will command His angels <u>concerning</u> you. <u>de with ablative case</u>
2. You will not strike your foot <u>against</u> a stone. <u>contra with accusative case; or in with accusative</u>
3. Jesus returned to Galilee and news <u>about</u> Him spread through the whole countryside. <u>de with ablative case</u>
4. He went <u>to</u> Nazareth where He had been brought up. <u>ad with accusative case</u>
5. The eyes of everyone in the synagogue were fastened <u>on</u> Him. <u>in with ablative case</u>
6. He walked <u>along</u> the road <u>with</u> the disciples. <u>per with accusative case; cum with ablative case</u>

7. Some of the men were sitting <u>at the foot of</u> the large tree. <u>sub with ablative case</u>
8. The hungry men said that they were <u>without</u> food. <u>sine with ablative case</u>
9. When Father works, he does it <u>on behalf of</u> his family. <u>pro with ablative case</u>
10. The children ran <u>down from</u> the hill because it was so fun. <u>de with ablative case</u>
11. <u>On account of</u> your lovely singing, you are going to study at Julliard. <u>ob or propter with accusative case</u>
12. The storm headed <u>toward</u> our city. <u>ad with accusative case</u>
13. The storm came <u>into</u> our city. <u>in with accusative case</u>
14. Then the storm headed <u>out of</u> our city. <u>e or ex with ablative case</u>
15. As it blew <u>into</u> Nevada, it was far <u>away from</u> our city. <u>in with accusative case; ab with ablative case</u>
16. High winds blew <u>over</u> the desert. <u>trans with accusative case</u>
17. Put the wood <u>behind</u> the house <u>in</u> the storage shed. <u>post with accusative case; in with ablative case</u>
18. We learn Latin <u>with</u> a great teacher. <u>cum with ablative case</u>
19. He gave money to the organization <u>on behalf of</u> the blind. <u>pro with ablative</u>
20. We are definitely <u>against</u> wrongdoing. <u>contra with accusative</u>

DRILL SHEET AFTER CHAPTER SEVEN.
TRANSLATE INTO LATIN:
1. under the stars   <u>sub stellis (Abl. Place Where)</u>
2. through the forest   <u>per silvam</u>
3. on account of the common crowd   <u>ob turbam (or, *propter turbam*)</u>
4. into the eye   <u>in oculum</u>
5. with the apostles   <u>cum apostolis</u>
6. against the nations   <u>contra populos</u>
7. about the whales   <u>de balaenis</u>
8. behind the farmhouse   <u>post villam</u>
9. away from the boys   <u>a pueris</u>
10. toward the homeland   <u>ad patriam (Acc. Place to Which)</u>
11. out of Italy <u>ex Italia (Abl. Place from Which)</u>
12. across the earth <u>trans terram</u>
13. into Gaul   <u>in Galliam</u>
14. out of (from) water   <u>ex aqua (Abl. Place from Which)</u>
15. on behalf of the family <u>pro familia</u>
16. on the tunic   <u>in tunica</u>
17. among the women   <u>inter feminas</u>
18. between the stars   <u>inter stellas</u>
19. with the boys and the girls   <u>cum pueris puellisque (or *pueris et puellis*)</u>
20. against the earth   <u>contra terram</u>

Latin to English. Translate these phrases and sentences.
These are <u>some</u> possible answers.

21. de provinciā <u>from the province, down from the province</u>
22. de terrā <u>from the earth, concerning the earth</u>
23. de iustitiā <u>concerning justice</u>
24. ad Italiam <u>toward Italy, to Italy</u>
25. ad carrum <u>near the wagon, at the cart</u>
26. ad magistros   <u>to the teachers, to the masters</u>
27. ante equos <u>in front of the horses, before the horses</u>

<u>**Latin in the Christian Trivium – Volume I Teacher's Guide**</u>

28. ante raedam <u>in front of the carriage, before the carriage</u>
29. ante villam <u>in front of the farmhouse</u>
30. contra turbas <u>against the crowds</u>
31. contra puellas <u>against the girls</u>
32. contra Davum <u>against David</u>
33. contra nuntios <u>against the messengers</u>
34. in mundum <u>into the world</u>
35. in mundo <u>in the world</u>
36. in silvā <u>in the forest</u>
37. in silvis <u>in the forests</u>
38. inter feminas <u>among women, between women</u>
39. inter raedas <u>among (or *between*) the carriages</u>
40. ob iustitiam <u>on account of justice</u>
41. ob stellas <u>on account of stars</u>
42. per turbam <u>through the crowd</u>
43. per aquam <u>through the water</u>
44. per Christum <u>through Christ</u>
45. per vias <u>through the roads (or *along the roads*)</u>
46. post turbas <u>behind the crowds</u>
47. post ancillas <u>behind the handmaidens</u>
48. post balaenam <u>behind the whale</u>
49. post discipulos <u>behind the disciples</u>
50. propter sapientiam <u>on account of wisdom</u>
51. propter familiam <u>on account of the family</u>
52. sub provinciam <u>at the foot of the province</u>
53. de viā <u>down from the road (*concerning the road*)</u>
54. sub terrā <u>under ground</u>
55. sub raedā <u>under the carriage</u>
56. sub oculis <u>under the eyes</u>
57. sub equo <u>under the horse</u>
58. trans viam <u>across the road</u>
59. trans provincias <u>across the provinces</u>
60. trans Romam <u>across Rome</u>
61. trans Europam <u>across Europe</u>
62. trans patrias <u>across the homelands</u>
63. ab Italiā <u>from Italy</u>
64. a patriā <u>from the country, homeland</u>
65. a Galliā <u>from Gaul</u>
66. a turbā <u>from the crowd</u>
67. a viis <u>from the roads</u>
68. a silvā <u>from the forest</u>
69. ab apostolo <u>from the apostle</u>
70. cum magistro <u>with the teacher</u>
71. cum viris feminisque <u>with men and women</u>
72. cum Tito <u>with Titus</u>
73. cum viro <u>with a man</u>
74. cum numero virorum <u>with a group of men</u>
75. cum servis <u>with servants</u>
76. de raedā <u>about the carriage</u>
77. de raedis <u>about the carriages</u>
78. de naturā <u>about nature</u>
79. epistula de Deo <u>a letter about God</u>
80. epistula de ancillis servisque <u>a letter about (or *from*) handmaidens and servants</u>
81. de balaenā <u>about a whale</u>
82. de stellis <u>about stars</u>
83. e silvā <u>from the forest</u>
84. e tunicā <u>from the tunic</u>
85. e familiā <u>from the family</u>
86. ex aquā <u>from water</u>
87. ex aquis <u>from waters</u>
88. e villis <u>from the farmhouses</u>
89. ex agro <u>from the field (or *out of the field*)</u>
90. sine iustitiā <u>without justice</u>
91. sine sapientiā <u>without wisdom</u>
92. sine aquā <u>without water</u>
93. sine terrā <u>without land</u>
94. sine oculis <u>without eyes</u>
95. pro Romā <u>for Rome</u>
96. pro patriā <u>for the homeland</u>
97. pro Christo <u>for Christ</u>
98. pro mundo <u>for the world</u>
99. pro ludis <u>for the games (or *schools*)</u>
100. pro Domino <u>for the Lord</u>

Chapter Eight Objectives:

At the end of the lesson students will be able to:

- recite the endings for second declension neuter nouns.
- say which word is used with questions expecting the answer "yes" and which one is used expecting the answer "no."
- use **ita vero** and **minime** when answering questions.
- solve different problems translating dates from the Roman calendar to our calendar.
- understand the derivatives' meanings.

<u>**Chapter Eight**</u>

1. Enter the chapter phrase into the notebook in the "Phrase" section, as well as one from the Teacher's Guide.
2. Read and discuss section **I A-Paradigm.**
3. Copy the Latin paradigm and memorize it.
4. **II Vocabulary**. See past lessons if you need any instructions.
6. Do all of **Exercise A** either orally or written.
7. **Study Sheet.**
8. **Drill Sheet**.
9. Read and discuss **I B**.
10. **Exercise B**.
12. **Exercise C**.
13. **Reading Lesson V.**
16. Read and discuss **VI**. Do the exercise listed there.
17. Students need to memorize the list of the seven hills in section **VII.**

The first hill that the Roman farmers settled on was the Palatine, which became the hill where the nobility lived. A mnemonic device to learn the Seven Hills of Rome is:

"**C**an **Q**ueen **V**ictoria **E**at **C**old **A**pple **P**ie?

[**C**aelius, **Q**uirinalis, **V**iminalis, **E**squilinus, **C**apitolinus, **A**ventinus **P**alatinus]

[Caelian Quirinal Viminal Esquiline Capitoline Aventine Palatine]

18. Review for the test the day before the test is given.
19. Give **Test Four**.
20. Correct the test, grade it, and go over any problem areas.

Chapter Eight

Second Declension Neuter nouns;
Questions; <u>On the Road to Rome</u>

Neuter nouns of the second declension end in **-um** in the nominative singular, instead of the **-us, - ir,** or **-er** ending which signifies a masculine second declension noun. All neuter nouns, no matter which declension have one similarity: the nominative is always the same as the accusative, and in the plural these two cases always end in **-a.**

I. Grammar

A. Paradigm

The following paradigm shows the declension of a neuter noun. When you copy it, put it into your notebook on a page titled <u>Second Declension</u> in the "Cases/Declensions" section. Memorize each ending.

māndā′tūm, *commandment*

Cases	Singular		Endings
Nom.	manda′t**um**	a (the) commandment	**-um**
Gen.	manda′t**i**	of a (the) commandment	**-i**
Dat.	manda′t**o**	to, for a (the) commandment	**-o**
Acc.	manda′t**um**	a (the) commandment	**-um**
Abl.	manda′t**o**	(by, with) the commandment	**-o**
	Plural		
Nom.	manda′t**a**	the commandments	**-a**
Gen.	mandato′**rum**	of the commandments	**-orum**
Dat.	manda′t**is**	to, for the commandments	**-is**
Acc.	manda′t**a**	the commandments	**-a**
Abl.	manda′t**is**	(by, with) the commandments	**-is**

B. Questions

There are two types of questions. One is expecting the answer *yes* or *no*; the other is seeking information.

> *Are you coming with me?*
> *What is your name?*

Roman Imperial Eagle

Put the following chart into your notebook in the section titled "Grammar" on the <u>Latin Syntax</u> page.

To ask a question which expects a yes or no answer, add the suffix **-ne** to the first word in the sentence. The suffix is properly called an enclitic, which means a word that "falls upon" another word.

To ask a question seeking information, do not add the **-ne**.
Quis est vir? *Who is the man?*

To ask a question which expects the answer *yes*, **nonne** is placed first in the sentence.
Nonne puella est parva? *Isn't the girl small?* or *The girl is small, isn't she?*

To ask a question which expects the answer *no*, **num** is placed first in the sentence.
Num puella est parva? *Is the girl small?* or *The girl isn't small, is she?*

Since there are no words in Latin for *yes* or *no*, you may either answer with a positive response or a statement.
       Laborasne? *Are you working?* **Laboro.** *I am working.* **Non laboro.** *I am not working.*
However, you may also use these idioms: **Ita vero,** *so true,* meaning *yes,* or **minime,** *the very least,* meaning *no.*

II. Vocabulary   English Derivatives

Use yellow cards with black ink for neuter nouns (14). Write the conjunctions on white cards with purple ink (4). Write enclitics, interrogative particles, and idioms on white cards with black ink (5).

bel′lūm, bel′lī, n., *war*	(bellicose, belligerent)
cae′lūm, cae′lī, n., *sky, heaven*	(celestial)
dō′nūm, dō′nī, n., *gift*	(donation)
fīrmamen′tūm, fīrmamen′tī, n., *prop, support, atmosphere*	
frūmen′tūm, frūmen′tī, n., *grain*	
māndā′tūm, māndā′tī, n., *commandment, mandate, order*	
op′pīdūm, op′pīdī, n., *town*	
peri′cūlūm, peri′cūlī, n. *danger, risk*	(peril)
princi′pīūm, princip′ī, n., *beginning*	(principal)
reg′nūm, reg′nī , n., *kingdom, royal power*	(interregnum)
Sabbā′tūm, Sabbā′tī, n., or **Sabbā′ta, Sabbātōrūm,** n., *The Sabbath*	
stīpen′dīūm, stīpen′dī, n., *payment, wage*	(stipend)
testimōn′īūm, testimōn′ī, n., *testimony, witness*	(testimonial)
ver′būm, ver′bī, n., *word*	(verbal, verbose)
quō′nīām, conjunction, *because, since*	
quōd, conjunction, *because*	

Some conjunctions when used in Latin are placed second in the sentence, and are called postpositive conjunctions, but in English, they are first in the sentence.
       au′tem, conjunction, *moreover, but* (postpositive)
       ē′nim, conjunction, *for* (postpositive)

-nē, enclitic, expecting a *yes* or *no* answer
nōn′nē, interrogative particle expecting a *yes* answer
nūm, interrogative particle expecting a *no* answer
ī′ta ve′rō, idiom, *so true, yes*
min′ īmē, idiom, *the very least, no*

THE COLOSSEUM, ROME, ITALY 2001

III. Exercises

A. Decline the new nouns in the vocabulary lesson.

stipendium	stipendia
stipendi	stipendiorum
stipendio	stipendiis
stipendium	stipendia
stipendio	stipendiis

B. English to Latin

1. to or for the Sabbath (dat. pl.) <u>Sabbatis</u>
2. wages (nom. pl.) <u>stipendia</u>
3. of the towns (gen. pl.) <u>oppidorum</u>
4. wars (nom. pl.) <u>bella</u>
5. testimonies (acc. pl) <u>testimonia</u>

6. <u>We do</u> not <u>praise kingdoms</u>, do we?
    Num regna laudamus?

7. <u>He praises</u> the <u>kingdom</u> (of God), doesn't he?
    Nonne regnum Dei laudat?

8. Is the <u>lieutenant telling</u> (about the wars)?
    Legatusne de bellis narrat?

9. <u>You</u> (pl.) <u>are not thinking</u> (about the dangers) (of war), are you?
    Num de periculis belli putatis.

10. The <u>son</u> and <u>daughter think</u> (about heaven and God's commandments).
    Filius et filia de caelo et de Dei mandatis putant.

11. The <u>horse is carrying</u> the <u>boys</u>, isn't it?
    Nonne equus pueros portat ?

12. <u>Does</u> the <u>man give gifts</u> (to the woman)?
    Donane feminae vir dat?

1/pl.   dat. pl.   (de + abl. s.)   1/pl.

13. Since we are telling the men (about the Lord), we are singing, aren't we?

     Nonne quoniam viris de Domino narramus, cantamus?

    (inter + acc. pl.)   nom.s. 3/s. nom.s. gen.s.

14. (Among the apostles), Peter is the man (of God).

     Inter apostolos Petrus est vir Dei.

   nom.s.   3/s.   infinitive

15. The prophet is preparing to sing, isn't he?

     Nonne propheta cantare parat?

C. Latin to English

Translate. Notice that word order is not always the traditional one.

   acc. s. gen.s. 3/pl. nom.pl.

1. Regnum Dei amant viri.

  (Mentally change to:) Viri amant regnum Dei.

     Men love the kingdom of God.

     nom.s. gen.s. 3/s. (in + abl.s.) conj. (in + abl.s.)

2. Nonne regnum Dei est in caelo etiam in terrā?

     The kingdom of God is in heaven and also on earth, isn't it?

  conj.   1/pl.   (in + abl.s.) 1/pl.   (de + abl. pl.) gen.s.

3. Quoniam habitamus in terrā, putamus de mandatis Domini.

     Since we live on earth, we think about the commandments of the Lord.

    (trans + acc.s.) nom.pl. nom.pl.   3/pl.

4. Nonne trans regnum puellae puerique laborant?

     Across the kingdom the girls and boys work, don't they?

   2/s.   acc. s.   dat.s.

5. Dasne tunicam puellae?

     Are you giving a tunic to the girl?

  adv. 3/s. nom.s.   (in + abl.s.)

6. Non est periculum in Italiā.

     There is not danger in Italy.

   3/s.   nom.s.   (in + abl.s.)

7. Estne frumentum in carro?

     Is the grain in the wagon?

   nom.pl. 3/pl. acc.s.

8. Ubi viri parant periculum?

     Where are the men preparing for danger? (or, *when*)

   acc. s. dat.pl. conj. 3/pl.   1/pl.

9. Stipendium pueris quod laborant damus.

  Change to: Damus stipendium pueris quod laborant.

     We are giving a payment to the boys because they are working.

nom.pl. (de + abl.s.) acc.s.   3/pl.

10. Angeli de caelo testimonium dant.
       Angels give (their) testimony from heaven.

     3/s.   acc. pl.   gen.s. gen.s.

11. Auscultatne verba Petri Davique?
       Is he listening to the words of Peter and David?

       3/pl. nom.pl. (in + abl.s.)

12. Nonne sunt oppida in Italiā?
       There are towns in Italy, aren't there?
     (or, *They are the towns in Italy, aren't they?* or *Are there towns are in Italy?*)

     3/s. nom.s.   3/s.   nom.s.

13. Ubi est patria? Estne America?
       Where is the homeland (or, *country*)? Is it America?

      (ante + acc.s.) 1/pl.

14. Num ante carrum ambulamus?
       We aren't walking in front of the wagon, are we?

     3/pl.   nom.s. dat.s.

15. Vocant, "Gloria Deo."
       They call, "Glory to God."

IV. Reading Lesson Read aloud and translate.

In Via *(ad) Romam

    Aquila vocat, "Tempus est excitare *(It is time to get up)*!" Clara vocat Priscillam et Fideliam, "Auscultatisne Aquilam? Tempus est excitare!" Philippus vocat Davum Titumque, "Tempus est excitare!" Servi parant equos ut portent *(to carry)* familiam ad Romam.

    Servi carros, raedasque parant. Raedae Aquilam et puellas et ancillas portant. Equus Fidelium ad Romam portat. Servi puellas et Aquilam in raedā et pueros in equis curant. Servi gladios portant et familiam contra periculum servant.

    Servi ad raedas ambulant. Equi nonnullos *(some)* servos portant.

    Servi frumentum portant. Pueri vocant, "Ad Romam!"

    Equi et raedae familiam portant in viā ab oppido Vercellis in provinciā Galliae. Via ad Romam est per oppida. Oppida sunt Placentia, Bononia, Florentia, Clusium, Veiique, tandem *(finally)* via ducit *(leads)* ad Romam!

Recognition Vocabulary

Towns are named Placentia, Bononia, Florentia, Clusium and Veii in English.

---

*We are putting the "ad" in parentheses to help with the translation.

On the Road to Rome

Aquila calls, "It is time to get up! " Clara calls Priscilla and Fidelia, "Are you are listening to Aquila? It is time to get up! " Philip calls David and Titus, "It is time to get up." The servants prepare the horses to carry the family to Rome. The servants prepare the wagons and carriages.

The carriages carry Aquila, the girls, and the handmaidens. The horse carries Fidelius to Rome. The servants take care of the girls and Aquila in the carriage, and the boys on the horses. The servants carry swords and they guard the family against danger.

Servants walk near the coaches. The horses carry some (of) the servants.

The servants carry the grain. The boys call, "To Rome! "

The horses and the coaches (carriages) carry the family on the road from the town of Vercellae in the province of Gaul. The way to Rome is through the towns. The towns are Placentia, Bononia, Florentia, Clusium, and Veii; finally, the road leads to Rome!

Responde Latine. Answer in a complete sentence.

1. Quis Priscillam Fideliamque vocat?
2. Quis Davum Titumque vocat?
3. Ubi equi familiam portant?
4. Quos *(Whom)* servi curant?
5. Per quot *(how many)* oppida equi et raedae familiam portant? (Give the number in English.)

Questions

1. Who is calling Priscilla and Fidelia? Clara vocat Priscillam Fideliamque.
2. Who is calling David and Titus? Philippus vocat Davum Titumque.
3. Where are the horses carrying the family? Portant familiam ad Romam.
4. Whom do the servants take care of? Curant Aquilam et puellas puerosque.
5. Through how many towns do the horses and coaches carry the family? Per quinque oppida familiam portant.

V. Vercellae is in Transalpine Gaul, across the Alps. It is 75 miles northwest of Placentia. Placentia
is in Cisalpine Gaul, south of the Alps, and 80 miles north of Bononia.
Give the total mileage for their trip.

If the family can only travel 30 miles per day, how many days will it take to get to Roma?

Vercellae in northwest Gallia to Placentia in Cisalpina - 75 miles
Placentia to Bononia in Cisalpina - 80 miles
Bononia down to Florentia - 45 miles
Then on to Clusium - 60 miles
On to Veii - 73 miles
Then Roma at last - 20 miles

<u>Map Study</u>
Total mileage is 353 miles, and takes approximately 12 days.

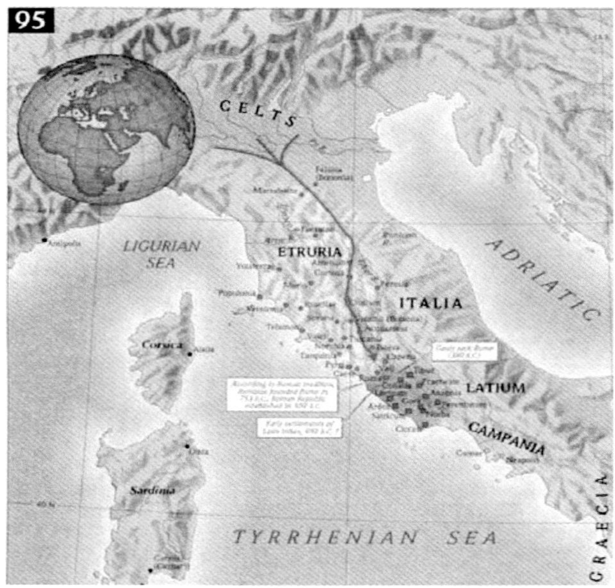

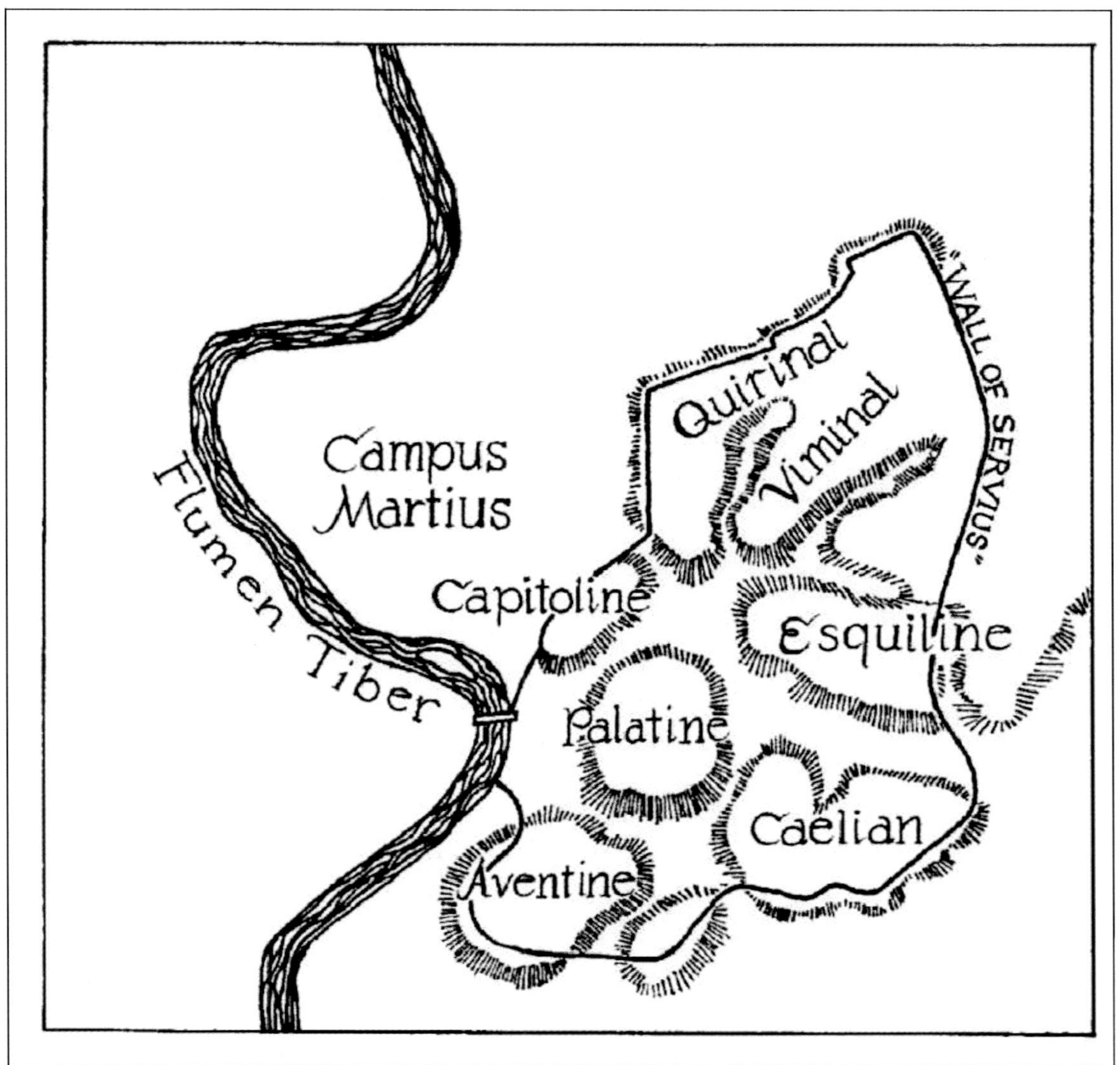

Campus Martius, the Field of Mars, was used as a training ground for soldiers and private citizens who wanted to become physically fit.   It was dedicated to Mars, the Roman god of war. In later times it was also used for military celebrations.

Name ____Date __________________________

Latin in the Christian Trivium
Study Sheet
Chapter Eight

Grammar

1. What two cases of neuter nouns are always alike? <u>Nominative and accusative cases are always alike.</u>

2. What is the ending of these two cases in the plural? <u>-a</u>

3. Decline **verbum** or **stipendium** and give meanings for each case.

CASE	SINGULAR	MEANING	PLURAL	MEANING
Nom.	verbum	word	verba	words
Gen.	verbi	of the word	verborum	of the words, the words'
Dat.	verbo	to/for the word	verbis	to/for the words
Acc.	verbum	the word	verba	words
Abl.	verbo	by/with the word	verbis	by/with words
Nom.	stipendium	wage	stipendia	wages
Gen.	stipendi	of a wage	stipendiorum	of the wages, wages'
Dat.	stipendio	to/for a wage	stipendiis	to/for wages
Acc.	stipendium	wage	stipendia	wages
Abl.	stipendio	by/with a wage	stipendiis	by/with wages

Practice

4. Write the case, number, and meaning of each noun:

a. Sabbatorum	<u>genitive</u>	<u>plural</u>	<u>of the Sabbaths</u>
b. caeli	<u>genitive</u>	<u>singular</u>	<u>of heaven, the sky's</u>
c. dona	<u>nominative</u>	<u>plural</u>	<u>gifts</u>
	<u>accusative</u>	<u>plural</u>	<u>gifts</u>
d. stipendiis	<u>dative</u>	<u>plural</u>	<u>to/for payments</u>
	<u>ablative</u>	<u>plural</u>	<u>by/with payments</u>
e. principia	<u>nominative</u>	<u>plural</u>	<u>beginnings</u>
	<u>accusative</u>	<u>plural</u>	<u>beginnings</u>
f. frumentorum	<u>genitive</u>	<u>plural</u>	<u>of grains</u>
g. caelis	<u>dative</u>	<u>plural</u>	<u>to/for skies</u>
	<u>ablative</u>	<u>plural</u>	<u>by/with skies</u>
h. testimonio	<u>dative</u>	<u>singular</u>	<u>to/for a witness</u>
	<u>ablative</u>	<u>singular</u>	<u>by/with a witness</u>
i. dono	<u>dative</u>	<u>singular</u>	<u>to/for a gift</u>
	<u>ablative</u>	<u>singular</u>	<u>by/ with a gift</u>
j. periculum	<u>nominative</u>	<u>singular</u>	<u>danger</u>
	<u>accusative</u>	<u>singular</u>	<u>danger</u>

k. mandatis   dative   plural   to/for commandments

                       ablative   plural   by/with commandments

5. Write the required forms of each noun or phrase.

   a. toward town   ad oppidum
   b. in the beginning   in principio
   c. among the men   inter viros
   d. j ustice (as a direct object) iustitiam
   e. of heaven   caeli
   f. of wars   bellorum
   g. into Italy   in Italiam
   h. under the stars   sub stellis
   i. to or for kingdoms   regnis
   j. the lands (as a subject)   terrae

6. Underline the English sentence which is the best translation for the Latin sentence.

  a. **In viā est turba.** (1) On the road there are crowds. (2) There is a crowd in the farmhouse. <u>(3) There is a crowd on the road.</u>

  b. **Virine bellum parant?** <u>(1) Are the men preparing for war?</u> (2) They prepare the men for battle. (3) Who is preparing for wars?

  c. **Putamus de Dei sapientiā et iustitiā.** (1) God is thinking about giving us wisdom and righteousness. <u>(2) We do think about God's wisdom and righteousness.</u> (3) The wisdom and righteousness of God is our desire.

  d. **Ubi balaenae habitant?** <u>(1) Where do whales live?</u> (2) Do the whales live here? (3) What do whales have?

  e. **Apostoline animos** *(hearts)* **virorum confirmant?** (1) The apostles have strong hearts. (2) Do the men strengthen the hearts of the apostles? <u>(3) Do the apostles strengthen the hearts of men?</u>

Sentence Work

7. *Men love gifts.* The word *men* is used as the <u>subject</u>; therefore it is in the <u>nominative</u> case. It is a noun of the <u>second</u> declension, <u>plural</u> in number and <u>masculine</u> in gender; therefore the ending should be <u>-i</u> and the complete word is <u>viri</u>. The word *gifts* is used as the <u>direct object</u>; therefore it is in the <u>accusative</u> case; it is a noun of the <u>second</u> declension, <u>plural</u> in number and <u>neuter</u> in gender; therefore the ending should be <u>-a</u>, and the complete word is <u>dona</u>. The word *love* is in the present tense; its subject is <u>viri</u>, with which it must agree in the <u>plural</u> number and the <u>third</u> person; therefore the ending should be <u>-nt</u> and the complete verb is <u>amant.</u>

Translation: <u>Viri dona amant.</u>

        nom. pl.   nom. pl. 3/pl. (in + abl.)
8. The <u>prophets</u> and the <u>apostles</u> <u>are</u> (in Italy).
      Prophetae et apostoli in Italia sunt.

       2/s.   infinitive   acc. pl.
9. <u>Do</u> <u>you</u> <u>like</u> <u>to look at</u> the games?
      Amasne spectare ludos?

10. <u>They</u> <u>are setting</u> the <u>books</u> <u>apart</u> for God's purpose.
      Libros sanctificant.

11. The <u>slaves</u> <u>are</u>   not the <u>messengers</u> (of God), but the <u>angels</u> <u>are</u>.
      Servi nuntii Dei non sunt, sed angeli.

12. The <u>Word</u> (of God) <u>gives</u> <u>wisdom</u> (to men and women).
      Verbum Dei viris et feminis sapientiam dat.

13. <u>We</u> <u>love</u> <u>God,</u> because <u>God</u> <u>loves</u> <u>men</u> and <u>women.</u>
      Deum amamus quod Deus viros et feminas amat.

14. Moreover, <u>you do listen to</u> the <u>disciples.</u> (Teacher, the "to" is part of the verb in
      Latin.) Discipulos autem auscultas.

15. <u>They</u> <u>are</u> (in the country), but <u>they</u> <u>do</u> not <u>like</u> <u>horses.</u>
      Sunt in patria, sed equos non amant.

DRILL SHEET AFTER CHAPTER EIGHT
TRANSLATE INTO ENGLISH:

Remember that these are some of the possible correct answers; there may be variations which are still correct.

1. e regno <u>out of the kingdom, from the kingdom</u>
2. in oppido <u>in town</u>
3. ad Galliam <u>toward Gaul, near Gaul, to Gaul</u>
4. de epistulā <u>concerning the letter</u>
5. sub silvam <u>up to the forest, or up to the foot of the forest</u>
6. in bello <u>in the war</u>
7. inter feminas <u>among women, between women</u>
8. a mandatis <u>from the commandments</u> (not "by/with" because **mandatis** is not a person)
9. ob stipendia <u>on account of the wages, payments</u>
10. ad caelum <u>to heaven, toward the sky, toward heaven</u>
11. pro regno <u>for the kingdom, on behalf of the kingdom</u>
12. de memoriā <u>concerning the memory, about the memory</u>
13. cum discipulis <u>with the disciples</u>
14. post villam <u>behind the farmhouse</u>
15. post oculos <u>behind the eyes</u>
16. pro testimoniis <u>for the witnesses</u>
17. e turbā <u>from the crowd, out of the crowd</u>
18. ex aquā <u>from the water, out of the water</u>
19. propter naturas <u>because of the natures, on account of the natures</u>
20. pro sapientiā <u>on behalf of wisdom, for wisdom</u>
21. ob periculum <u>on account of danger, because of the danger</u>
22. de caelo <u>down from heaven, about heaven, concerning heaven</u>

23. de donis concerning gifts, about the gifts
24. a firmamento from the support, away from the support (or *atmosphere*)
25. sine frumento   without grain
26. sine periculo without danger
27. in principio in the beginning
28. verba discipulorum the words of the disciples, the speech of the disciples
29. principium sapientiae the beginning of wisdom
30. principium iustitiae the beginning of justice
31. Estis puellae. You are girls.
32. Non estis pueri. You are not boys.
33. Sunt discipuli. They are disciples. There are disciples.
34. Habito quod habitat I live because he lives
35. Sum discipulus Christi enim puto. I am a disciple of Christ for I think.
36. Putamus de verbis Philippi. We think about the words of Philip.
37. Putasne de verbis Philippi? Do you think about the words of Philip?
38. Puto de caelo. I think about heaven. I think about the sky.
39. Spectat caelum. He is looking at the sky.
40. Spectas stellas in caelo. You are looking at the stars in the sky.
41. Spectamus pueros in ludo. We are looking at (*watching*) the boys in school.
42. Amo ma gistrum in ludo. I like the teacher in school.
43. Pueri non habitant in ludo. The boys do not live in school.
44. Numerum librorum portare temptamus. We are trying to carry a number of books.
45. Ambularene temptas? Are you trying to walk?
46. Prophetae poetas in Italiā honorant. Prophets honor the poets in Italy.
47. Puella feminas honorat. The girl honors the women.
48. Dat eius *(his)* verbum! He gives (his) word!
49. Sum beatus *(happy)* quoniam amas me *(me)*. I am happy since you love me.
50. Vir enim Sabbata amat For the man loves the Sabbaths…
51. Temptamus enim equos curare. For we are trying to take care of the horses.
52. Sunt pericula in Italiā. There are dangers in Italy.
53. Puellae autem non laborant. But the girls are not working (*suffering*).
54. Regnum Dei in terrā est. The kingdom of God is on the earth.
55. De caelo angeli gladios portant. Down from heaven the angels carry swords.
56. Frumenta sunt in carris. The grains are in the carts.
57. Agricola viris stipendia dat. The farmer gives wages to the men.
58. Paramus bellum. We are preparing for war.
59. Paratis bellum. You are preparing for war.
60. Paro bellum. I am preparing for war.
61. Dominus viris feminisque Sabbata dat. The Lord gives the men and women Sabbaths.
62. Ioannes pro populis mundi lacrimat. John is crying on behalf of the nations (*peoples*) of the world.
63. Apostoli animum Iacobi confirmant. The apostles strengthen the heart of James. (may translate "*encourage*")
64. Dominus viros feminasque mundi liberat. The Lord sets the men and women of the world free.
65. Deus enim mandata dat… For God gives the commandments…
66. Amamus mandata Dei. We love the commandments of God.
67. Mandata populos liberant. The commandments set the nations free.
68. Viae ad oppidum sunt. The roads are near the town (They are the roads to town).
69. Sunt bella in terrā. There are wars on the earth.

70. Stellae in caelo sunt, non in terrā. <u>Stars are in the sky, not on earth.</u>

Test Four to be taken after the completion of Chapter Eight

Grammar Section
1. What is the part of speech called that shows how a noun or a pronoun is connected to another word in the sentence? <u>A preposition</u>
2. Which case is used to express Place to Which, indicating motion toward a place? <u>accusative</u>
3. Which case is used to express Place from Which? <u>ablative</u>
4. What is the ending (two letters) added to the most important word in the sentence when we ask a question which can be answered "yes" or "no"? <u>-ne</u>

Preposition Work. Translate each phrase.

5. trans oppidum <u>across town</u>
6. sub caelo <u>under heaven</u>
7. per silvam <u>through the forest</u>
8. ante bellum <u>before the war</u>
9. in principio <u>in the beginning</u>
10. sine stipendio <u>without payment</u>
11. inter feminas <u>among women</u>
12. contra testimonium <u>against the testimony</u>
13. ex oppido <u>out of town, from town</u>
14. de insulā <u>about the island, from the island</u>

Noun Work
15. Decline one of these two second declension neuter nouns: **kingdom** or **w ord**.

CASE	SINGULAR	PLURAL	SINGULAR	PLURAL
NOM.	regnum	regna	verbum	verba
GEN.	regni	regnorum	verbi	verborum
DAT.	regno	regnis	verbo	verbis
ACC.	regnum	regna	verbum	verba
ABL.	regno	regnis	verbo	verbis

Translation Exercise Mark and translate the Latin sentence into English.

    nom.s. acc.s. 3/s.
16. Deus mundum amat.
    God loves the world.

    acc.pl. dat.pl.   (per + acc. s.) nom.s. 3/s.
17. Mandata viris feminisque per Verbum Deus dat.
    God gives the commandments to men and women through the Word.

    nom.pl. (de + abl.s.) acc.s. 3/pl.
18. Angeli de caelo populum spectant.
    Angels from heaven are looking at the people.
    (Or: Angels are looking down from heaven at the people.)

19. Amamus Deum quoniam nos *(us)* amat.
      We love God because He loves us.

20. Virne testimonium de Deo dat?
      Does the man give a (meaning "his") testimony (witness) about God?

21. Filius in silvā ambulat. <u>The son is walking in the forest.</u>
22. Filius in silvam ambulat. <u>The son is walking into the forest.</u>
23. Filius e silvā ambulat. <u>The son is walking out of the forest. (also, *from*)</u>
24. Filius a silvā ambulat. <u>The son is walking away from the forest. (also, *from*)</u>
25. Propter mandatum puella pro raedā non ambulat. <u>Because of the commandment, the girl does not walk in front of the carriage.</u>
26. Puellae ambulant cum amicis. <u>The girls are walking with (their) friends.</u>

Word Work
Write the Latin word from which the underlined word is derived **and** write a brief meaning or synonym of the underlined word.

27. The medicine drops were to be administered <u>sublingually.</u> <u>sub + lingua. under the tongue</u>
28. Oliver Cromwell ruled England in the absence of a king during the <u>interregnum</u> period. <u>inter + regnum . between the kingdom(s)</u>
29. We have enjoyed the <u>celestial</u> view on these clear winter nights. <u>caelum, heavenly</u>
30. The president feels he has a <u>mandate</u> from the people to clean up government. <u>mandatum, commandment</u>
31. Stefanie receives a <u>stipend</u> for tutoring. <u>stipendium, wage, payment</u>
32. The teacher was extremely <u>verbose</u>, and we were tired. <u>verbum, wordy</u>

33-40. Translation Exercise

      Davus e villā ambulat. Stellas in caelo spectat. Stella de caelo cadit *(falls)*!
Puellis de stellā narrat. Estne in periculo? Minime! Stella non cadit ad terram. Eheu! *(Whew!)*

David is walking out of the farmhouse. He is looking at the stars in the sky. A star falls down from the sky! Is he in danger? No! The star does not fall to the earth. Whew!

40-50. Another translation. Translate **nuntium** as *message.*

In viā ante villam est vir. Vir Iesus est. Testimonium turbae virorum, feminarum, puerorum et puellarum dat. Turba virum amat et pro regno Dei laborat. Mandata laudant. Cum Domino sunt discipuli, apostoli. Et vitam et verba Dei honorant. Iesus nuntium ad populum portat. Nuntium est: "Sapientia verbaque Dei mundum superant. Deus est vita mundi. Prophetae viam parant. Regnum Dei principium iustitiae pro patriis terrae est." Legatus autem in equo epistulam trans agrum portat. Nuntium periculi contra Dominum et amicos est. Vir gladium Domino dare temptat, sed gladium non cupit *(want)*. Lacrimat, consecrat populum et ab villā ad oppidum ambulat.

NOTE: This story is an original story written by Dr. Frank Bain of New Jersey and used with permission.

On the road in front of a farmhouse (or *villa*) is a man. The man is Jesus. He gives testimony to a crowd of men, women, boys and girls. The crowd loves the man and works on behalf of the kingdom of God. They praise the commandments. With the Lord are the disciples, the apostles. They honor both the life and words of God. Jesus carries a message to the people. The message is: The wisdom and words of God are overcoming the world. God is the life of the world. The prophets are preparing the way. The kingdom of God is the beginning of righteousness for the nations of the earth. However, a lieutenant on a horse carries a letter across the field. It is a message of danger against the Lord and friends. A man tries to give the Lord a sword, but he does not want a sword. He weeps, blesses the people and walks away from the farmhouse (or *villa*) toward town.

Chapter Nine Objectives:

At the end of the lesson students will be able to:

- define an adjective.
- tell how to find the stem of a first and second declension adjective.
- state the rule for Ablative of Means.
- recite from memory the declension of the personal pronouns.
- know who built the Appian Way.

Chapter Nine

The primary thing for you, as teacher, to remember is that with adjectives, the first adjective in the vocabulary list is masculine; the second one is feminine, and the third is neuter. All nouns must be modified by an adjective of the same gender as its noun. Often they have the same ending, but not always.

Example: Agricola altus… Endings are not the same because agricola is masculine within a "feminine" declension, first. But its adjective is masculine, declined like the second declension masculine nouns.

1. Enter the chapter phrase into the notebook. One of the secular ones you want to be sure to learn is **Carthago delenda est**. It is a good beginning point to study the Punic Wars and Hannibal. The Senator who said this famous phrase was Cato the Elder. He was afraid that Carthage would continue to build up militarily, and then eventually defeat Rome. No one listened to him for a long, long time.

   Hannibal of Carthage was a brilliant general, using many strategies, such as ambushes and choosing the time and place for his battles. He began the war by attacking Saguntum, which was an ally of Rome and very distant from Rome, thereby calling out Rome to the battle site of HIS choosing.

Note: Look for Abbott's extremely interesting story of Hannibal and the Punic Wars at www. abe.com and anything else written by Jacob Abbott. *Famous Characters of History, Hannibal.* St. Huberts Guild, 1906.

(This is a place you might want to introduce Theodore Roosevelt's slogan, "Walk softly and carry a big stick." What is the significance of that saying?)

2. Read and discuss **I Grammar.**

3. Enter **II Ablative of Means** description into the student notebook.
Some have trouble understanding this concept. Ask them: What do you use to do something? Do you use a computer to type? Do you use stove to cook? Do you use a whistle to call the team? Do you use a horse (not a person) to get home safely? All those things you USE are Ablative of Means. Be sure to note that you normally do not use persons in this construction, although sometimes this is an exception done in advanced Latin.

4. **III Vocabulary** Work. Continue to make flash cards and/or vocabulary sheets. Drill and quiz student on vocabulary words, even if on a casual basis.

5. In the back of the Teacher's Guide is a chart which is titled "Objective Genitive." Copy that and make it available for the students. They do not yet know all of the information on it, but it will help them when deciding when to use
nostrum or **nostri**, and **vestrum** or **vestri**.

6. Learn the personal pronouns in this way: ego, mei, mihi, me, me. nos, nostrum (nostri) nobis, nos, nobis. tu, tui, tibi, te, te, vos, vestrum (vestri), vobis, vos, vobis.

7. **Exercise B**
8. **Drill Sheet**.
9. **Exercises D** and **E**..
10.   **Reading Lesson VI.**

res iudicata

(race you-dee-KAH-tuh)

A QUESTION DECIDED BY COMPETENT LEGAL PROCEEDINGS, WHICH CANNOT AGAIN BE RAISED

Monday	Tuesday	Wednesday	Thursday	Friday

Chapter Nine

Adjectives ending in -us or - er, Personal Pronouns, Ablative of Means; <u>Roman Roads</u>

I. Grammar
A. Adjectives

Adjectives are words used to modify nouns or words or word groups used as nouns. Some adjectives in English are *black, large, thin,* and *healthy.* Numbers can also be adjectives when used to describe nouns, *fifteen boys.*

Copy this chart and put it on a page titled <u>Adjectives</u> in the "Grammar" section of your notebook.

Adjectives

Functions. Adjectives are used to:
1. **describe** a quality of a noun: *beautiful morning, red flag*
2. **limit** a noun: this includes **possessives** *(my, your)*; **demonstratives** *(this car, that recipe)*; **interrogatives** *(what year? whose dinner?)*

Agreement. In Latin adjectives which end in **-us, -a,** or **-um** belong to the first and second declension. Some also end in **-er** and belong to the same declensions. They are learned in all three genders because they must agree with the noun they modify in gender, number and case. Often the ending for the adjective is the same as the ending for the noun it modifies, but this is not always true.

Poetae sunt beati. *Poets are happy.*
Feminae sunt amicae. *The women are friendly.*

In the first example **beati** has the masculine ending to agree with **poetae**, which is masculine.

Adjectives Used as Nouns. Any adjective may be used as a noun. Its translation is determined by the gender of the adjective. Make flash cards for these adj ectives.

bonus, *a good man*   **boni,** *good men, the good*
bona, *a good woman*   **bonae,** *good women*
bonum, *a good thing*   **bona,** *good things, good*

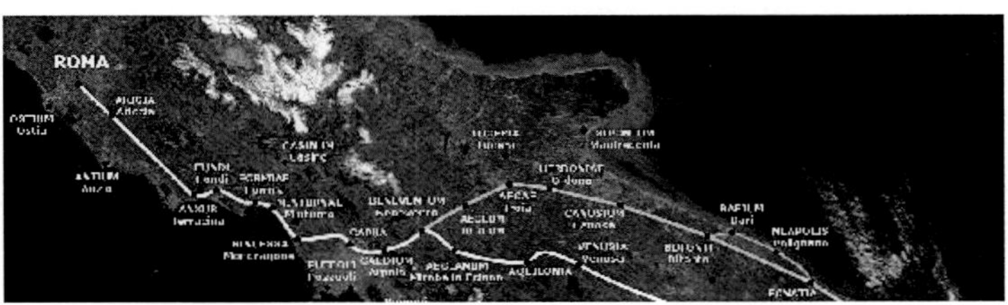

Via Appia

Remember, adjectives are NOT necessarily placed after the noun. They can be anywhere.

malus, *a bad man*	**mali,** *bad men*
mala, *a bad woman*	**malae,** *bad women*
malum, *a bad thing*	**mala,** *bad things*
(none)	**multi,** *many men*
	multae, *many women*
	multa, *many things*

In English we might say, "The poor you will always have with you," and "The meek will inherit the earth."

Finding the stem. When you learn this vocabulary, you are learning the nominative singular forms for masculine, feminine and neuter adjectives. To find the stem, remove the **-a** ending from the feminine singular form. The part which is left is the stem to which you add the endings. Sometimes the **e** is kept, and sometimes it is dropped; by looking at the feminine singular form you can see if the **e** is kept.

In Latin, adjectives may be placed either before or after the noun modified. The general rule is that the most important word is placed first in a phrase or a sentence. For that reason, numeral adjectives, adjectives which indicate quantity and interrogative adjectives tend to be placed before the nouns which they modify.

B. Paradigm

Enter the following paradigm on a page titled <u>First and Second Declension Adjectives</u> in the "Grammar" section.

	gra′tus, *pleasing*			**li′ber,** *free*		
			Singular			
	M	F	N	M	F	N
Nom.	gra′tus	gra′ta	gra′tum	li′ber	li′bera	li′berum
Gen.	gra′ti	gra′tae	gra′ti	li′beri	li′berae	li′beri
Dat.	gra′to	gra′tae	gra′to	li′bero	li′berae	li′bero
Acc.	gra′tum	gra′tam	gra′tum	li′berum	li′beram	li′berum
Abl.	gra′to	gra′tā	gra′to	li′bero	li′bera	li′bero
			Plural			
Nom.	gra′ti	gra′tae	gra′ta	li′beri	li′berae	li′bera
Gen.	grator′um	gratar′um	grator′um	libero′rum	libera′rum	libero′rum
Dat.	gra′tis	gra′tis	gra′tis	li′beris	li′beris	li′beris
Acc.	gra′tos	gra′tas	gra′ta	li′beros	li′beras	li′bera
Abl.	gra′tis	gra′tis	gra′tis	li′beris	li′beris	li′beris

The Appian Way

II. Ablative of Means or Instrument

Enter the following chart in your notebook on the page titled <u>Ablative Case</u> in the section, "Cases and Declensions".

The means by which an action is formed, not the person by whom, is expressed by the ablative case without a Latin preposition.

Normally, use the English preposition, *with,* or sometimes *by,* or *in,* to translate.

Viri gladiis oppugnant.

The men attack with swords.

NOTA BENE: In Latin, you can often identify Ablative of Means if you are able to substitute mentally, "by means of" or "using" before the noun.

Example: The boys carry the books by means of or using the wagon.

III. VocabularyEnglish Derivatives

Adjectives are put on green flash cards with black ink (32). Pronouns are to be put on blue cards with red ink (4). The first one in each listing is the masculine one; the second is the feminine one, and the third is the neuter form.

āl′bus, āl′ba, āl′būm, *white* — (albino)

āl′tūs, āl′ta, āl′tūm, *high, deep, tall* — (altitude, altimeter)

amī′cūs, amī′ca, amī′cūm, *friendly* — (amiable, amicable)

bēā′tūs, bēā′ta, bēā′tūm, *happy, blessed* — (beatitude)

bō′nūs, bō′na, bō′nūm, *good, kind* — (bonus)

dēf es′sūs, dēfes′sa, dēfes′sūm, *tired, weary*

fe′rūs, fe′ra, fe′rūm, *fierce, wild, savage* — (feral)

grā′tūs, grā′ta, grā′tūm, *pleasing, welcome, grateful* — (gratitude)

inimī′cūs, inimī′ca, inimī′cūm, *unfriendly, hostile* — (inimical)

lā′tūs, lā′ta, lā′tūm, *wide, broad* — (latitude)

lī′ber, lī′bera, lī′berūm, *free* — (liberty)

lon′gūs, lon′ga, lon′gūm, *long, tall*

māg′nūs, māg′na, māg′nūm, *large, great, big* — (magnify)

mā′lūs, mā′la, mā′lūm, *bad, evil* — (malice)

mē′dīūs, mē′dīa, mē′dīūm, *middle of* *

mē′ūs, mē′a, mē′ūm, *my, mine, my own*

mī′ser, mī′sera, mī′serūm, *unhappy, sad, miserable*

mŭl′tūs, mŭl′ta, mŭl′tūm, *much,* pl. *many* — (multiply)

nī′ger, nī′gra, nī′grūm, *black*

nōs′ter, nōs′tra, nōs′trūm, *our*

nō′vūs, nō′va, nō′vūm, *new* — (novelty)

pārā′tūs, pārā′ta, pārā′tūm, *prepared, ready*

pār′vūs, pār′va, pār′vūm, *small, little*

prox′īmūs, prox′īma, prox′īmūm, *neighboring* — (approximate, proximity)

pŭl′cher, pŭl′chra, pŭl′chrūm, *beautiful, pretty, noble, fine, handsome*

pū′rūs, pū′ra, pū′rūm, *pure* — (purify)

sā′cer, sā′cra, sā′crūm, *sacred, holy, consecrated, dedicated, accursed***

sānc′tūs, sānc′ta, sānc′tūm, *pure, holy, virtuous* — (sanctify)

sū′ūs, sū′a, sū′ūm, *his own, her own, its own*

tū′ūs, tū′a, tū′ūm, *your, yours, your own* (singular)

vē′rūs, vē′ra, vē′rūm, *true* — (verily, verify)

ves′ter, ves′tra, ves′trūm, *your, yours, your own* (plural only*)*

***medius** is not followed by the genitive; the "of" is part of the meaning.

** **sacer** can mean *set aside to be cursed*

ē′go, mē′ī, *I, me* — (egotist)

nōs, nōs′trūm, *we, us*

tū, tū′ī, *you*

vōs, ves′trūm, *you (all)*

<blockquote>
Notice the effect of the prefix **in-** with the word **inimicus**. What would **ingratus** mean?
</blockquote>

IV. Personal Pronouns

A pronoun is a word used in place of a noun. Personal pronouns are obviously those pronouns which refer to persons. They include *I, you, he, she, it, we you (plural)* and *they*. In this lesson we are going to memorize the different forms for some of these.

First Person Pronouns

Cases	Singular	Plural
Nom.	ē′go, *I*	nōs, *we*
Gen.	mē′ī, *of me*	nōstri,
Dat.	mī′hī, *to, for me*	nō′bīs, *to,*
Acc.	mē, *me*	nōs, *us*
Abl.	mē, *(by, with) me*	nō′bīs, *(by with us)*

Second Person Pronouns

Nom.	tū, *you*	vōs, *you*
Gen.	tū′ī, *of you*	ves′tri, ves′trūm, *of you*
Dat.	tib′ī, *to, for you*	vōbīs, *to, for you*
Acc.	tē, *you*	vōs, *you*
Abl.	tē, *(by, with)* you	vōbis *(by, with)* you

The genitive of personal pronouns is not used to show possession. Instead we use the adjectives, **meus, noster, tuus,** and **vester**. Translate **vestri** and **vestrum** as *of you*, and **nostri**, and **nostrum** as *of us*.

When we use **cum** with personal pronouns it is placed after the pronoun and the two words are combined into one word: **mecum, nobiscum, tecum, vobiscum.** The usual order in Latin is to say "I and you", rather than "you and I", as it is done in English.

You use pronouns as the subject when you want to add emphasis. Otherwise, the ending of the verb is sufficient to show who is the subject.

Amas puellam. *You love the girl.*

<u>**Tu**</u> **amas puellam**. <u>*You*</u> *love the girl.*

V. Exercises

> Further explanation of the use of adjectives as nouns: In English we rarely use adjectives as nouns. In Latin, we <u>often</u> do.
>
> And, one reason we did not give the paradigm for **multi** in the singular is because you don't really translate it as a noun. In the plural, you could say, "many (men) sunt hic", **multi sunt hic**, but in the singular, it would not be realistic to say "much (man) is here", **multus est hic**.

A. Forms. Decline two of the adjectives from the vocabulary in all forms, singular and plural.

Answer A. Follow the paradigm in the lesson.

B. Pronouns. Translate only the italicized words.

> Remember, in Latin, the order of pronouns is different than it is in English. Where we would say, " you and I", in Latin it would be "I and you."

1. Give the book *to me*. 2. He saw *you and us*. 3. *We* have been friends for a long time.
4. *You* (pl.) *and I* love your father. 5. They were going *with us*.
6. The servants will be working *with you* (pl.).

> 1. mihi
> 2. nos et te
> 3. nos
> 4. ego et vos
> 5. nobiscum
> 6. vobiscum

C. Adjectives

1. parvum oppidum	6. ferorum equorum	11. album equum
2. cum amicis apostolis	7. liber sacer	12. balaenas magnas
3. proxima oppida	8. tuis prophetis	13. beatis viris
4. stellae novae	9. in mediā viā	14. Raeda est parata.
5. liberos populos	10. Sancta Sabbata	15. puerorum altorum

> 1. a small town
> 2. with the friendly apostles
> 3. the neighboring towns
> 4. new stars (or *the new star's*, or *to/for the new star*)
> 5. free peoples (or *free nations*)
> 6. of the wild horses (or *the wild horses'*)
> 7. a sacred book
> 8. to/for your prophets, or by/with your prophets
> 9. in the middle of the road
> 10. Holy Sabbath (or *Sabbaths*)
> 11. a white horse
> 12. large whales
> 13. to/for the happy men, or by/with the happy men
> 14. The carriage is ready.
> 15. of the tall boys (or *the tall boys'*)

D. Mark each sentence and then translate.

> **NOTE:** Underline the adjective which goes with each noun because it will be in the same case, number, and gender as the noun it modifies. From now on, it is important that students mark the gender of the noun whenever they have an adjective modifying a noun.

    1/pl.   (in + abl. s. fem.)   1/pl. nom. pl.
1. We are walking (in the middle of the road) and we are tired.
      In media via ambulamus et sumus defessi. (or, *defessae*)

    2/s.   nom.s. fem.   gen.s.
2. Are you a holy woman (of God)?
      Esne sancta femina Dei? (or *sacra*)

    nom.s. 3/s. acc. (abl. means, fem.)
3. The man calls me (with a beautiful trumpet).
      Vir tuba pulchra me vocat.

    nom.pl. neut. 3/pl. nom.pl.neut. nom.pl.neut.
4. Your gifts are pleasing and beautiful.
      Tua dona sunt grata et pulchra. (or if speaking to more than one person, **vestra**)

    nom.s.masc. 3/s.   acc.pl.fem.   (dat.pl. masc.)
5. The tall farmer gives the new carriages (to the good men).
      Agricola altus viris bonis raedas novas dat.

    1/pl.   nom.sg.fem.   conj. 2/s. or pl. nom.pl.fem.
6. The neighboring handmaiden and you are true friends, aren't you?
      Nonne proxima ancilla et tu es (or *vos estis*) verae amicae?

    gen.s. nom.s neut. 3/s. nom.s.n. nom.s.n.
7. God's Word is pure and true.
      Dei verbum est purum et verum.

    nom.pl. m. nom.pl.m.   3/pl. (in + abl. s.)
8. Many (and) good men sing (in Italy).
      Multi et boni in Italia cantant. (or *boni viri*)

    nom.s.   3/s.   acc. sg. fem.   (Abl.Means/s.)   dative
9. My teacher honors our little family (by means of a kind letter) (to us)
      Meus magister nostram parvam familiam bona epistula nobis
          honorat. (or, *Mea magistra…bonis litteris*)

    nom.s. fem.   3/s. nom.s. fem. dat.
10. Your small country is neighboring (to us).
      Tua patria parva est proxima nobis.

E. Translate. Latin to English.

    nom.pl.m.   acc.pl.n.   3/pl.
    1. Multi   magna dona amant.   Many (*men*) love large gifts.

From now on, just m., f., or n. will mean masculine, feminine, or neuter.

Why not say *between many women*? It is because *between* indicates only two women. The sentence says "many".

(inter + acc. pl. f.)   2/s.   nom.s. f.
2. Inter feminas multas, es beata.
     Among many women, you are blessed.

   nom. s. m.   acc. s. m.   3/s.
3. Meus filius gladium portat.
     My son is carrying a sword.

   nom. s. m.   3/s. nom. s. m.
4. Tuus filius agricola est paratus.
     Your son the farmer is ready.

   nom. s. m.   acc. s.n.   3/s.
5. Proximus populus bellum amat.
     The neighboring nation loves war (or *neighboring people love war)*.

   infinitive   (cum + abl.pl.m.) adv.   nom. pl.m.   1/pl.
6. Pugnare cum magnis viris non   parati   sumus.
     We are not prepared to fight with large men.

   nom. pl. n.   3/pl. nom.pl.n. dat.
7. Dona tua sunt grata mihi.   (or *vestra*, if plural)
     Your gifts are pleasing to me.

   nom.pl.f.   dat.s.m.   3/pl.
8. Purae puellae gratae Domino sunt.
     Pure girls are pleasing to the Lord.

   nom.s.m.   3/s. nom.s. m.   conj.   nom.s.m.
9. Iesus   est meus Dominus et meus sanctus Deus.
     Jesus is my Lord and my holy God.

   nom.pl. m.   acc.s.   3/pl. conj. 3/pl.   nom. pl.m.
10. Liberi viri Deum amant quod sunt boni.
     Free men love God because they are good (men).

   nom. pl. m. (in + abl. pl.) 3/pl.   3/pl.   nom.pl. m.
11. Agricolae in agris laborant, quod non sunt mali.
     The farmers work in the fields because they are not bad men.

   nom. s. m.   (in + abl.s.f.)   3/pl.
12. Miseri poetae in mediā magnā silvā habitant.
     The unhappy poets live in the middle of a large forest.

   nom. s. n. 3/s. nom.s. n.
13. Num caelum est nigrum?
     The sky isn't black, is it?

   nom.s. n.   gen.pl.   3/s. nom.s. n.
14. Testimonium discipulorum est verum.
     The witness of the disciples is true.

VI. Reading Lesson

Romanae Viae

Sunt multae viae (ad) Romam. Viae conveniunt Romae. Viae sunt Via Appia et Via Aurelia et Via Flaminia et Via Latinia et Via Ostiensis et Via Tivolia et Via Tusculia. Via Ostiensis ducit ad oppidum Ostiam. Est occidentale Romae et portus pro Romanis navibus. Via Tivolia est via ad Tivoliam, oppidum orientali Romae.

Romani nonnullas vias appellant nominibus notorum. Via Appia est magna via (ad) Romam. Romani viam Appiam Viam propter Appium Claudium appellant. Appius Claudius est vir Romae qui vias et aquaeducta aedificavit.   Aquaeducta aquam ad oppida et familias portant. Multa aquaeducta in Appia Via sunt.

Via Flaminia est via ab oppido Vercellis quae est in septentrionali. Fidelii familia iter facit in Viā Flaminiā. Familia magnum numerum agricolarum qui per Viam Flaminiam habitant spectat. Multi agricolae in viā ambulant et frumentum carris portant. Amicos salutant.

Aquila et Clara et puellae iam ambulant inter raedas et carros. Puellae cantant dum ambulant. Multos qui etiam per viam ambulant spectant. Familia locum ut requiescat ad viam invenit. Sedere et spectare viros et feminas etiam ambulantes in viā amant. Aquila fabulam de vitā in Romā narrat.

Raedae Fidelium et familiam ad insulam in Viā Flaminiā portant. Vita est bona Fidelio et familiae. Sunt beati!

Responde Latine.

1. Quid (*what*) notam et magnam viam ad Romam appellant? 2. Quis (*who*) magnas vias et aquaeducta aedificavit? 3. Quem (*whom*) agricolae salutant? 4. Quos (*whom*) familia spectat?

Recognition Vocabulary

aedī′ficāvit, *built* (in the past time, long ago)

āmbūlān′tēs, *walking*

āquaedūc′tūm, -i, n., *aqueduct*

convē′nīūnt, *come together*

dū′cit, *leads*

dūm, *while*

invē′nit, *finds*

iām, *already, now*

ī′ter fā′cit, *is traveling*

lō′cus, lō′cī, m., *place*

nā′vībūs, *ships*

nōmin′ībūs, *with names*

nonnūl′las, *some*

nō′tūs, nō′ta, nō′tūm, *famous*

quī, *who*

occīdentā′lē, *west*

orīentā′lē, *east*

por′tūs, *harbor*

quae, *which*

quō′quē, *also*

Rō′mae, *at Rome*

Rōmā′nī, *the Romans*

septentrīōnā′lī, *north*

ūt rēquīē′scāt, *in order that they might rest*, or *to rest*

Street Names:

Vī′a Āp′pīa, *Appian Way*

Vī′a Aurē′līa, *Aurelian Way*

Vī′a Flāmin′īa, *Flaminian Way*

Vī′a Lātin′īa, *Latinian Way*

Vī′a Tīvo′līa, *Tivolian Way*

Vī′a Tuscū′līa, *Tusculian Way*

Vī′a Ostīen′sis, *Ostian Way*

Roman Roads

There are many roads to Rome. The roads come together at Rome. The roads are the Appian Way, Aurelian Way, Flaminian Way, Latinian Way, Ostian Way, Tivolian Way and Tusculian Way. The Ostian Way leads to the town of Ostia. It is west of Rome and is the harbor for Roman ships. The Tivolian Way is a road to Tivoli, a town east of Rome.

The Romans name some roads with the names of famous men. The Appian Way is a large road to Rome. The Romans call the road the Appian Way because of Appius Claudius. Appius Claudius is (*was*) a man of Rome who built roads and aqueducts. Aqueducts carry water to the towns and the families. Many aqueducts are on the Appian Way.

The Flaminian Way is the road from the town of Vercellae which is in the north. The Fidelius family is traveling on the Flaminian Way. The family is looking at a large number of farmers who live along the Appian Way. Many farmers walk on the road and carry grain with carts. They greet friends.

Aquila, Clara and the girls are already walking between the carriages and carts. The girls are singing while they walk. They are watching many who also are walking along the road. The family finds a place to rest near the road. They like to sit and look at the men and women also walking on the road. Aquila tells a story about life in Rome.

The carriages carry Fidelius and the family to the apartment on the Flaminian Way. Life is good for Fidelius and the family. They are happy!

Questions
1. What do they call the fam ous large road to Rome? Appellant Viam Appiam.
2. Who built large roads and aqueducts? Appius Claudius aedificavit.
3. Whom do the farmers greet? Agricolae amicos salutant.
4. Whom does the family watch? Familia viros et feminas spectat.

A bridge across the
Tiber River in Rome

As the city was on a river, about fifteen miles from the sea, Ancus thought it would be a very good thing to have a seaport connected with it; so he built a harbor at Ostia, a town at the mouth of the Tiber. Between the city and the port there was a long, straight road, which was built with the greatest care, and made so solidly that it is still in use today.

To last so long, a road had to be made in a different way from those which are built today. The Romans used to dig a deep trench, as long and as wide as the road they intended to make. Then the trench was nearly filled with stones of different sizes, packed tightly together. On top of this thick layer they laid great blocks of stone, forming a strong and even pavement. A road like this, with a solid bed several feet deep, could not be washed out by the spring rains, but was smooth and hard in all seasons. Little by little the Romans built many other roads, which ran out of Rome in all directions. From this arose the saying, which is still very popular in Europe, and which you will often hear, "All roads lead to Rome."

The most famous of all the Roman roads was the Appian Way, leading from Rome southeast to Brundusium, a distance of three hundred miles. This road, although built about two thousand years ago, is still in good condition, showing how careful the Romans were in their work.

PICTURE DRAWN BY TEACHER MARY JOY JOHNSON

From Story of the Romans.

Name ____Date _____________________

Latin in the Christian Trivium
Study Sheet
Chapter Nine A

Grammar

1. Why do Latin adjectives have three forms in every case? <u>There is one for masculine, one for feminine, and one form for neuter nouns.</u>

2. With what does an adjective agree? <u>It agrees with the noun it modifies in gender, number and case.</u>

3. Therefore, does the ending of an adjective always agree with the ending of the noun it modifies? <u>No, it often does, but not necessarily.</u>

4. What kind of adjectives may be used as nouns in Latin? <u>Any adjective may be used as a noun.</u>

5. How do we translate **multi** when it is used as a noun? <u>Many men.</u>

6. Complete these vocabulary words, writing the feminine and neuter forms completely.

MASCULINE	FEMININE	NEUTER	MEANING
albus	alba	album	white
amicus	amica	amicum	friendly
altus	alta	altum	high, deep
beatus	beata	beatum	blessed, happy
bonus	bona	bonum	good
defessus	defessa	defessum	tired
ferus	fera	ferum	wild, fierce, savage
gratus	grata	gratum	pleasing
inimicus	inimica	inimicum	unfriendly
latus	lata	latum	wide, broad
liber	libera	liberum	free
longus	longa	longum	long
magnus	magna	magnum	large, great
malus	mala	malum	bad, evil
medius	media	medium	in the middle of
meus	mea	meum	my, mine
multus	multa	multum	much, in pl., many
niger	nigra	nigrum	black
novus	nova	novum	new
paratus	parata	paratum	prepared, ready
parvus	parva	parvum	small, little
proximus	proxima	proximum	neighboring
pulcher	pulchra	pulchrum	beautiful, pretty
purus	pura	purum	pure
sacer	sacra	sacrum	holy, sacred
sanctus	sancta	sanctum	pure, holy, virtuous
suus	sua	suum	his own, her own, its own

tuus	tua	tuum	your, yours
verus	vera	verum	true
vester	vestra	vestrum	your, yours (pl.)

Practice

7. Decline **patria pulchra,** *beautiful homeland.*

SINGULAR	PLURAL
patria pulchra	patriae pulchrae
patriae pulchrae	patriarum pulchrarum
patriae pulchrae	patriis pulchris
patriam pulchram	patrias pulchras
patria pulchra	patriis pulchris

8. Decline **liber sacer,** *holy book.*

SINGULAR	PLURAL
liber sacer	libri sacri
libri sacri	librorum sacrorum
libro sacro	libris sacris
librum sacrum	libros sacros
libro sacro	libris sacris

9. Write the declension of the following personal pronouns.

SINGULAR		PLURAL	
ego	tu	nos	vos
mei	tui	nostri, nostrum	vestri, vestrum
mihi	tibi	nobis	vobis
me	te	nos	vos
me	te	nobis	vobis

10. Write in Latin:

with me	mecum	with us	nobiscum
with you *(sing.)*	tecum	with you *(pl.)*	vobiscum

Practice with pronouns

11. Underline the Latin pronoun which is the correct translation for the italicized word.

    a. My friend gave *me* a new dictionary. (**me, ad me, <u>mihi</u>, nos**)
    b. Her horse ran *to you.* (**<u>ad te</u>, te, vos, vestrum**)
    c. His brother is going *with us.* (**<u>nobiscum</u>, cum nos, mihi, noster**)
    d. Give *me* liberty or give *me* death. (**tui, ad me, ego, <u>mihi</u>**)
    e. God sees me and everything *I* do. (**me, <u>ego</u>, mihi, mecum**)
    f. That was so kind *of you.* (**tecum, <u>vestri</u>, vobis, mihi**)

g. *We* love God's Law for its expression of holiness. **(nobis, ego, <u>nos</u>, vobiscum)**
h. The Lord be *with you*! **(mecum, <u>vobiscum</u>, vester, teipsum)**
i. Angels have not appeared *to me*. **(ad te, <u>mihi</u>, mecum, nostrum)**
j. He has spoken *to you* and your friends as well. **(ad me, ad te, <u>tibi</u>, vos)**

Using Ablative of Means

12. *Pretend you were able to translate these into Latin. Underline any prepositional phrases that would be Ablative of Means in Latin. Two are done for you.*

Example: He did his math homework <u>using a pencil.</u>
He was able to attend college <u>with his full scholarship</u>.

a. We learn about the news each day <u>by means of the radio.</u>
b. Nick became fit <u>by means of daily exercise.</u>
c. Her voice was clear and strong <u>using a new microphone.</u>
d. Rob checked the car's oil <u>with a dip stick.</u>
e. Uncle John wrote *Stone Fox,* <u>using his new computer.</u>

Name ____ Date ___________________

Latin in the Christian Trivium
Supplementary Study Sheet 9B
Chapter Nine

Grammar

Some of you may be wondering where the personal pronouns are for *he*, *she*, and *it*.
You will learn them later again as demonstrative pronouns and adjectives, but you can be introduced to them now.

	is, ea, id			**ei, eae, ea**		
	Masc.	*Fem.*	*Neuter*	*Masc.*	*Fem.*	*Neuter*
Nom.	**is,** *he*	**ea**, *she*	**id,** *it*	**ei**, *they*	**eae**, *they*	**ea**, *they*
Gen.	**eius**, *his, of him*	**eius**, *her, of her*	**eius**, *its, of it*	**eorum**, *of them, their*	**earum**, *of them, their*	**eorum**, *of them, their*
Dat.	**ei**, *to/for him*	**ei**, *to/for her*	**ei**, *to/for it*	**eis**, *to/for them*	**eis**, *to/for them*	**eis**, *to/for them*
Acc.	**eum**, *him*	**eam**, *her*	**id**, *it*	**eos**, *them*	**eas**, *them*	**ea**, *them*
Abl.	**eo**, *by/with him*	**eā**, *by/with her*	**eo**, *by/with it*	**eis**, *by/with them*	**eis**, *by/with them*	**eis**, *by/with them*

Let's try using them in sentences now. Here are English sentences, and you put the correct form of **is, ea**, or **id** in place of the blank. Use the English gender; don't worry about translating the entire sentence into Latin.

Put the proper Latin pronoun in place of the italicized English ones. Sometimes there are two.

1. Give your money *to him.*   __*ei*__

2. *He* likes *her.*   __*is*__   __*eam*__

3. *She* likes *him.*   __*ea*__   __*eum*__

4. My friend likes *her.*   __*eam*__

5. *Her* house is red.   __*eius*__

6. *Its* coat is soft.   __*eius*__

7. We will go with *them.*   __*eis*__

8. *She* found *them.*   __*ea*__   __*eos, eas,* or *ea*__

9. *Their* hearts were pure.   __*eorum* or *earum*__

10. *To him* we gave the honors.   __*ei*__

This time, substitute in a pronoun in place of the italicized noun; just use one Latin word. Here are two example sentences:

a. *A good name* is to be more desired than great riches.
   Mentally change to: <u>It</u> is to be more desired than riches.

   <u>Id</u> is to be more desired than great riches.

b. *The rich man* rules over the poor.
   Mentally change to: <u>He</u> rules over the poor.
   <u>Is</u> rules over the poor.

Now you do yours.

1. A wise man guards *his tongue.*
    A wise man guards <u>*id.*</u>

2. The way *of a guilty man* is crooked.
    (Change to: The way *of him* is crooked.)
    The way of <u>*eius*</u> is crooked.

3. The Lord is the maker *of them* all.
    The Lord is the maker <u>*eorum*</u> all.

4. The execution *of justice* is joy for the righteous.
    The execution <u>*eius*</u> is joy for the righteous.

Latin in the Christian Trivium – Volume I Teacher's Guide

5. The execution of justice is joy *for the righteous.*
   The execution of justice is joy _eis._

6. Better is a poor man who lives with *integrity.*
   Better is a poor man who lives with _eo._

7. It is by *his deeds* that a boy distinguishes himself.
   It is by _eis_ that a boy distinguishes himself.

8. He offered help *to a woman.*
      He offered help _ei._

9. His friends have gone far from *Peter.*
   His friends have gone far from _eo._

10. The Lord has made both *of them.*
    The Lord has made both _eorum (or, earum)._

DRILL SHEET AFTER CHAPTER NINE
MARK AND TRANSLATE INTO LATIN:

1. the good boys (nom.) pueri boni
2. neighboring towns (nom.) oppida proxima
3. your friends (acc.) tuos amicos (or *tuas amicas*)
4. the great commandment (nom.) magnum mandatum
5. of pure water aquae purae
6. to/for pretty eyes oculis pulchris
7. in the middle of the island in media insula
8. to us ad nos (or in dative: *nobis*)
9. true words (acc.) verba vera
10. a black horse's equi nigri
11. Holy God (nom.) Sanctus Deus (or *Sacer Deus*)
12. of our new books librorum nostrorum novorum
13. for blessed women pro feminis beatis, or feminis beatis
14. evil men (nom.) mali (or *mali viri*)
15. a pleasing word (acc.) verbum gratum
16. his own school (acc.) ludum suum
17. with many angels cum multis angelis
18. a new commandment (acc.) mandatum novum
19. My friend is a true friend. Meus amicus est verus amicus.
20. We honor the memory of your friend. Memoriam tui amici honoramus.
21. Large whales live near the long island. Magnae balaenae ad longam insulam habitant.
22. A man is thinking about his (own) homeland. Vir de sua patria putat.

> Just a reminder. There are often several ways to translate. Only one is usually given. When no gender is specified, the masculine is used.

1/s.   acc. pl. n.

23. I <u>am listening to</u> your (pl.) <u>good words</u>.
       Vestra (or if speaking to only one person, *tua*) verba bona ausculto.

nom.pl. n.   3/pl.   dat.s.m.

24 .<u>Your words</u> <u>are pleasing</u> (to my friend).
       Tua (or if to more than one person, *vestra*) verba meo amico grata sunt.

1/pl.   dat.   acc.pl.   (de + abl. pl. f.)

25. <u>We</u> <u>are telling</u> you <u>stories</u> (about the blessed women).
       Fabulas tibi (or if pl., *vobis*) de feminis beatis narramus.

3/s.   (dat. sing.)   gen.s.

26. <u>She</u> <u>is singing</u> (to the Lord) (of heaven).
    Domino caeli cantat.

nom. s. f.   3/s.   nom.s. f. (dat.s.)

27. A <u>pure girl</u> <u>is</u> <u>pleasing</u> (to God).
       Puella pura est grata Deo.

nom.s. m.   3/s.   nom.s. m.

28. The <u>small book</u> <u>is</u> <u>black</u>.
       Liber parvus est niger.

nom.s. m.   3/s.   (ad + acc. s.)

29. An <u>unfriendly servant</u> <u>is</u> (near the farmhouse).
       Servus inimicus est ad villam.

nom.s. f.   3/s.   acc. pl. f.   acc. pl. m.

30. The <u>good handmaiden</u> <u>takes care of</u> <u>the small girls and boys</u>.
       Ancilla bona puellas parvas et pueros parvos curat.

nom.s. masc.   3/s.   acc. pl. neut.   (abl. means. s. masc.)

31. <u>His</u> (own) <u>servant</u> <u>carries</u> the <u>white gifts</u> (in a black wagon).
       Servus suus alba dona carro nigro portat.

1/pl.   (in + abl.s. n.)   (in + abl. s. f.)

32. <u>We</u> <u>live</u> (in a neighboring town) (in the middle of Gaul).
       In proximo oppido in media Gallia habitamus.

nom. pl. n.   3/pl.   nom. pl. n.

33. <u>Your words</u>   <u>are</u> <u>true</u>.
       Tua (or vestra) verba sunt vera.

nom. pl. n.   3/pl.   nom.pl. n.   (dat.)

34. <u>Evil words</u>   <u>are</u> not <u>pleasing</u> (to us).
       Mala verba grata nobis non sunt.

nom.pl.m.   3/pl. nom.pl. m. (dat.)

35. The <u>apostles</u> <u>are</u> <u>sacred</u> (to God).
       Apostoli sacri Deo sunt.

nom.pl. m.   3/pl. nom.pl. m. gen.s. (in + abl. s.)

36. The <u>boys</u>   <u>are</u> <u>tall</u>   (in the poet's family), aren't they?
       Nonne pueri alti in poetae familia sunt?

Latin in the Christian Trivium – Volume I Teacher's Guide

  3/pl.   nom.pl. n.   (in + abl.)
37. <u>Are</u> there <u>many dangers</u> (in Italy)?
       Suntne multa pericula in Italia?

  3/s.   nom.s. masc.   infinitive   acc. s. masc.
38. <u>Is</u> the <u>little boy</u> <u>ready</u> **to greet** the messenger?
       Parvus ne puer nuntium salutare paratus est?

  1/pl.   nom.pl. m.   1/pl.   nom.pl. m.
39. Because <u>we</u> <u>are</u> <u>free</u>,   <u>we</u> <u>are</u> <u>happy</u>.
       Quoniam sumus liberi, sumus beati. (or *liberae*)

  3/pl.   nom.pl. f.   (in + abl.s. n.)
40. There <u>are</u> <u>many stars</u> (in the black sky).
       Sunt multae stellae in caelo nigro.

  nom. pl. m.   3/pl.   acc. pl. m.   (in + abl. s.)
41. The <u>unfriendly men</u> <u>are attacking men</u>   (in the kingdom).
       Inimici (**viri** may or may not be added here) viros in regno oppugnant.

  1/s.   acc. s. f.
42. I <u>am asking for</u> a new <u>carriage</u>.
       Raedam novam rogo.

  nom.s. 3/s.   acc. pl m.   3/s. nom.s. m.
43. The <u>boy</u> <u>is listening to</u> his (own) good friends, and <u>he</u> <u>is</u> <u>happy</u>.
       Puer suos amicos bonos auscultat et est beatus.

  nom.s. f.   nom.s. f.   3/s. (ad + acc.s.)
44. A <u>broad</u> and <u>long province</u> <u>is</u> (near Italy).
       Provincia lata et longa ad Italiam est.

  nom.pl. m. 3/pl.   nom.pl. m.
45. The <u>friends</u> <u>are</u> not <u>fierce</u>.
       Amici non sunt feri. (or, *amicae non sunt ferae*)

  2/s.   infinitive   acc.s.
46. <u>Do</u> <u>you</u> <u>like</u> **to guard** the <u>kingdom</u>?
       Regnumne servare amas ? (or *amatis*)

Deus nobis linguam dedit.

At the end of the lesson students will be able to:

- count in Latin.
- know the difference between cardinal and ordinal numerals.
- understand the Roman calendar.
- have memorized the names of the seven hills of Rome.

Chapter Ten

1. Enter the phrase first page of Chapter Ten into the student notebook. This is the name of a hymn which you might want to find in your hymnal and translate. It will be easy for your student now.
2. Read and discuss Section **I Grammar**.
3. Copy the numeral paradigms.
4. Memorize numerals. Learn across: **unus, una, unum**, etc.
5. **Vocabulary II**. Make vocabulary cards and/or vocabulary sheets for your notebook. Be sure your students are able to deduce the meaning of each derivative from the Latin root. Some students are interested in the "math connection" with words from this lesson. Would a Latin student know how many angles are in a nonagon? How many is sextillion anyway? What are primary, secondary, and tertiary industries in the United States? (Answer: Primary: farming, lumber, etc., Secondary: manufacturing, and Tertiary: service industries.)
6. Read and discuss **Section III**. This is very important. Emphasize the giving, showing, and telling verbs which take the dative case.
7. Do all of the **Study Sheet**.
8. Section **IV**, **Exercise A**.
9. Do the **Drill Sheet**.
10.   Section **IV**, **Exercise B**, quickly done orally if the teacher has time.
11.   Learn the song in **IV C**.
12.   Read and discuss **V Our Calendar**. Suggestion for a report: all the various types of calendars.
13.   **V Reading Lesson**. Rome considered itself to be a living thing, like a person or a god.
14.   Color the map in section **VIII**; Color the Flumen Tiber (Tiber River) blue; the Circus Maximus, the Forum, and the Castra Praetoria red. (Teacher note: The Forum Romanorum is just south of the Temple of Jupiter.) After reading the story, see if you can find where the Fidelius family lives, and put an X on the spot.
15.   Review for the test.
16.   Give **Test Five**.
17.   Correct the test.

Te Deum (Laudamus).
(We Praise) Thee, God.

Numerals, Dative of Indirect Object; Calendar;
<u>The Great Town of Rome</u>

Numerals, which are also adjectives, are both cardinal and ordinal numerals. *Cardinal* means "of first importance"; it is the primary way to express a number. *Ordinal* (from **ordo**, rank) shows the order or rank of something. Of the cardinal numerals, only *one, two* and *three* are declined.

I. Grammar
Numerals

Unus, *one*, is declined as follows. Notice that **unus** is only singular because there could not be a plural form for one of anything. These endings will be used again for irregular adjectives in Chapter 15. Please write the following charts and put them in your notebook under <u>Adjectives</u> in the "Grammar" section.

	MASCULINE	FEMININE	NEUTER
Nom.	u′nus	u′na	u′num
Gen.	uni′us	uni′us	uni′us
Dat.	u′ni	u′ni	u′ni
Acc.	u′num	u′nam	u′num
Abl.	u′no	u′na	u′no

Duo, *two*. At one time, Latin had a separate set of forms for two of anything, so there were three grammatical numbers: singular, dual, and plural. Because of that, the declension of **duo** is irregular. Memorize it. Copy it, and put it below the declension for **unus**.

	MASCULINE	FEMININE	NEUTER
Nom.	du′o	du′ae	du′o
Gen.	duo′ rum	dua′rum	duo′rum
Dat.	duo′bus	dua′bus	duo′bus
Acc.	du′os	du′as	du′o
Abl.	duo′bus	dua′bus	duo′bus

Tres, *three*, is of course, only declined in the plural. These endings are similar to third declension endings also found in Chapter 15. Add this chart to the previous two.

	MASC. and FEM.	NEUTER
Nom.	tres	tri′a
Gen.	tri′um	tri′um
Dat.	tri′bus	tri′bus
Acc.	tres	tri′a
Abl.	tri′bus	tri′bus

II. Vocabulary   English Derivatives

Put these numerals on green cards with black ink (25).

A. Cardinal Numerals

ū′nūs, ū′nă, ū′nūm, *one* (I)   (unify, unit)
dū′ō, dū′æ, dū′ō, *two* (II)   (duet, dual, double)
trĕs, trī′ă, *three* (III)   (trinity, triangle)
quāt′tūōr, *four* (IV)   (quadruplets, quadratic)
quĭn′que, *five* (V)   (quintuplets)
sĕx, *six* (VI)   (sextuplets)
sĕp′tĕm, *seven* (VII)   (September)
ŏc′tō, *eight* (VIII)   (October, octagon)
nō′vĕm, *nine* (IX)   (November)
dē′cĕm, *ten* (X)   (December, decimate)
ūn′dēcĭm, *eleven* (XI)
dūō′dēcĭm, *twelve, dozen* (XII)
vīgĭn′tī, *twenty* (XX)
cĕn′tūm, *one hundred, a hundred* (C)   (century, centurion, cent, percent)
mĭl′lē, *one thousand, a thousand* (M)   (millimeter)

Only the numerals meaning one, two or three are declined. The others up to one hundred remain in the same form no matter what case the noun is in that they modify.

quattuor equi, *four horses*
octo feminarum, *of eight women*

B. Ordinal Numerals

prī′mūs, -ă, -ūm, *first*   (primary)
sēcūn′dūs, -ă, -ūm, *second*   (secondary)
tĕr′tīūs, -ă, -ūm, *third*   (tertiary)
quār′tūs, -ă, -ūm, *fourth*   (quarter)
quĭn′tūs, -ă, -ūm, *fifth*   (quintillion)
sĕx′tūs, -ă, -ūm, *sixth*   (sextillion)
sĕp′tīmūs, -ă, -ūm, *seventh*   (September)
ŏctā′vūs, -ă, -ūm, *eighth*   (October)
nō′nūs, -ă, -ūm, *ninth*   (nonagon)
dĕ′cīmūs, -ă, -ūm, *tenth*   (decimate)

C. More nouns. Feminine nouns of the first declension (I) go on pink cards (7) except **campus,** which is masculine and goes on a blue card (1). Genitive forms are abbreviated. The Roman numeral tells you to which declension each noun belongs.

audā′cīa, - ae, I, f., *boldness, daring, audacity*
cām′pus, -i, II, m., *field, plain*
cau′sa, - ae, I, f., *reason, cause*
cō′pīa, - ae, I, f., *abundance, supply, plenty*   (copious, cornucopia)
    copiae, copia′rūm, f., *forces, troops*
cū′ra, - ae, I, f., *care, anxiety*   (sinecure)
fā′ma, - ae, I, f., *rumor, report, reputation, fame*
hō′ra, - ae, I, f., *hour*
nau′ ta, -ae, I, m., *sailor*   (nautical)
pōr′ta, - ae, I, f., *gate*   (portal)

III. Latin Syntax

On your notebook page titled Dative Case copy the following information.

> **Dative of Indirect Object**   You have noticed previously that the dative case is usually translated, "to" or "for" someone or something. Sometimes in English the words "to" or "for" are left out of the sentence and understood to be there. This is a usage called the *indirect object*. You use the dative case after verbs of *giving, showing*, and *telling*. Use **ad + accusative** when there is motion expressed.
> **Ancilla mihi donum dat.** *The handmaiden gives <u>me</u> a gift. The handmaiden gives a gift <u>to me</u>.*
> **Puer equo frumentum portat.** *The boy carries grain <u>for the horse</u>.*
> **Ad oppidum puer frumentum portat.** *The boy carries grain <u>to town</u>.*

IV. Exercises

A. Numerals

1. unus equus 2. unius puellae 3. duobus viris 4. quinque dona 5. cum octo parvis pueris
6. una ancilla 7. septem pura verba 8. mille stellae 9. viginti raedae 10. octo libros
11. primum oppidum 12. prima femina 13. primus vir 14. nonus agricola 15. quinque linguae
16. quarta porta 17. cum tribus discipulis 18. decem amici 19. quattuor epistulae 20. octavus nauta

1. one horse	11. the first town
2. of one girl, or one girl's	12. the first woman
3. to/for two men, or by/with two men	13. the first man
4. five gifts	14. the ninth farmer
5. with eight small boys	15. five tongues, or five languages
6. one handmaiden	16. the fourth gate
7. seven pure words	17. with three disciples
8. a thousand stars	18. ten friends
9. twenty carriages	19. four letters
10. eight books	20. the eighth sailor

Some of these are repeats of earlier vocabulary words.

B. Translate, noting each case.

    acc. pl. f.   (in + abl.s.) 1/ pl.
1. Septem parvas puellas in viā spectamus
      We are looking at seven small girls on the road.

    3/pl. nom. pl. (in + abl.s.) (prope + acc. s.)
2. Sunt octo equi in oppido prope Romam.
      There are eight horses in the town near Rome.

    3/s. nom. s. m.
3. Est unus Deus.
      There is one God.

    3/pl. (inter + acc. pl. f.)
4. Navigant inter duas insulas.
      They are sailing between two islands.

  nom. s. m.   3/s. nom.s. m. nom.s. m.   3/s. nom.s.m.
5. Primus equus est niger et secundus est albus.
      The first horse is black, and the second is white.

    nom. pl. m.   acc. s. f.   3/pl.
6. Viginti servi puram aquam rogant.
      Twenty servants are asking for pure water.

  nom.s. f. gen. pl.   gen. s. 3/s. nom.s.f.
7. Vita discipulorum Christi est bona.
      The life of the disciples of Christ is good.

    nom.s. gen.s. 3/s. (in + abl. s.)
 8. Copia aquae est in oppido.
      A supply of water is in town .

  nom. s. (ad + acc. s. m.)   3/s.
9. Legatus ad tertium virum ambulat.
      The lieutenant is walking toward (or *near*) the third man.

   conj. nom.s. conj. nom.s. 3/s.
10. Neque vir neque femina lacrimat.
      Neither man nor woman is crying. (Colloquially, neither are crying)

C. A song in Latin

Can you sing this song to the tune of "Ten Little Indians"?

**Unus parvus, duo parvi, tres parvi liberi;
Quattuor parvi, quinque parvi, sex parvi
liberi; Septem parvi, octo parvi, novem parvi
liberi; Decem parvi liberi.**

Then sing it in reverse.

Decem Parvi Liberi

Gail Busby; Tune "Ten Little Indians"

V. Our Calendar

The Romans' early calendar was what is called an agrarian calendar. It began in March, when the planting season began, and ended in the autumn, after the harvest. Days during the wintertime were not on the calendar; they were kept track of only by counting backward from the beginning of the year. ("Today is the 83rd day before March 1.")

Later, the calendar was changed to cover the whole year. But that new calendar was still very inaccurate, and it had whole months called "intercalary" months - they didn't happen every year, they were just added in some years to bring the calendar back into the right relationship to the seasons.

Gaius Iulius Caesar reformed the calendar, creating the Julian calendar. His calendar was much more accurate. It still began in March, though. The 12 months of Caesar's calendar were named Martius, Aprilis, Maius, Iunius, Quinctilis, Sextilis, September, October, November, December, Ianuarius, and Februarius. You can see here that September really is the seventh month.

When Caesar was killed, the month of Quinctilis (fifth) was renamed Iulius (July) to honor him, and later Sextilis (sixth) was renamed Augustus (August) to honor the Emperor Augustus. Later still, in the 6th century, the Gregorian calendar replaced the Julian. It had the same months, but the new calendar started with January instead of March because January is the month when days begin to grow noticeably longer.
~FROM TEACHER BURBO, ACADEMIC ASSISTANCE CLASSROOM ON AMERICA ONLINE.

Some additional information: January - Ianus, the god of beginnings; February - februa, a Roman ceremony of purification; March - Mars, god of war; April - aperio, to open (as of buds); May - Maia, daughter of Atlas; June - Iunius, a Roman family name. The remaining were named after the numbers, seven through ten.

VI. The City of Rome

Rome was a city built on twenty hills, but only seven are well known. They are the <u>Aventine, Caelian, Capitoline, Esquiline, Palatine, Viminal,</u> and <u>Quirinal.</u> The Forum of the city is the central marketplace. The amphitheater is the place where shows were performed, and the Circus Maximus was the large racetrack, where chariots raced. The city itself is located 17 miles inland from the Tyrrhenian Sea and sits on the banks of the Tiber River.

Because of its long history, Rome is called the Eternal City, *Roma Aeterna.* Eventually the Romans considered the city to be sort of a god, to be worshipped itself. They worshipped the city, then the state, and later the Emperor.

In downtown Rome, this statue was designed byt Giuseppe Sacconi in 1885.

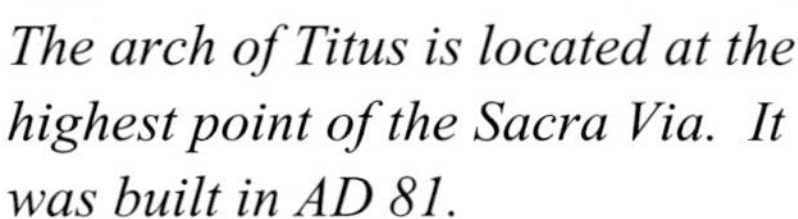

The arch of Titus is located at the highest point of the Sacra Via. It was built in AD 81.

VII. Reading
The names of the hills are underlined in the English passage above and also in this Reading Lesson in Latin.

Magnum Oppidum
Roma

In medio campo Lati habitat populus e magno oppido Romā. Roma est in viginti clivis. Multi sunt parvi, sed septem sunt magni. Magnum oppidum est septendecim milia passuum *(seventeen miles)* ab Tyrhenneno Mare *(Sea)* in Flumine *(river)* Tibere. Populus Romae putat, "Roma est sacra, et dei Romam amant."

<u>Palatinum</u> est in medio oppido. Forum et Amphitheatrum et Circus Maximus circum id *(it)* sunt, et <u>Aventinus, Caelius,</u> et <u>Esquilinus</u> sunt circum Forum et amphitheatrum et Circum Maximum. <u>Capitolinus</u> est ad Tiberem.

Viri feminaeque ad <u>Capitolinum</u> habitant ubi hostes *(enemy)* oppugnant. Porta Capena est inter Clivum <u>Caelium</u> et Clivum <u>Aventinum.</u> Campus Martius est inter Flumen Tiberem et Clivum <u>Capitolinum.</u> Magnum oppidum est latum et longum et pulchrum.

Familia Fideli nunc *(now)* in Romā in novā et pulchrā insulā in medio oppido in Viā Flaminiā ad templum ad Clivum Capitolinum habitat.

Recognition Vocabulary

    āmphīthēā′trūm, āmphīthēā′trī, n., *amphitheatre*
    Cām′pūs Mār′tīūs = *Camp Mars* or *Field of Mars*
    Cāpitōlī′nūs, *the Capitoline Mountain*
    Cīr′cūs Mā′xīmūs, *Circus Maximus,* the racetrack
    clī′vūs, clī′vī, m., *hill*
    flū′men, *river*
    Lā′tī ūm, Lā′tī, n., *Latium* the district in west central Italy where Rome is located
    Palā′tīūm, Palā′tī, n., *the Palatine Hill,* where the wealthy Romans lived
    Pōr′ta Cāpē′na, *Porta Capena,* the gate in the Servian Wall marking the beginning of
        the Via Appia

TEACHER: *Palace* and *palatial* are derived from **palatium.**

VIII. Detailed Map of the City of Rome

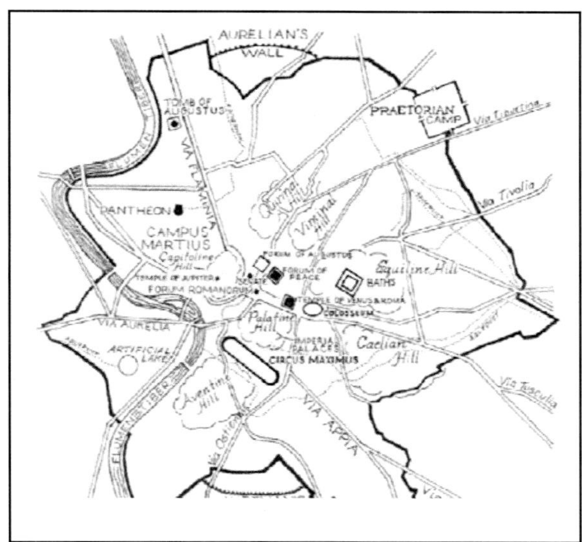

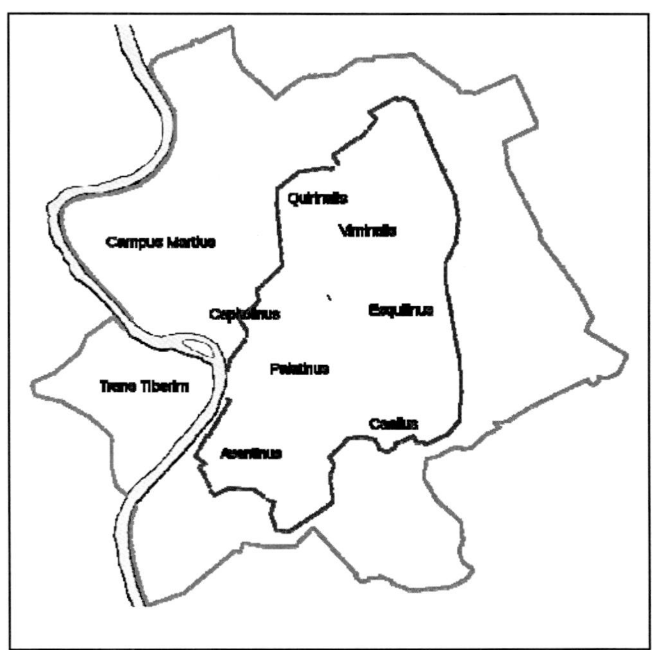

Richardprins via Wiki Commons

<u>Reading Lesson</u>

Rome, A Great Town

In the middle of the plain of Latium lives a people from the great town (of) Rome. Rome is (located) on twenty hills. Many are small, but seven are large. The large town is seventeen miles from the Tyrhennian Sea on the Tiber River. The people of Rome think, "Rome is sacred, and the gods love Rome."

The Palatine is in the middle of the town. The Forum, the Amphitheatre, and the Circus Maximus are around it, and the Aventine, Caelius, and Esquiline are around the Forum, the amphitheatre, and the Circus Maximus. The Capitoline is near the Tiber (River).

Men and women live near the Capitoline when the enemy attacks. Porta Capena is between the Caelian Hill and the Aventine Hill. Camp Mars is between the Tiber River and the Capitoline Hill. The large town is wide, long, and beautiful.

Fidelius' family now lives in Rome in a new beautiful apartment in the middle of town on Via Flaminia near the temple near the Capitoline Hill.

Responde Latine. Answer in a complete sentence.
1. Magnum oppidum Roma est in medio _______________________ . (Fill in the blank.)
2. In quot *(how many)* clivi est Roma?
3. Quae nomina *(What… names)* septem magnorum clivorum sunt? (See map on previous page.)
4. Quid est nomen *(name)* fluminis?
5. In qua via Fideli familia habitat?

Questions.
1. In medio campo Lati. 2. On how many hills is Rome? Roma est in viginti clivis. 3. What are the names of the seven great hills? Capitoline, Quirinal, Viminal, Esquiline, Caelian, Aventine, Palatine. 4. What is the name of the river? Nomen fluminis est Tiber. 5. On what street does the Fidelius family live? Habitant in Via Flaminia ad Forum.

Can Queen Victoria Eat
Cold Apple Pie?

Name ____Date ____________________

Latin in the Christian Trivium
Study Sheet
Chapter Ten

Grammar

1. Which cardinal numerals are declinable? <u>One, two, and three.</u>

2. Decline **duo** and **tres.**

	MASCULINE	FEMININE	NEUTER
Nom.	duo	duae	duo
Gen.	duorum	duarum	duorum
Dat.	duobus	duabus	duobus
Acc.	duos	duas	duo
Abl.	duobus	duabus	duobus

	MASCULINE and FEMININE	NEUTER
Nom.	tres	tria
Gen.	trium	trium
Dat.	tribus	tribus
Acc.	tres	tria
Abl.	tribus	tribus

PRACTICE WITH NUMERALS

Practice One *Fill in the remaining blanks of this table below.*

ROMAN NUMERAL	CARDINAL	ORDINAL
1. I	unus	primus
2. II	duo	secundus
3. III	tres	tertius
4. IV	quattuor	quartus
5. V	quinque	quintus
6. VI	sex	sextus
7. VII	septem	septimus
8. VIII	octo	octavus
9. IX	novem	nonus
10. X	decem	decimus
11. XI	undecim	(not given)
12. XII	duodecim	(not given)

Practice Two *Identify the following as cardinal or ordinal numerals and translate. Use the nominative case unless another case is indicated.*

1.	my second report	ordinal	mea secunda f ama
2.	with one friend	cardinal	cum uno amico
3.	eight reasons	cardinal	octo causae
4.	the fourth island	ordinal	quarta insula
5.	with 100 angels	cardinal	cum centum angelis
6.	four carriages	cardinal	quattuor raedae
7.	the seventh kingdom	ordinal	septimum regnum
8.	two eyes	cardinal	duo oculi
9.	the third language	ordinal	tertia lingua
10.	the first disciple	ordinal	primus discipulus

Practice Three *Translate these short phrases into English.*

1.	viginti equi	twenty horses
2.	undecim litterae	eleven letters
3.	mille viri	a thousand men
4.	octava causa	the eighth reason
5.	nona epistula	the ninth letter
6.	decimus vir	the tenth man
7.	sextus filius	the sixth son
8.	sexta filia	the sixth daughter
9.	primus liber	the first book
10.	quarta porta	the fourth gate

Practice Four

   nom.s. dat.   acc.s. 3/s.
1. Deus mihi vitam dat.
     God gives me life.

   nom.s.   nom.s. gen.s. 3/s.
2. Christus Filius Dei est.
     Christ is the Son of God.

   nom. pl. dat.   (de + abl.s.) 3/pl.
3. Angeli nobis de Domino nuntiant.
     The angels report to us about the Lord.

   nom.pl.   conj. nom.pl. acc. s. acc.s. 3/pl.
4. Agricolae et poetae Christum Dominum amant.
     Farmers and poets love Christ the Lord.

English Derivatives
Give 1) the Latin origin for these words and 2) use each in an intelligent sentence. An example sentence is given.

1. **sinecure**
sine = without; cura   anxiety   His job as a sales clerk is a sinecure.

2. **linguistics**   lingua = language or tongue
     She is a volunteer for the linguistics department at the mission.

3. **copious**   copia = abundant supply
   We have a copious supply of grapes in the Napa Valley.

4. **ancillary**   ancilla = handmaiden
   The main factory and its ancillary plant both do manufacturing.

5. **sublingual**   sub = under; lingua = language or tongue
   The medication is to be admininstered sublingually.

WORD STUDY Write the translation. (Can you count in Latin?)

Una raeda et una raeda sunt duae raedae; duo angeli et unus angelus sunt tres angeli; duo apostoli et duo apostoli sunt quattuor apostoli; tres discipuli et duo discipuli sunt quinque discipuli; quattuor balaenae et duo balaenae sunt sex balaenae; sex mandata et unus mandatum sunt septem mandata; quinque dona et tria dona sunt octo dona; septem gladii et duo gladii sunt novem gladii; sex ancillae et quattuor ancillae sunt decem ancillae.

<table>
<tr><td>

Can you count in Latin?

One carriage and one carriage are two carriages; two angels and one angel are three angels; two apostles and two apostles are four apostles; three disciples and two disciples are five disciples; four whales and two whales are six whales; six commandments and one commandment are seven commandments; five gifts and three gifts are eight gifts; seven swords and two swords are nine swords; six handmaidens and four handmaidens are ten handmaidens.

</td></tr>
</table>

DRILL SHEET AFTER CHAPTER TEN
TRANSLATE INTO LATIN:

1.	eight boys (nom.)	octo pueri
2.	five gates (acc.)	quinque portas
3.	twenty whales (nom.)	viginti balaenae
4.	seven memories (abl.)	septem memoriis
5.	eleven messengers (dat.)	undecim nuntiis
6.	ten poets (gen.)	decem poetarum
7.	three towns (abl.)	tribus oppidis
8.	three nations (acc.)	tres populos
9.	nine lives (nom.)	novem vitae
10.	nine lives (acc.)	novem vitas
11.	the sixth son (nom.)	sextus filius
12.	the eighth kingdom (dat.)	octavo regno
13.	the first Sabbath (nom.)	primum Sabbatum (or prima Sabbata)

14. the second boy (gen.)   <u>secundi pueri</u>
15. the fourth man (dat.)   <u>quarto viro</u>
16. the third country (nom.)   <u>tertia patria</u>
17. the third sailor (nom.)   <u>tertius nauta</u>
18. the fourth tunic (dat.)   <u>quartae tunicae</u>
19. the tenth road (nom.)   <u>decima via</u>
20. the seventh province (abl.)   <u>septima provincia</u>

Translate into English.
21. fama trium virorum   <u>the report of three men</u>
22. quattuor equi   <u>four horses</u>
23. septima memoria   <u>the seventh memory</u>
24. secundum bellum   <u>the second war</u>
25. vitae unius pueri quinque parvarum puellarumque
                                    <u>the lives of one boy and (of) five small girls</u>
26. Deus est Unus.   <u>God is One.</u>
27. mille litterae   <u>a thousand letters</u>
28. decimum oppidum   <u>the tenth town</u>
29. tertiā horā   <u>at the third hour</u>

    nom.pl   3/pl. (sine + abl.s.)
30. Viginti nautae sunt sine curā.
      Twenty sailors are without anxiety.

    nom.pl.m.   (ad + acc.s.) gen.s.   3/pl.
31. Novem servi magni ad villam agricolae ambulant.
      Nine big servants walk to the farmer's house.

    acc.s. (ob + acc.s.) 1/pl.
32. Virum ob audaciam laudamus.
      We praise the man because of (his) boldness.

    nom.s. dat.pl. acc.pl.   3/s.
33. Magister pueris duos libros dat.
      The teacher gives the boys two books.

    nom.s.m. (in + abl.s.f.)   3/s.
34. Legatus in magnā villā habitat.
      The lieutenant lives in a large house (or *farmhouse*).

    nom.pl. nom.pl.   (ab + abl.s.) (ad + acc.s.) 3/pl.
35. Quinque feminae sex puellaeque ab agro ad oppidum ambulant.
      Five women and six girls are walking from the field to town.

    nom.s.f. gen.pl.   gen.pl.   adv. 3/s. nom.s. f.   nom.s.m. acc.pl. 3/s.
36. Natura virorum feminarumque non est *bona,   sed Deus   nos amat.
      The nature of men and women is not good, but God loves us.

    abl. means pl.   1/pl.
37. Tribus linguis cantamus.
      We sing in three languages.

---

*Meaning *not perfect*. Naturally, we try to do good things, but fall short of perfect.

38. Iesus (Jesus) discipulis vocat, "Hora adest." (adest = *ad* + *est*)
  Jesus calls to the disciples, "The hour is near."

39. Suntne quinque filii quattuor filiaeque in tuā familiā?
  Are there five sons and four daughters in your family?

40. Sumus liberi viri liberae feminaeque quod sumus Christiani. (*Christians*)
  We are free men and women because we are Christians.

Test Five to be taken after the completion of Chapter Ten
Grammar Section

1. Which case is used to express the "means" by which an action is performed?
Ablative case.
2. How do you find the stem of an adjective to which you add the endings?
Remove the ending from the nominative singular feminine form . (For first and second declension adjectives that is **-a**.)
3. Which numerals are declinable in Latin? unus, duo, tres, or *one, two*, and *three*

Declensions
4-5. Decline **unus** in the singular only of course.

Nom.	unus	una	unum
Gen.	unius	unius	unius
Dat.	uni	uni	uni
Acc.	unum	unam	unum
Abl.	uno	una	uno

6-7. Decline **duo** in the plural only of course.

Nom.	duo	duae	duo
Gen.	duorum	duarum	duorum
Dat.	duobus	duabus	duobus
Acc.	duos	duas	duo
Abl.	duobus	duabus	duobus

8-9. Decline **tres** in the plural only of course.

Nom.	tres	tria
Gen.	trium	trium
Dat.	tribus	tribus
Acc.	tres	tria
Abl.	tribus	tribus

Adjective Usage Give the required forms in Latin of the following adjectives and numeral adj ectives.

10. **large** (abl. sing. f.) magna

11. **prepared** (dat. pl. m.) <u>paratis</u>
12. **pleasing** (nom. sing. neu.) <u>gratum</u>
13. **pure** (acc. pl. neu.) <u>pura</u>
14. **happy** (nom. pl. fem.) <u>beatae</u>
15. **your** (nom. pl. neu.) <u>vestra or tua</u>
16. **fourth** (dat. pl. fem.) <u>quartis</u>
17. **third** (abl. pl. masc.) <u>tertiis</u>
18. **twenty** <u>viginti</u>
19. **tenth** (gen. pl. masc.) <u>decimorum</u>
20. **five** <u>quinque</u>
21. **seven** <u>septem</u>

Sentence Work

Mark and translate the Latin sentence into English.

1/pl. nom.pl. m. (in + abl.) gen.s.
22-23. Sumus puri in oculis Dei.
       We are pure in the eyes of God.

1/pl.   acc. s. conj. acc. 3/s.
24-25. Amamus Deum quod nos amat.
       We love God because He loves us.

conj. nom.s.m. 3/s. acc. nom.s. 3/s.
26-27. Quoniam bonus est, nos Christus servat.
       Since He is good, Christ saves us.

nom.pl. acc. pl. (abl.means/pl.)   1/pl.
28-29. Nos   libros nostris oculis spectamus.
       We are looking at the books with our eyes.

3/s. nom.s.f.   (ante + acc.s.)
30-31. Est una hora ante cenam (*dinner*).
       It is one hour until dinner.

3/s. nom.s.f.   (in + abl.s.f.)
32-33. Est quinta filia in nostrā familiā.
       She is the fifth daughter in our family.

Word Work

Write the Latin word from which the italicized word is derived **<u>and</u>** write a brief meaning or synonym of the italicized word.

34. Romans used to *decimate* the troops if one soldier disobeyed.
<u>decim. destroy every tenth person, or destroy (in general)</u>
35. It is *approximately* four miles to my home from town.
<u>proximus. nearly</u>
36. Our cousins are very *amiable* people.
<u>amo. (or amicus, or amicitia) loving</u>
37. If we *interrogate* the students we shall know if they have studied.
<u>rogo. ask ; inter, among</u>
38. Service industries are *tertiary* industries, while both farming and logging are primary industries and manufacturing is a secondary one.
<u>tertius. third (in importance)</u>

At the end of the lesson students will be able to:

- tell the difference between past tense in English and imperfect tense in Latin.
- say the tense signs of the imperfect and future tenses.
- list in order each king of Rome.
- state the difference between a democracy and a republic.

General Sequence of Instruction: Use each chapter's instructions for detailed plan, but a general plan is the following:
1.) Read the grammar.
2.) Learn the vocabulary.
3.) Do Study Sheet to reinforce.
4.) Do Drill Sheet for practice.
5.) Complete the Exercises in the chapter including the Reading Lesson
6.) Quiz orally or use bi-chapter tests to evaluate.

<u>**Chapter Eleven**</u>

1. Enter the chapter phrase into the notebook. Discuss the meaning, and explain why we needed a Savior.
2. Read and discuss **I Grammar A, B,** and **C**. Learn the paradigms.
Memorize in this way: amabam, amabas, amabat, amabamus, amabatis, amabant.
You will notice that the imperfect tense sign is –**ba**-. Some teachers help the students memorize by asking, "What do imperfect sheep say?" Answer: Ba, ba, ba. To learn the future tense signs, there are a few ways. When Bo Jackson was a famous baseball player, people would say, "B<u>o</u> will B<u>u</u>nt" Another way is to think of owing someone some money. <u>I-O-U</u> some money, and will repay it in the FUTURE.

3.
3. **Do the Study Sheet.**
4. **Exercises A, B,** and **C**, either as written work or orally with teacher.
5. **Drill Sheet**.
6. **Exercise D**. Unless your student is very quick and accurate, he or she still needs to mark the sentences. More difficult sentences will come later and they will continue to have to mark them.
7. Read and discuss **III History**. The three types of government need to be explained, because there is a vast difference between them. Emphasize that a <u>**Republic is Rule by Law**</u>, our Law being the Constitution of the land, and not by majority rule.
8. **Reading Lesson IV**.

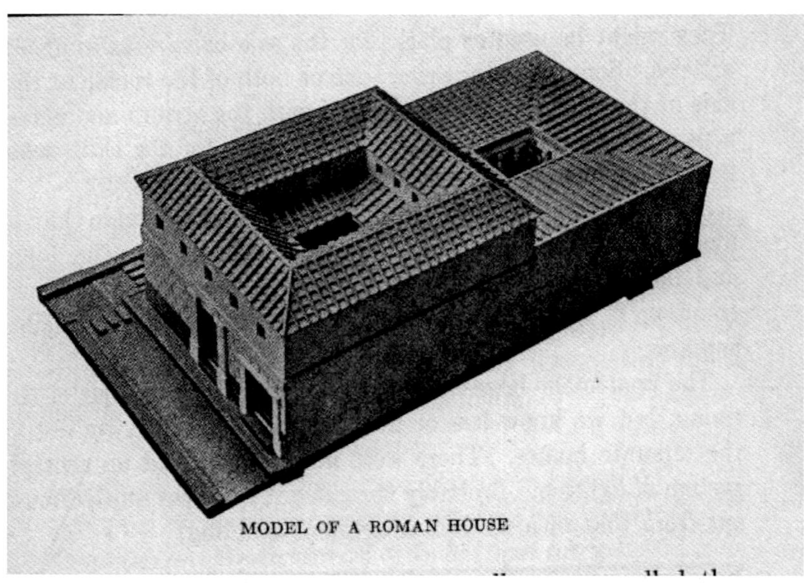
MODEL OF A ROMAN HOUSE

Chapter Eleven

Omnes enim peccaverunt et egent gloriam Dei.
For All have sinned, and come short of the Glory of God.

Imperfect and Future Tenses;
The Monarchy and the Republic; <u>At the Circus Maximus</u>

I. Grammar

There are three tenses formed on the present stem of a verb: the *present*, the *imperfect*, and the *future* tenses. You recall that the present stem of a first conjugation verb is found by removing the **-re** ending from the second principal part of the verb.

am′o ama′re ama′vi ama′tus

Remove the **-re** and your present stem is **ama-**.

A. The Present Tense

This chart is already on the page in the "Conjugations" section of your notebook.

> The present tense is formed by adding the personal endings, **-o, -s, -t, -mus, -tis, -nt**, to the present stem, omitting the **-a** before the first person singular form.
>
> | | SINGULAR | PLURAL |
> |---|---|---|
> | FIRST PERSON | ā′mo, *I love* | amā′**mus**, *we love* |
> | SECOND PERSON | ā′mas, *you love* | amā′**tis**, *you love* |
> | THIRD PERSON | ā′mat, *he, she, it loves* | ā′ma**nt**, *they love* |

B. The Imperfect Tense

The imperfect tense is one which has no exact duplicate in English. It is an action which occurred in the past, and may or may not be continuing on. There are several ways to translate the imperfect tense from Latin to English: the usual translation of **amabat** is *he was loving* or *he used to love*, but it may sometimes be translated as *he loved*. You will choose which translation sounds best in the sentence.

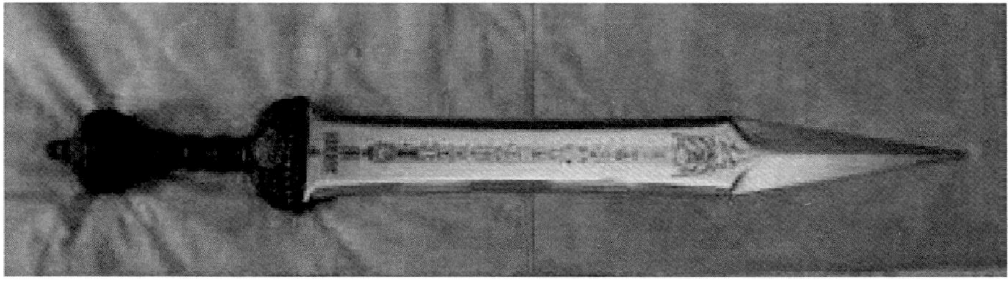

Copy this chart and put it below the Present tense chart already in your notebook. Add the words *Indicative Mood* at the top of the page above the three charts.

To form the <u>imperfect</u> tense in Latin, we add the tense-sign **-ba** to the present stem, and then add the personal endings **-m, -s, -t, -mus, -tis,** and **-nt.**

	SINGULAR	PLURAL
FIRST PERSON	ama′**bam,** *I was loving*	amaba′ **mus,** *we were loving*
SECOND PERSON	ama′**bas,** *you were loving*	amaba′**tis,** *you were loving*
THIRD PERSON	ama′**bat,** *he, she, it was loving*	ama′**bant,** *they were loving*

C. The Future Tense

The future tense, as in English, states a fact which is to occur in the future. In the first person, we use *shall* because it is considered a promise. In all others, we use *will* because it means, he *will* do something if he *wills* to do it. However, language changes over time, so it is not wrong to use *will* instead of *shall.*

The <u>future</u> tense is formed in Latin by adding the tense sign, <u>-bi-</u>, to the present stem, and then adding the personal endings, **-o, -s, -t, -mus, -tis, -nt.** In the first person singular the ′i′ is dropped, and in the third person plural the ′i′ is changed to a ′u′.

	SINGULAR	PLURAL
FIRST PERSON	ama′**bo,** *I shall love*	ama′**bimus,** *we shall love*
SECOND PERSON	ama′**bis,** *you will love*	ama′**bitis,** *you will love*
THIRD PERSON	ama′**bit,** *he, she, it will love*	ama′**bunt,** *they will love*

The Imperfect and Future Tenses of **Sum** are irregular. Write these down and put them in your section titled "Conjugations" on the page titled <u>Irregular Verbs.</u>

Imperfect Tense

	SINGULAR	PLURAL
FIRST PERSON	er′**am,** *I was*	era′**mus,** *we were*
SECOND PERSON	er′**as,** *you were*	era′**tis,** *you were*
THIRD PERSON	er′**at,** *he, she, it was, there was*	er′**ant,** *they were, there were*

Future Tense

	SINGULAR	PLURAL
FIRST PERSON	e′**ro,** *I shall be*	er′**imus,** *we shall be*
SECOND PERSON	er′**is,** *you will be*	er′**itis,** *you will be*
THIRD PERSON	er′**it,** *he, she, it will be, there will be*	er′**unt,** *they will be, there will be*

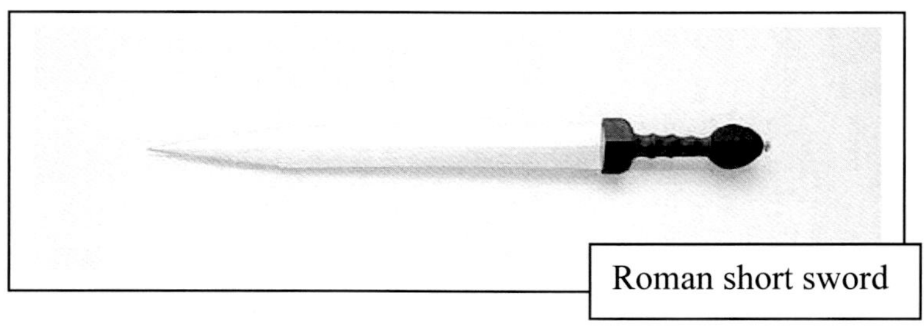

Roman short sword

II. Exercises

A. Analyze each form and translate.

1. putabam, nuntiabitis, cantat, eris 2. curat, erant, lacrimamus, portabunt 3. eramus, honoramus, vocabat, spectabunt 4. servabis, sanctificabamus, rogo, erunt 5. narratis, erit, narras, sanabant 6. eratis, confirmatis, auscultabatis, dabam 7. do, amabant, parabas, ero 8. laudabamus, curabant, eram, oppugnabant 9. puto, putant, erant, spectabitis 10. amabo, portabis, dant, eramus

NOTE TO TEACHER: Remember, these are some of the possible translations. The imperfect tense may be translated like a simple past tense, **amabat**, *he loved*, but it seems to confuse students at this point. Do not mark it wrong if they translate that way, but encourage them to translate the imperfect as *he was loving* or *he used to love* until Volume II, when they learn the Perfect Tense.
The perfect tense is a past tense implying that an action was done in the past, and is completed. If you said *he loved* in the perfect tense, you would mean, "he loved and he does not love anymore." In the imperfect tense, *he loved* means "*he loved and he probably still does.*" It is more precise than the simple English past tense.

	PERSON	NUMBER	TENSE	TRANSLATION
1.	1	sg.	imp.	I was thinking, I used to think, I thought
	2	pl.	fut.	you will announce
	3	sg.	pres.	he, she or it is singing, he sings
	2	sg.	fut.	you will be
2.	3	sg.	pres.	he cares for, she takes care of
	3	pl.	imp.	they were, there were
	1	pl.	pres.	we are crying, we do cry, we cry
	3	pl.	fut.	they will carry
3.	1	pl.	imp.	we were
	1	pl.	pres.	we honor, we are honoring, we do honor
	3	sg.	imp.	he, she or it was calling, called, used to call
	3	pl.	fut.	they will look at
4.	2	sg.	fut.	you will guard, you will save
	1	pl.	imp.	we were setting apart for God's purpose
	1	sg.	pres.	I ask, I am asking, I do ask
	3	pl.	fut.	they will be, there will be
5.	2	pl.	pres.	you tell, you are telling, you do relate
	3	sg.	fut.	he will be, she will be, it will be
	2	sg.	pres.	you are relating, you are telling, you tell
	3	pl.	imp.	they were healing, they were curing, they healed
6.	2	pl.	imp.	you were
	2	pl.	pres.	you strengthen or you declare
	2	pl.	imp.	you were listening to, you were overhearing, listened to, overheard
	1	sg.	imp.	I was giving, I used to give, I gave
7.	1	sg.	pres.	I give, I am giving, I do give
	3	pl.	imp.	they were loving, they did love, they loved
	2	sg.	imp.	you were preparing, you prepared
	1	sg.	fut.	I shall be

8.	1	pl.	imp.	we were praising, we praised, we used to praise
	3	pl.	imp.	they used to care for, they cared for, were caring for
	1	sg.	imp.	I was
	3	pl.	pres.	they were attacking, they attacked
9.	1	sg.	pres.	I am thinking, I do think, I think
	3	pl.	pres.	they think, they do think, they are thinking
	3	pl.	imp.	they were, there were
	2	pl.	fut.	you will look at, you will watch
10.	1	sg.	fut.	I shall love
	2	sg.	fut.	you will carry
	3	pl.	pres.	they give, they do give, they are giving
	1	pl.	imp.	we were

B. Translate.

1. they will greet - <u>salutabunt</u>
   you are suffering – <u>laboras</u>
   we shall attack - <u>oppugnabimus</u>
2. he will announce - <u>nuntiabit</u>
   I am thinking - <u>puto</u>
   we will cry - <u>lacrimabimus</u>
3. they were carrying - <u>portabant</u>
   they are telling - <u>narrant</u>
   they were living- <u>habitabant</u>
4. you (pl.) were greeting - <u>salutabatis</u>
   we shall strengthen - <u>confirmabimus</u>
   they sing - <u>cantant</u>
5. I shall greet - <u>salutabo</u> you
   are asking for - <u>rogas</u> they
   will praise - <u>laudabunt</u>
6. he was greeting - <u>salutabat</u>
   we shall call - <u>vocabimus</u>
   they will guard - <u>servabunt</u>
7. you (pl.) relate- <u>narratis</u>
   we were looking at - <u>spectabamus</u>
   I shall ask - <u>rogabo</u>
8. they will suffer - <u>laborabunt</u>
   we were calling – <u>vocabamus, or appellabamus</u>
   she was curing - <u>sanabat</u>
9. I shall attack - <u>oppugnabo</u>
   he sets apart for God's purpose - <u>sanctificat</u>
   we were living - <u>habitabamus</u>
10. you honor - <u>honoras</u>
    I am announcing - <u>nuntio</u>
    I shall announce - <u>nuntiabo</u>

C. Latin to English.

nom.s.   3/s.   imperf.
1. Quintus equus ambulabat.
    The fifth horse was walking. (or *walked*)

acc.pl. gen. pl. m.   2/pl. imperf.
2. Nonne animos puerorum parvorum confirmabatis?
    You were encouraging the small boys, weren't you? (literally, *You were strengthening the hearts of the small boys, weren't you?*)

nom. pl. m.   dat. 3/pl. pres. acc. 3/pl. pres.
3. Mei amici boni mihi sunt et   me amant.
    My friends are good to me and they like me.

acc.pl. gen.s. m.   1/s. imperf.
4. Verba poetae amici auscultabam.
    I was listening to the words of the friendly poet. (or *I was listening to the words of the poet's friend.* It depends on the context of the paragraph it may be in.)

nom.pl. m.   nom.pl. m. (in + abl.s.f.) 3/pl. fut.
5. Neque mali neque inimici in meā villā habitabunt.
    Neither evil nor unfriendly men will live in my farmhouse. (or, *my house*)

nom.s. 2/s.pres.   nom.s.m.
6. Tu es   meus verus amicus.
    You are my true friend.

nom.s. acc.s.m. 3/s. imperf.
7. Ioannes filium suum curabat.
    John was taking care of his (own) son. (John took care of…)

1/s. fut. acc.s.   acc. 3/s.fut. 3/s. fut.
8. Honorabo Deum et me curabit et servabit.
    I shall honor God and He will take care of me and save me.

nom.pl. gen.s.m.   acc. adv. 3/pl. fut. conj. acc.s. gen.s. 1/pl. pres.
9. Verba mali unius   nos non superabunt quod Verbum Dei auscultamus.
    The words of one evil man will not overcome us because we listen to the Word of God.

nom.pl. f. (in + abl.s.f.) (ad + acc.s.) 3/pl.imperf.
10. Viginti balaenae albae in altā aquā ad insulam erant.
    Twenty white whales were in the deep water near the island.

D. Mark each sentence first, then translate.

     nom.s.f.   (ante + acc. pl. n.)   3/s. fut.   acc.pl.f.
1. The tall gate (in front of the neighboring towns) will protect the common crowds
        (a + abl.s.)
        (from danger).

    Porta alta ante proxima oppida (or *pro proximis oppidis*) turbas a periculo servabit.

     nom.s.m.   3/s. imperf.   acc.s.f.   dat. s.
2. The friendly sailor was giving his own tunic (to the man).
    Nauta amicus viro tunicam suam dabat.

     nom.s. m.   3/s. im perf.   indecl.   acc.pl. f.   (ad + acc.pl.)   gen.s.
3. The evil teacher was carrying one thousand unfriendly letters (to the men) (of the town).
    Magister malus ad viros oppidi mille epistulas inimicas portabat.

     nom.pl. m.   gen.s.   3/pl. fut.   acc.pl. m.   gen.s.
4. The savage men (of Gaul) will attack the unfriendly men (of Italy).
    Viri feri Galliae viros inimicos Italiae oppugnabunt.

     2/s. imperf.   dat.   acc.s.   gen.pl. m.
5. You were giving us the testimony (of the three servants).
    Dabas nobis testimonium trium servorum .

     nom.s.f.   (a + abl.s. f.)   3/s. fut. (abl. of means- s.f.)
6. The family (from your homeland) will sing (in your language).
    Familia a tua (or *vestra*) patria tua (or *vestra*) lingua cantabit.

     nom. pl. f.   3/pl. imperf. acc. s. n.   (trans + acc. pl. f.)   (ad + acc.s.)
7. The three coaches were carrying much grain (over the broad roads) (to the town).
    Tres raedae multum frumentum trans vias latas ad oppidum portabant.

     (propter + acc.s.)   nom.s.   3/s. fut.   acc.s.   gen.pl.
8. (Because of the commandment) the trumpet will announce the beginning (of the Sabbath).
    Propter (or ob) mandatum tuba principium Sabbati nuntiabit.

     nom.s. 3/s.pres. nom.s.m. gen.s.   3/s. pres.   acc.
9. Christ is the   Son   (of God) and He takes care of us.
    Christus est Filius Dei et nos curat.

     (post + acc.s.)   nom.s. 3/s. imperf. acc.s. nom.pl. nom.pl. 3/pl. imperf.   acc.s.
10. (After the war) the nation was praising God; the men and women were asking for wisdom.
    Post bellum populus Deum laudabat; viri et feminae sapientiam rogabant.

III. Additional Roman History: First, the Monarchy...

Rome had three forms of government: monarchy, republic, and empire. The monarchy was established by the Etruscans after they had organized Italy. According to legend, Romulus was the first of seven kings. Several legends surround his life if he even existed, the most famous regarding the death of his brother.

Rome did not choose to set up a democracy because it had seen the problems with democracy in Athens. They knew that a pure democracy, "rule by the majority", would set the stage for mob rule, and that a stable society must be maintained based upon an unbiased law. In a true democracy, a crowd could be convinced to vote for things as a group that they would never do on an individual basis. An example of that is the way that the Jews were convinced to demand the release of Barabbas instead of Christ. Individually, many of those people knew that Barabbas was a criminal and that Christ had only shown kindness and compassion to them. But when they were manipulated by a few well-placed agitators in the crowd, they screamed for the release of Barabbas.

In the century preceding Christ's birth, Julius Caesar seized power and effectively changed the Republic into an Empire. He was an excellent general and strategist whose goal was to make a name for himself by conquering much of Europe. He was killed before he could set himself up as Emperor, and his nephew (and adopted son) Octavian actually is considered to be the first of the Roman Emperors, giving himself the name Augustus Caesar in 27 B.C. He began an era called the Pax Romana, where the language, laws, roads and aqueducts of the Romans spread throughout the known world. Unfortunately, the Pax Romana (Peace of Rome), while it did usher in an era of peace, brought a peace which meant absolute tyranny.

IV. Reading Lesson
Ad Circum Maximum

Davus et Titus Philippusque certamen ad Circum Maximum spectant. Circus Maximus est circus magnus inter Palatinos Aventinosque clivos. Duo centum milia *(two hundred thousands)* virorum feminarumque certamina spectant. Certamen est mirus ludus.

Ante certamen Philippus et pueri sacerdotes spectant. Sacerdotes ambulant et certamen consecrant. Equi ad circum *(at the racetrack)* ambulant. Sunt quattuor equi qui ambulant cum uno curru. *(chariot, abl. case)* Equi circum circum septies ambulant.

Claustrum altum est in medio circo. Est periculosum equis. Viri feminaeque longam tubam auscultant. Statim *(suddenly)* certamen incipit *(is beginning).* Davus Titusque aurigam qui est in albā tunicā spectant.

Aurigae certamen sine periculo complent *(finish).* Davus Titusque clamant et aurigam quod erat primus laudant. Pueri sunt beati ubi *(when)* Aquilam et puellas ad Forum salutant quod auriga, quem *(whom)* laudabant, est primus.

Recognition Vocabulary

        auʹrīga, aurīʹgae, m., *driver*
        certāʹmen, (singular) **certāmīʹna**, (pl.) *race*
        cīrʹcūs, cīrʹcī, m., *racetrack*
        clausʹtrūm, clausʹ trī, n., *barrier*
        cūrʹrūs, cūrʹrūs, (4th declension) *chariot*
        mīʹrūs, -ā, -ūm, *amazing, spectacular*
        perīcūlōʹsus, -a, -ūm, adj., *dangerous, risky*
        sācerdōʹtēs, *priests*, (nom. and acc. case)
        sepʹtīēs, adverb, *seven times*

<u>Reading Lesson</u>

At the Circus Maximus

David, Titus, and Philip are watching the race at the Circus Maximus. The Circus Maximus is a large racetrack between the Palatine and Aventine hills. Two hundred thousand men and women (literally *two hundred thousands of men and women*) are watching the races. The race is a spectacular game.

Before the race Philip and the boys are watching the priests. The priests are walking and blessing the race. The horses are walking at the racetrack . There are four horses [24] which are walking with one chariot. The horses walk around the racetrack seven times.

A tall barrier is in the middle of the racetrack . It is dangerous for the horses. The men and women are listening to the long trumpet. Suddenly the race is beginning. David and Titus are watching the driver who is in the white tunic.

The drivers finish the race without danger. David and Titus are shouting and praising the driver because he is first. The boys are happy when they greet Aquila and the girls at the Forum because the driver, whom they were praising, is first.

Responde Latine. Answer in a complete sentence.

1. Ubi est Circus Maximus?
2. Quot *(How many)* certamina spectant?
3. Cur *(why)* sacerdotes circum Circum ambulant?
4. Cur Titus Davusque pro auriga in alba tunica clamant et eum *(him)* laudant?
5. Cur pueri beati sunt, ubi Aquilam et puellas post certamen salutant?

Circus Maximus today

---

[24]Not *who* because they were animals, not people.

Questions.
1. Where is the Circus Maximus? Est inter Palatinos et Aventinos clivos.
2. How many are watching the races? Duo centum milia virorum feminarumque
    certamina spectant.
3. Why are the priests walking around the racetrack? Consecrant certamen.
4. Why are Titus and David shouting for the driver in the white tunic and praising him?
    Laudant quod erat primus.
5. Why are the boys happy when they greet Aquila and the girls after the race? Beati sunt
    quod auriga erat primus.

Name ____Date _____________________

Latin in the Christian Trivium
Study Sheet
Chapter Eleven

Grammar

1. What tenses are formed on the present stem of a verb? <u>present, imperfect, and future tenses</u>
2. How is the present tense of a verb formed? <u>by adding the personal endings to the stem</u>
3. What is the tense sign of the imperfect tense? <u>-ba-</u>
4. What is the tense sign of the future tense? <u>-bo, -bi-, and -bu-</u>

Practice. Fill in the blanks.

WORD	PERSON	NUMBER	TENSE	TRANSLATION
5. rogabimus	1	pl.	future	we shall ask
6. sanctificabo	1	sg.	future	I shall set apart for God's purpose
7. putant	3	pl.	pres.	they think
8. portabam	1	sg.	imp.	I was carrying, I used to carry
9. narrabat	3	sg.	imp.	he, she, or it was relating, telling
10 lacrimatis	2	pl.	pres.	you cry, you are crying, you do cry
11. laudabis	2	sg.	fut.	you will praise
12. parant	3	pl.	pres.	they prepare
13. navigabunt	3	pl.	fut.	they will sail
14. nuntiabis	2	sg.	fut.	you will announce
15. laboramus	1	pl.	pres.	we suffer, we work, we labor
16. vocabo	1	sg.	fut.	I shall call

Underline the Latin word which is the correct translation for the English.

17. You will strengthen	**confirmas**	**confirmabatis**	<u>**confirmabis**</u>
18. I was taking care of	<u>**curabam**</u>	**curabat**	**curabo**
19. We shall be hard pressed	**laborabunt**	**laboramus**	<u>**laborabimus**</u>
20. They will listen to	**auscultabant**	<u>**auscultabunt**</u>	**auscultabo**
21. They are giving	<u>**dant**</u>	**dabant**	**dabunt**
22. She was honoring	**honorabam**	<u>**honorabat**</u>	**honorabit**

23. I shall relate   **narro**   **narrabam**   <u>**narrabo**</u>

24. I was thinking   <u>**putabam**</u>   **putabat**   **putabo**

25. He used to ask for   **rogat**   <u>**rogabat**</u>   **rogant**

26. He was guarding   **servabam**   <u>**servabat**</u>   **servabant**

Sentence Work   Mark all sentences, and then translate.

        nom.s. m.   gen.s.m.   3/s.imperf.   acc.s. f.

27. The <u>second son</u> (of the good man) <u>used to guard</u> the <u>family.</u>
       Filius secundus viri boni familiam servabat.

        nom.pl. 3/pl. imperf.   acc. pl. m.

28. The <u>words</u> <u>were strengthening</u> our hearts (Use **animos** for *hearts*).
       Verba animos nostros confirmabant.

      nom.pl. m.   3/pl.pres.   acc.s.   3/pl. fut.   (in + abl.s.)

29. <u>Many men</u> <u>honor</u> the <u>Lord,</u> and <u>they</u> <u>will live</u> (in heaven).
       Multi (viri) Dominum honorant et in caelo habitabunt.

        nom.pl   3/pl. fut.   acc.pl. m.

30. The <u>good men</u> <u>will</u> not <u>attack</u> the <u>little boys.</u>
       Boni (viri) pueros parvos non oppugnabunt.

31. On a separate sheet of paper write a journal (diary) entry for one of your days this week. You may tell about your family or your school, or what you did today. Begin with "Dear Diary,". **Cara Emphemeris.** Write it in Latin, of course!

TEACHER: Give this assignment as "credit/no credit."

DRILL SHEET AFTER CHAPTER ELEVEN
TRANSLATE INTO LATIN.

1. we shall praise <u>1/pl. fut. - laudabimus</u>
2. they were loving <u>3/pl. imperf. - amabant</u>
3. you (pl.) are carrying <u>2/pl. pres. - portatis</u>
4. there is <u>3/s. pres. - est</u>
5. you will give <u>2/s. fut. - dabis</u>
6. you are telling <u>2/s. pres. - narras</u>
7. he was telling <u>3/s. imperf. - narrabat</u>
8. they will walk <u>3/pl. fut. - ambulabunt</u>
9. she will think <u>3/s. fut. - putabit</u>
10. we were suffering <u>1/pl. imperf. - laborabamus</u>
11. they are <u>3/pl. pres. - sunt</u>
12. we were crying <u>1/pl. imperf. - lacrimabamus</u>
13. he is attacking <u>3/s. pres. - oppugnat</u>
14. I prepare <u>1/s. pres. - paro</u>
15. you prepare to work <u>2/s. pres – paras; infinitive – laborare; Paras laborare.</u>
16. we like to work <u>infinitive – laborare; 1/pl. pres. amamus; Amamus laborare.</u>

17. he will ask <u>3/s. fut.- rogabit</u>
18. they set apart for God's purpose <u>3/pl. pres. - sanctificant</u>
19. will you (pl.) listen to? <u>2/pl. fut. - auscultabitisne?</u>
20. he does announce, doesn't he? <u>nonne; 3/s. pres. - nuntiat?; Nonne nuntiat?</u>
21. I love you. <u>te; 1/s. pres. – amo; Te amo.</u>
22. Do you love me? <u>amas, 2/s. pres. – Amasne me?</u>

Chapter Twelve Objectives:

At the end of the lesson students will be able to:

- tell the difference between an adjective and an adverb.
- state the general rule for forming adverbs from adjectives in Latin.
- recite the meanings of the irregular adverbs given in this lesson.
- describe the character of the Roman.

Chapter Twelve

1. Put the chapter phrase into the notebook. Who now has everything under His feet? What does that mean? Learn a secular phrase as well.
2. Read and explain section **I Grammar**. The adverbs in this lesson are NOT those regularly formed, but are exceptions.
3. Copy the box in section **I A.**
4. Learn **II Vocabulary**. There are good derivatives listed here; **ubiquitous** is one which is seen often in newspaper articles. Ask your student to use this word in conversation this week.
5. Do the **Study Sheet**. You will notice that the Study Sheet is work on English adverbs only, because many people are confused with the use of adverbs and adjectives.
    Especially emphasize that you use **really** not **real** to modify an adjective.
    A common error is saying **real good** instead of **really good**.
6. **Exercise A**.
7. **Drill Sheet**.
8. **Exercise B**.
9. Read and discuss **IV The Roman Character**. Our professor (both of us studied Latin from the same professor) used to say when he saw a child playing with blocks, neatly stacking them in columns, "How very Roman of him!" What nations today have this characteristic of being methodical and disciplined, paying attention to detail?
10.   This is a good time to use library books or the internet and show students more examples of Roman art. They will really enjoy drawing columns, and making tesserae (described in their Activity Book). If you have the facilities, you could assign the students to do a mosaic, build a Roman arch, or design a Roman home complete with furniture.
11.   **Reading Lesson VI**.
12.   Review for the test.
13.   Give the **Test Six**.
14.   Then correct the test.

Chapter Twelve

Et omnia subiecit sub pedibus eius.
And He has put all things under His feet.

Adverbs; Roman Character; Roman Art; <u>Life in Rome</u>

I. Grammar

Adverbs are modifiers that describe, restrict, or otherwise qualify the words to which they relate. They describe verbs, adj ectives, and other adverbs.

This chart must be put on the page titled <u>Adverbs</u> in the section "Grammar."

Formation of Adverbs
Most adverbs made from adjectives of the first and second declension adjectives are formed by adding **–e** to the feminine base. This rule holds true whether tor not the adjective is one which ends in **–us** or **–er**.

āl′tē,	*on high, deeply*	**lon′gē,**	*far off, by far*
lā′tē,	*widely, broadly*	**mī″serē,**	*wretchedly, desperately*
lī″berē,	*freely, frankly*	**pūl′chrē,**	*beautifully, nobly*

Not all first and second declension adjectives have regularly formed adverbs. Some exceptions are listed in this vocabulary lesson.

II. Vocabulary

Put these adverbs on white cards with orange ink (26).

bē′nē, *well*	(benediction)	
crās, *tomorrow*	(procrastinate)	**mā′lē,** *badly*
cūr, *why*		**mā′nē,** *early in the day*
dī′ū, *for a long time*		**mox,** *soon, immediately*
dūm, *while*		**nūnc,** *now*
he′rī, *yesterday*		**pōs′tēa,** *afterwards*
fŭr′tim, *stealthily*	(furtively)	**prī′mūm,** *first*
hic, *here*		**sae′pē,** *often*
hō′dīē, *today*		**sem′per,** *always*
iām, *now, already*		**tān′tūm,** *only, so much, greatly*
ī′bī, *there, in that place*		**tūm,** *then, at that time*
in′terim, *meanwhile*		**tūnc,** *then*
lon′gē, *far, far away*		**ū′bī,** *where, when* — (ubiquitous)
		ves′perē, *in the evening* — (vespers)

III. Exercises

A. Form adverbs from the following adjectives. Remember that sometimes translations will be in a phrase instead of just a word. For example, **amice**, *in a friendly manner.*

Then translate.
1. beatus 2. gratus 3. magnus 4. pulcher 5. verus 6. liber 7. inimicus 8. longus
9. altus 10. malus

1. **beate**, happily, in a blessed way
2. **grate**, gratefully, pleasantly, in a pleasing way
3. **magne**, greatly
4. **pulchre**, beautifully
5. **vere**, truly
6. **libere**, freely, generously
7. **inimice**, in an unfriendly manner
8. **longe**, far
9. **alte**, highly, deeply
10. **male**, badly

B. Translate from Latin to English.

nom. pl. (sine + abl.s.) adv. 3/pl. imperf.
1. Equi sine aquā heri erant.

   The horses were without water yesterday.

2/pl. fut.   dat. pl.   adv.   acc.s. f.
2. Dabitisne pueris cras **vestram** amicitiam?

   Will you (pl.) give the boys your friendship tomorrow?

CORRECTION: The student book may have **tuam**, but it should be **vestram**.

adv.   (ad + acc.s.) acc.s. (de + abl. pl. m.)   3/s. imperf.
3. Postea ad villam nuntium de defessis apostolis portabat.

   Afterwards he (or *she*) was carrying the message about the tired apostles
   to the farmhouse.

nom.s.m. (de + abl. pl. f.)   adv. 3/s. imperf.
4. Legatus de Romanis copiis heri putabat.

   The lieutenant was thinking about the Roman troops yesterday.

nom.pl. m.   (circum + acc.s.)   adv.   3/pl. fut.   adv.   3/pl. fut.
5. Centum viri circum oppidum cras ambulabunt et tunc oppugnabunt.

   One hundred men will walk around the town tomorrow and then they will attack (*it*).

nom.s.m. nom.s.f. acc.s.f. acc.s.f.   3/pl. imperf.
6. Vir feminaque filiam Iuliam *(Julia)* appellabant.

   The man and woman (or *husband and wife*) were calling (*their*) daughter Julia. (*or named*)

nom.s.f. acc.s.m. adv. 3/s. pres.
7. Femina filium tantum amat.

   The woman loves only the (meaning *her*) son.

    adv.   nom.pl. m. acc.s.   acc.s. 3/pl. imperf.

8. Postea discipuli puerum aquam rogabant.
      Afterwards the disciples were asking the boy for water.

    adv.   nom.pl. f. adv. 3/pl. pres.

9. Ubi septem puellae primum cantant?
      Where are the seven girls singing first?

    nom.s.m.   acc. pl.f.   adv. 3/s. fut.

10. Dominus nostras familias mox sanabit.
      The Lord will soon heal our families.

    nom.s. n.   adv. (a + abl.s.f.) 3/s. pres.

11. Nostrum oppidum longe a tuā villā est.
      Our town is far from your farmhouse.

    adv. nom.s. f.   3/s. imperf.

12. Cur parva puella lacrimabat?
      Why was the little girl crying?

    nom.pl.f. acc.pl. m. adv. 3/pl. imperf.

13. Copiae nostros furtim oppugnabant.
      The troops stealthily were attacking our (men).

    nom.pl.m. adv. adv. 3/pl. imperf.

14. Duo amici heri male cantabant.
      The two friends were singing badly yesterday.

    adv. nom.pl.m. (in + abl.pl) adv. 3/pl. imperf.

15. Interim servi in agris saepe laborabant.
      Meanwhile the servants were often working in the fields.

    dat. pl.m.or f. acc.pl.n. adv. 1/s. fut.

16. Servis   dona   libere dabo.
      I shall freely give the servants gifts. (or ...*give gifts to the servants*)

    dat.s.m. acc.s. m.   2/s. pres.

17. Legato tuum gladium das.
      You are giving the lieutenant your sword. (or...*giving your sword to the lieutenants*)

    (propter + acc. pl.) adv. (in + abl.s.) adv. 1/pl. fut.

18. Propter malos ibi in oppido non habitabimus.
      On account of the evil men there, we shall not live in town.

    nom.s. gen.s.m. nom.s.f. adv. 3/s. pres.

19. Iustitia Dei   bona semper est.
      The righteousness of God is always good.

    nom.pl.m. adv. 1/pl. fut.

20. Amici semper erimus.
      We shall always be friends.

IV. The Roman Character

The character of the ancient Roman could be summed up in three words: **organized, practical**, and **disciplined**. He showed this organizational skill in his methodical expansion of the Roman Empire. In 264 B.C. Rome intervened to stop the Carthaginians from controlling the Strait of Messina (between Italy and Sicily), and this began the First Punic War. The Romans, you recall, were farmers, and the Phoenicians were accomplished sailors and merchants who controlled the Mediterranean Sea. The Romans had no ships at that time, but because the Romans had this type of methodical character, they realized that the best way to build a navy was to capture a Carthaginian ship, strip it, and make a pattern. Then they used that model to build an entire fleet of warships. They found an abandoned ship and proceeded to do just that.

Within a few hundred years, the Romans had systematically expanded their empire, by simply marching to an unconquered territory and devising a method of attack, attacking, conquering, and then assimilating the conquered peoples into their empire. They were practical in that they allowed conquered people (except those taken as slaves) to keep their own customs and religions, but simply to pay a tribute each year to Rome, and to house the Roman occupation army. Then the Roman army built a road from each province captured back to Rome. This began the expression used even today, "All roads lead to Rome."

Discipline was absolute. When laws were made, they were enforced totally. No mercy was shown, even if the perpetrator of the crime had had extenuating circumstances. The Romans prided themselves on being unsentimental, but more than that, they were brutal. Their laws were not based on God's Law, but on the whims of the Senate and, later, the Emperor. This very discipline was used by God though, to help us understand why we know that the Roman soldiers could not have fallen asleep as they guarded Christ's tomb. Falling asleep on duty was punishable by death.

V. Culture: Art in Rome

No study of Latin or Rome would be complete without a commentary on Rome's art. As you just learned, Romans were very practical people. Today, we often joke that people are divided into two types: Engineers and Salesmen. I would suggest to you that we who are like Romans become the math majors and engineers in America. Salesmen are generally more the artistic type, preferring to see the flow in everything and to appreciate beauty just for itself.

Now we know that the Greeks were definitely more interested in the arts. But, while the Romans preferred to concentrate on maintaining law and order, and to build useful things, or to provide food, they could appreciate the contributions made by Greeks. They often purchased Greek art and also often had Greek tutors for their children.

Most artisans were Greek slaves at that time, or hired workers. Because of that, their art was done anonymously. The coins, vases, statues, and pictures were catalogued by type, but not by originator.

Homes of the wealthy were often built with marble floors or mosaics, which were filled with tiny multicolored cubes called **tesserae**. Furniture was beautifully designed, although not as comfortable as we are used to seeing. Tables, chairs, benches, couches, beds, and lamps were inlaid with ivory, tortoise shell, bronze or precious stones.

Jewelry was designed for beauty, using stones imported from Africa, Arabia and India. Every person wore at least one ring, some wore them on all fingers. They used their rings, remember, to sign their documents by pressing their ring into a wax seal.

Romans learned the art of making glass too, and some of their glass cups are displayed today in the British Museum and the Metropolitan Museum of Art. The historian Will Durant said that the Romans had no superior in glass making[*].

Sculpture began by using baked clay to form small statues and imitations of fruit. Their sculptures were beautiful in that they were realistic representations of figures. One such sculpture was erected after Augustus returned from a campaign in Spain and Gaul in 13 B.C. Titled *Ars Pacis Augustae,* it is considered to be the finest of all the sculptures which still remain in Rome.

When Rome became the ruler of the Mediterranean, Greek artists brought in their works, and often copied works of art to adorn the Roman homes. The Romans conquered Greece, but they adopted much of Greek art, literature, and music, and spread it thoughout the empire.

This art is not in the student book.

---

[*]An excellent study about Roman art is found in Will Durant's *Caesar and Christ.*

VI. Reading Lesson

Vita in Romā

Mane primā luce (*at dawn*), Ioannes pro Fidelio qui *(who)* Tiberio reportat equos parat. Fidelius laborare cum copiis Romae amat. Copiae in Praetoriis Castris inter Viam Monentanam Viam Tiburtinamque sunt. Equi eum *(him)* et Ioannem ad insulam vespere portabunt.

Clara cum Aquilā et puellis interim laborat. Ad Forum ambulare parant et portabunt copiam frumenti. Forum ad insulam in Viā Flaminiā est. Tum vir ad Forum eos *(them)* curabit.

Philippus, servus qui pueros curat, ad Circum Maximum cum eis *(them)* ambulare parat. Ludos   spectare amant. Circus Maximus in Appiā Viā ante Palatinum est. Post ludos pueri et Philippus ad Forum ambulant. Pueri puellas et Aquilam et Claram salutant, ubi vident *(they see)* eos *(them)* ad Forum. Postea ad Forum omnes *(all)* ambulant.

Nunc omnis *(all)* familia per oppidum ambulat et pulchrum Flumen Tiberem spectat. Tum ad insulam ambulant et cras parant.

Recognition Vocabulary

Cīr′cūs Mā′xīmūs, The large racetrack in Rome
Praetō′rīa Cās′tra, *Praetorian Camp*
rēpōr′tāt, *reports*
Rōmā′nus, -a, -um, *Roman*
Tībe′rīus, the emperor of Rome (added to TG)

<u>Reading Lesson</u>

Life in Rome
Early in the day at dawn (*first light*) John is preparing the horses for Fidelius who reports to Tiberius. Fidelius likes to work with the troops of Rome. The troops are in the Praetorian Camp between the Via Monentana and the Via Tiburtina. The horses will carry him and John to the apartment in the evening.

Meanwhile Clara is working with Aquila and the girls. They are preparing to walk to the Forum and they will carry a supply of grain. The Forum is near the apartment on Via Flaminia. Then a man will take care of them at the Forum.

Philip, the servant who takes care of the boys, is preparing to walk with them to the Circus Maximus. They like to watch the games. The Circus Maximus is on the Appian Way in front of the Palatine (Hill). After the games the boys and Philip walk to the Forum. The boys greet the girls, Aquila and Clara, when they see them at the Forum. Afterwards, they all walk to the Forum.

Then all the family walks through the town and looks at the beautiful Tiber River. Then they walk to the apartment, and prepare for tomorrow.

Responde Latine. Answer in a complete sentence.
1. Cui *(To whom)* Fidelius reportat? *(report)*
2. Ubi sunt castra copiarum Fideli?
3. Ubi Aquila et puellae ambulare parant?
4. Cur ibi ambulant?
5. Ubi est Forum?

1.To whom does Fidelius report? Tiberio reportat.
2. Where is the camp of Fidelius' troops? Copiae in Praetoriis Castris inter Viam Monentanam Viam Tiburtinamque sunt.
3. Where are Aquila and the girls preparing to walk? Ad Forum ambulare parant.
4. Why are they walking there? Portabunt copiam frumenti.
5. Where est the Forum? Forum ad insulam in Via Flaminia est.

ROMAN RUINS

The Roman Training
Ground

The Story of the Romans by H.A. Guerber. p. 45.

TEACHER:

As you have seen, the Romans were generally victorious in the wars which they waged against their neighbors. They were so successful, however, only because they were remarkably well trained.

Not very far from the citadel there was a broad plain, bordered on one side by the Tiber. This space had been set aside, from the very beginning, as an exercising ground for the youths of Rome, who were taught to develop their muscles in every way. The young men met there every day to drill, run races, wrestle, box, and swim in the Tiber.

These daily exercises on the Field of Mars, as this plain was called, soon made them brave, hardy, and expert; and, as a true Roman considered it beneath him to do anything but fight, the king thus had plenty of soldiers at his disposal.

Ancus Martius had greatly encouraged the young men in all these athletic exercises, and often went out to watch them as they went through their daily drill. He also took great interest in the army, and divided the soldiers into regiments, or legions as they were called in Rome.

Name ____Date __________________________

Latin in the Christian Trivium
Study Sheet
Chapter Twelve

Grammar
1. What parts of speech do adverbs modify? <u>verbs, adjectives, or other adverbs</u>
2. How do you change most adjectives of the first and second declension to form them into adverbs?
<u>You remove the ending of the feminine form, and replace it with an **-e**.</u>

Adverb Work
To refresh your memory, read the following and then do the exercises:
Adverbs answer the questions, how, when, where, and to what degree.
     A. Use adjectives to modify nouns or pronouns. Use adverbs to modify verbs, adjectives or other adverbs.
         Michael is an *honest* employer. (adjective)
         Michael deals with his employees *honestly*. (adverb)
     B. Use predicate adjectives after linking verbs.
         Douglas seems *quick*. (adjective, not *quickly*)
         Douglas runs *quickly*. (adverb, answers the question "how")

Underline the correct word in parentheses.
3. After hearing the good news, David became (<u>happy</u>, happily).
4. You must wash your hair (<u>often</u>, frequent) to keep it shiny.
5. Tom is (real, <u>really</u>) fast on the football field.
6. Joe felt (<u>good</u>, well) about performing (good, <u>well</u>) on his new job.
7. Hillarie is (<u>surely</u>, sure) happy about being a mother.
8. We were given Eternal Life (free, <u>freely</u>)
9. He did really (bad, <u>badly</u>) on his algebra test, and is going to make it up.
10. The detective crept through the house (stealthy, <u>stealthily</u>).

Sentence Work
Identify adverbs in the following sentences and tell if they answer the question, (A) *how,* (B) *when,* or (C) *where.*

	ADVERB	WHICH KIND?
11. Brandon will arrive tomorrow.	<u>tomorrow</u>	<u>B when</u>
12. Send all the mail here.	<u>here</u>	<u>C where</u>
13. Frank answered angrily.	<u>angrily</u>	<u>A how</u>
14. The little girl sang sweetly to her tired mother.	<u>sweetly</u>	<u>A how</u>
15. Happily, children used the sprinklers to cool themselves on a warm day.	<u>happily</u>	<u>A how</u>
16. Wise parents stayed at the park where they could carefully watch their children play.	<u>carefully</u>	<u>A how</u>
17. The dogs slept soundly near the warm radiators, seldom going outside.	<u>soundly</u>	<u>A how</u>
	<u>seldom</u>	<u>B when</u>

For this part of the exercise, change each adjective below into an adverb. Then use the adverb in a sentence of your own.

18. kind   kindly, sentences vary
19. fortunate   fortunately, sentences vary
20. happy   happily, sentences vary

DRILL SHEET AFTER CHAPTER TWELVE
TRANSLATE INTO LATIN.

1. He was always greeting me. Semper me salutabat.
2. I am not living badly. Male non habito.
3. We shall attack first. Primum oppugnabimus.
4. Why are there new dangers? Cur sunt pericula nova?
5. Do you often sing? Cantasne saepe?
6. We like to walk to our farmhouse. Ad nostram villam ambulare amamus.
7. Afterwards he will heal the slaves. Postea servos sanabit.
8. In the evening Peter was telling us *(dative)* about the Lord. Petrus nobis de Domino vespere narrabat.
9. He was walking stealthily through the forest. Ambulabat furtim per silvam.
10. Men often used to think about life, and they were asking God for wisdom. Viri saepe de vita putabant et Deum sapientiam rogabant.
11. Since we always try to honor our family, we are happy. Quoniam semper nostram familiam honorare temptamus, sumus beati. (or *beatae*)
12. She was walking through the little town early in the day. Per parvum oppidum mane ambulabat.
13. Yesterday we were slaves; tomorrow we shall be free. Heri eramus servi; cras erimus liberi.
14. My farmhouse is far away from yours. Mea villa est longe a tua.
15. First, we were listening to the nine tall poets. Primum novem poetas altos auscultabamus.
16. Were there eleven apostles? Erantne undecim apostoli?
17. He was suffering, but he was always singing. Laborabat sed semper cantabat.
18. We live on a beautiful earth, don't we? Nonne in terra pulchra habitamus?
19. My daughter sings well, and she praises God always. Mea filia bene cantat et Deum semper laudat.
20. Meanwhile through the forest the messenger was walking. Interim per silvam nuntius ambulabat.

Test Six to be taken after the completion of Chapter Twelve

Grammar Section

1. What is the tense sign for the imperfect tense? <u>–ba-</u>
2. What three tenses are formed on the present stem of a verb? <u>present, imperfect, future</u>
3. What parts of speech do adverbs modify? <u>verbs, adjectives, and other adverbs</u>

Adverbs. Give the correct Latin word for each adverb.

4. now, already	<u>iam</u>	8. always	<u>semper</u>
5. yesterday	<u>heri</u>	9. first	<u>primum</u>
6. afterwards	<u>postea</u>	10. badly	<u>male</u>
7. far away	<u>longe</u>	11. often	<u>saepe</u>

Tense Usage. Give a correct translation for each of the following Latin words.

12. estis <u>you are</u>   17. curabit <u>he, she, it will take care of</u>
13. rogabant <u>they were asking, they used to ask</u>   18. putamus <u>we think, we do think, we are thinking</u>
14. oppugnabunt <u>they will attack</u>   19. erunt <u>they will be, there will be</u>
15. dabatis <u>you were giving, you did give</u>   20. erit <u>he, she, it will be</u>
16. eram <u>I was</u>   21. sunt <u>they are, there are</u>

Sentence Work. Mark and translate these sentences from Latin to English.

(TEACHER: these are not marked for you because they are fairly easy. If you have any questions, email me at <u>mary @latintrivium.com</u>.)

22. Ambulabamus ad oppidum vespere. <u>We were walking to town (in the) evening.</u>
23. Mali nostram villam et familiam furtim oppugnabant. <u>The evil men were stealthily attacking our farmhouse (or *house*) and family.</u>
24. Heri eramus; nunc sumus; cras erimus. <u>Yesterday we were; now we are; tomorrow we shall be.</u>
25. "Amo te tantum," vocabat puer. <u>"I love you only," the boy used to call. (or, *"I only love you," the boy was calling.*)</u>

26-30. **Translation.** Think! *Used to* and *were/was.*

Tres magni pueri in altā aquā navigare amabant. Ambulabant ad oram (*beach*) mane.
Aqua erat pulchra et navigium (*their little boat*) erat paratum. Aquam diu spectabant.
Marcus primum clamabat, "Spectatisne balaenas?"
Tunc Titus clamabat, "Specto balaenas nigras. Sunt magnae!"
Petrus clamabat, "Sum defessus. Ambulabo ad villam nunc."
Defessi et beati pueri ad villam ambulabant et narrabant familiae de balaenā magnā et
nigrā. Erat iam vespere.

> Three big boys liked (or *used to like*) to sail in the deep water. They walked to the beach early in the day. The water was beautiful and their little boat was ready. They looked (or *were looking*) at the water for a long time.
> First Marcus shouted (or *was shouting*), "Do you see the whales?"
> Then Titus shouted (or *was shouting*), "I see black whales. They are large (huge)."
> Peter shouted (or *was shouting*) then, "I am tired. I will walk to the farmhouse now."
> The weary and happy boys walked (or *were walking*) to the farmhouse and related to (or *told*) the family about the large black whale. It was already evening.

Chapter Thirteen Objectives:

At the end of the lesson students will be able to:

- state the names of two of the three moods of verbs.
- state the rule for Ablative of Time When, Time within When, and Accusative of Duration of Time.
- use the vocative case properly.
- describe the composition of the Roman army.
- know why Christians were persecuted by the Romans.

Chapter Thirteen

1. Enter the chapter phrase into the notebook or use one from the front of the Teacher's Guide.
2. Read and discuss section **I Grammar**. There are actually three moods for verbs: the indicative, imperative, and subjunctive. Adults like to learn by knowing the structure of any subject first (like, *how many there are*), but younger students learn best by just learning as they go along, on a "need to know" basis. The subjunctive mood is covered in Volume III. To preview the subjunctive mood if the students ask, it is the mood of conditions. These are the type of sentences or clauses you would find in the subjunctive mood: Let it rain! It might rain. We may go to the park. She might visit.

3. Copy the material from the boxes regarding the Imperative Mood, Locative Case, Vocative Case plus the different uses of the Accusative and Ablative cases which are important to know. Other languages such as Greek and Russian use these same cases.

4. Do the **Study Sheet.**

5. Exercises **A, B, C,** and **D**.

6. Read and discuss **III Rome's Relgious Beliefs**. Many people do not understand why there was a conflict between the Christians and the Roman government. A very good (short) book discussing this is *The "Atheism" of the Early Church* by R.J. Rushdoony.

7. Exercises **E** and **F.** Why would "amabo" mean "please"?

8. Do all of the **Drill Sheet.**

9. Reading Lesson **IV.** Younger students like to decorate a GI Joe or Ken-type doll with foil and make him look like a Roman soldier. Some of our students have done this. For older students, you might ask them who is the "Tenth Legion" today guarding *our* president? Another research project is to find out why Abraham Lincoln only had one bodyguard the night he was shot, and why that bodyguard was not even in the building at the time of the assassination.

10.   Extra: At this time, some teachers like to have the students review all uses of the Accusative and Ablative Case that they have learned so far. It can be overwhelming to try to remember them all without review. If you would like the students to review, have them make a chart on a flash card of each type.

Accusative	*Ablative*
1. *Direct Object*	1. *Place Where (in or on)*
2. *Place to Which*	2. *Place from Which (a, ab, de, e, ex)*
3. *Duration of Time*	3. *Means or Instrument (in, with, by, using)*
	4. *Time When*
	5. *Time Within Which*

Chapter Thirteen

Imperative Mood; Locative and Vocative Cases; Ablative of Time When; Ablative Time Within Which; Accusative of Duration of Time; At the Praetorian Camp

The mood of a verb shows the manner in which its message is given. Thus far, all verbs you have translated have been in the Indicative Mood, which is the mood for declarative or interrogative sentences. The Indicative Mood can be thought of as the mood of *reality*. Statements or questions about real things or events are in the Indicative Mood. Examples are: *The quartet sang a new song.* Or *Will you run the race swiftly?*

I. Grammar
A. Imperative Mood

As its name implies, the imperative mood is the mood which is used when giving a command (**imperium, -i**, *command*). The imperative form of a verb can be either singular or plural, but it has only two tenses, present and perfect. It is always in the second person, *(You) Come quickly.* The future tense is rarely used except in poetry and drama, legal language, and books of instruction, such as, *Thou shalt not murder.* In this lesson you will use the present tense.

This chart belongs in the notebook section, "Grammar", on the page titled <u>Verbs</u>. These general rules apply to the first and second conjugation verbs.

The Imperative Mood is used when giving a command. For the singular form, it is formed in Latin by removing the **-re** from the second principal part of the verb. For the plural form, it is formed by adding **-te** to that stem.

appel'lō appellā'rē appellā'vī appella'tūs

Present Imperative Active

Singular	Plural
appel'la, *name!*	**appellā'tē**, *name!*

B . Locative Case To express location, some writers do not use "in plus ablative." Put this chart in the "Cases/Declensions" section of your notebook on a page titled <u>Locative Case</u>.

Locative Case With <u>names</u> of cities, small islands, and towns, you <u>may</u> use the Locative Case to show location.
First and Second Declensions: same form as genitive case, **Romae**, *at Rome,* or **Canae**, *at Cana.* All other Declensions: same form as Ablative except for **ruri**, *in the country,* and **Carthagini**, *at Carthage,* **domi**, *at home.*

In the Latin Bible, the locative case is not always used; it is often "in Bethaniā" or "in Nazareth."

C. Vocative Case

The Vocative case is used for direct address. This chart belongs on the second half of the page titled <u>Locative Case</u>. Title the second half of the page, <u>Vocative Case</u>.

The vocative case is in the same form as the nominative case, except in the singular of nouns and adjectives of the second declension ending in **-us** or **-ius**. The vocative for nouns ending in **-us** of the second declension adds the ending, **-e**, to the base, as in Mar**cus**, Mar**ce**. The vocative for nouns ending in **-ius** merely drops the **-us** ending, as in Iuli**us**, Iuli. The masculine vocative singular of **meus** is **mi**.

Latin, unlike English, rarely places the vocative first in the sentence. It is usually placed second.

D. More Uses of the Ablatives

In your notebook, add the following two charts on the page titled <u>Ablative Case</u> in the "Cases/Declensions" section.

Ablative of Time When
The time when an action occurs is shown by the ablative without a preposition.
    Navigabant ad insulam sextā horā. *They* were *sailing to the island at the sixth hour.*

Ablative of Time Within Which
The time within which an action occurs is also expressed by the ablative without a preposition.
    Viri patriam uno anno occupabunt. *The men will seize the country within one year.*
    Tribus annis ab Italiā navigabunt. *They will sail from Italy within three years.*

E. Accusative of Duration of Time

This chart belongs in the same section on the page titled, <u>Accusative Case</u>.

Accusative of Duration of Time
This is slightly different than **Time When** or **Time Within Which**. This is referring to the length of time occurring. It is expressed also without a preposition, but in the accusative case.
    Quattuor annos laborabamus. *We were suffering for four years.*

II. Exercises

A. Give the present active imperative second person singular of the following:

puto, sanctifico, lacrimo, rogo, sano, porto

<u>**A.** puta, sanctifica, lacrima, roga, sana, porta</u>

B. Give the present active imperative second person plural of the following:

servo, amo, do, laboro, canto

<u>**B.** servate, amate, date, laborate, cantate</u>

Navigant ad insulam.

C. Give the vocative singular of the following nouns:

ancilla, poeta, Christus, Pharisaeius, dominus, nauta
<u>ancilla, poeta, Christe, Pharisaei, domine, nauta</u>

D. Give the vocative plural of the following nouns:

discipulus, legatus, poeta, familia, filia
<u>discipuli, legati, poetae, familiae, filiae</u>

E. Read the Latin and translate:

    adv. acc. pl.   3/pl. fut.
1. Cras oppida oppugnabunt.
      Tomorrow they will attack the towns.

    im pv. voc.   acc.s. dat.pl. 3/pl. pres. nom.pl.m.
2. Da, puer, aquam viris; sunt   defessi.
      Boy (or *Son*), give the men water; they are tired. (or, *give water to the men*)

    (per + acc.) adv.   nom.pl.   3/pl. imperf.
3. Per silvam diu discipuli ambulabant.
      The disciples were walking through the forest for a long time.

    im pv.   idiom   acc.s.f.   3/s. nom.s.f.
4. Spectate, amabo, balaenam; est nigra.
      Please look at the whale, it is black.

    impv.   voc.   acc.pl. m. 3/pl. nom.pl. m.
5. Libera, domine, servos; sunt boni.
      Master, free the servants; they are good (men).

    2/s. pres. voc.   acc.s.
6. Curasne, mi fili, familiam?
      My son, are you taking care of the family?

    adv. voc.   (cum + abl.pl. m.)   abl. pl. f. 2/pl. fut.
7. Cras, magistri, cum nostris filiis et filiabus ambulabitis.
      Tomorrow you will walk with our sons and daughters, Teachers. (Masters)

    nom.pl. (in + abl. s. m.) 3/pl.
8. Epistulae in albo libro sunt.
      The letters are in the white book.

    im pv.   acc.pl. gen.s.
9. Laudate mandata Dei.
      Praise the commandments of God.

---

amabo = *please*. Other words for *please* are **quaeso** and **si tibi placet**.

nom.pl. m.   acc. sg. n.   3/pl. imperf.
10. Inimici viri quartum oppidum oppugnabant.
        The unfriendly men were attacking (or, *used to attack*) the fourth town.

F. Mark each sentence and translate. (IMPV means "imperative.")

idiom impv.dat. (de + abl. s. f.)   voc. sg.
1. Please <u>tell</u> us (about your family), my daughter.
        Narra, amabo, mea filia, nobis de tua familia.

1/pl. pres. nom.pl.. impv.   acc.s.   voc. pl.
2. <u>We are</u> <u>ready</u>; <u>guard</u> the <u>house</u>, good servants.
        Sumus, boni servi, parati (or paratae); servate villam.

nom.s. f.   3/s. pres. nom.s.f. *(per + acc.)
3. <u>A happy life</u> <u>is</u>   <u>ours</u>   (by means of Christ.)
        Vita beata nostra per Christum est.

voc.pl.   im pv. acc.pl. f.   (in + acc. s.)   abl. time when
4. Women, <u>call your daughters</u> (into the farmhouse) in the evening.
        Vocate, feminae, vestras filias in villam vespere.

impv.s. acc.s.   (dat.pl.)   voc.s.
5. <u>Give</u> <u>water</u> (to the horses), son.
        Da, fili, equis aquam.

3/s. imperf.   nom.s.   dat. s.   acc. duration of time
6. <u>She</u> <u>was</u> the <u>handmaiden</u> (to the woman) (for three years).
        Erat ancilla feminae tres annos.

nom.pl. m. 3/pl. pres.   nom.pl. m.   nom .pl. m.   dat.s.
7. The <u>sailors</u> <u>are</u>   <u>pure</u> and <u>pleasing</u>   (to God).
        Nautae puri et grati Deo sunt.

abl. time when   nom.s. 3/s. fut.   acc.pl.
8. (At the ninth hour) the <u>master</u> will <u>set</u> the <u>servants</u> <u>free</u>.
        Nona hora dominus servos liberabit.

1/pl. im perf.   acc.pl.   abl. time when
9. <u>We</u> <u>were looking at</u> the <u>whales</u> (at the sixth hour).
        Spectabamus balaenas sexta hora.

voc.pl.   idiom impv.pl.   (de + abl. pl.)   gen.pl.m.
10. Girls, please <u>think</u> (about the commandments) (of your teachers).
        Putate, puellae, amabo, de mandatis vestrorum magistrorum .

---

* **note: amabo,** *I shall like (you),* is the word for *please.* It is an idiom.
        Portate, amabo, gladios. *Please carry the swords. = Carry the swords (and) I*
                                                            shall like (you).

---

*Not really ablative of means, but "through Christ".

III. Rome's Religious Beliefs

Jupiter, the god of the heavens, Mars, the god of war, and Quirinus, the god of the common people were the primary gods in the early republic. Most of the farmers of Italy believed in these three who were called the *archaic triad*. Between the 500's and 100's B.C. many other gods were added to their religion, mostly borrowed from the Greeks but with new Roman names. The people feared the gods because they were just glorified imaginary men who reacted with anger, bad tempers, and injustice. You could never predict what one might do to you based on his jealousies or desire for revenge against another god.

Later in the republic, many Romans used their beliefs in pagan gods as a cover for their political aspirations. Of course, *some* Romans sincerely believed in the power of their gods, but many people gave lip service to them, just as today, many people call themselves Christians, and do not do what God tells them to do.

The Romans had always tolerated any religion that conquered people wanted to practice, as long as it was licensed by the state and as long as a person's first loyalty was to the Roman state. The problem Christians faced was that their first loyalty was to God. They even had the boldness to pray *for* the emperor's salvation. This kind of faith could not be tolerated by the Roman emperor because he felt that he alone was the savior and governor of mankind. This loyalty to another God placed the Christian in a position of treason, according to Roman thinking. The battle was between Christ and Caesar for the hearts and minds of the people. Hence, the persecution of the Christians.

The emperor eventually called himself the "Savior of the people" and all the other titles which were reserved for Christ. Loyalty was either to Caesar or to Christ.

Jesus King of Kings and Creator of all things.

Jupiter, pagan god, omnipotens pater Romanorum

IV. Reading Lesson

Ad Praetoria Castra (Praetorian Camp)

Davus et Titus Philippusque ad Circum Maximum sunt, et Aquila et Fidelia et Priscilla Claraque ad Forum sunt. Sed Fidelius Ioannesque ad Praetoria Castra sunt.

Fidelius cum copiis novis laborat. Ambulant saepe diu; portant multa. Ubi copiae paratae erunt, ad Iudeam navigabunt.

Romanus exercitus *(army)* magna structura erat et fortissimus *(very strong)*. Multos populos in multis terris superabat.

Erant quadringenti et quinquaginta milia (*450,000*) virorum inter copias Romanas trans imperium. Octo viri appellabantur *(were called)* contubernium. Erant decem contubernia in centuriā. Fidelius est dominus centuriae.

Recognition Vocabulary

centū′rīa, centū′rīae, f., *century (a group of 100 men originally, later 80 men)*
cōntūbēr′nīum, cōntūbēr′nīa, n., *contubernium*
impē′rīum, impē′rī, n., *power, command, empire*
Iūdē′a, Iūdē′ae, *Judea*
Roma′nus, Roma′na, Roma′num, *Roman*
structū′ra, structū′rae, f., *organization, structure*

A **contubernium** was ten men who lived together in one tent and ate meals together. It was later reduced to <u>eight</u> men because the tents were too crowded. Ten contubernia made a **century**. Ten centuries made up a **cohort**, and ten cohorts made up a legion. So the approximate size of a legion was (8 X 10 X 10 X 10) about 8,000 to 10,000 men. One **legion** was a little larger, made up of the most trusted troops, and this legion guarded the general. During Julius Caesar′s command, it was the Tenth Legion.

<table>
<tr><td>

<u>Reading Lesson</u>

At the Praetorian Camp

David, Titus, and Philip are at the Circus Maximus, and Aquila, Fidelia, Priscilla and Clara are at the Forum. But Fidelius and John are at the Praetorian Camp.

Fidelius is working with the new troops. They often walk for a long time; they carry many things. When the troops are (literally, *will be*) ready, they will sail to Judea.

The Roman army was a great organization, and it was very strong. It used to defeat (*conquer*) many peoples (*nations*) in many lands.

There were 450,000 men among the Roman troops across the empire. Eight men were called a contubernium. There were ten contubernia in a century. Fidelius is the master of a century.

</td></tr>
</table>

Responde Latine. Answer in a complete sentence.
1. Ubi copiae navigare parant?
2. Quibuscum *(With whom)* Fidelius laborat?
3. Quot viri in exercitū Romano sunt?

Name ____Date ___________________

Latin in the Christian Trivium
Study Sheet
Chapter Thirteen

Grammar Review

1. The two moods of a Latin verb that you have learned so far are   indicative and imperative.
2. The three tenses of a Latin verb that you have learned so far are present, imperfect, and future.
3. The three persons of a Latin verb are first, second, and third. (I, you, someone else)
4. The two numbers of a Latin verb are   singular and plural.
5. The present active imperative singular form is the same as the present   stem.
6. The vocative case is used for   direct address.
7. The accusative case is used to show the duration of time in which something is occurring.
8. The ablative case is used to show the time when something occurs.
9. The ablative case is used to show the time within which something occurs.
10. Who were the three primary pagan gods that the Romans worshipped? Jupiter, Mars, and Quirinus.
11. Why were the Christians persecuted by the Romans? Because they wanted to worship Christ only, not the emperor. They also prayed FOR the emperor.

Practice

12. Give the present imperative active second person singular of the following verbs.

narro	narra	**do**	da
navigo	navig a	**nuntio**	nuntia

13. Give the present imperative active second person plural of the following verbs.

ausculto	auscultate	**servo**	servate
laudo	laudate	**ambulo**	ambulate

14. Give the vocative singular of the following nouns.

amicus	<u>amice</u>	**filia**	<u>filia</u>
filius	<u>fili</u>	**Davus**	<u>Dave</u>

15. Circle the Latin phrase that best translates the bracketed English words.

(a) My friend will walk to my house {within two hours.}
    (1) in duo horas   (3) duobus horis – (ablative of time within which)
    (2) duas horas   (4) a duobus horis

(b) The poet was giving a gift {to the woman.}
    (1) feminis   (3) ad feminam
    (2) femino   (4) feminae (dative case follows verb of giving)

(c) He was carrying the boys {with the carriage}.
    (1) in raedis   (3) raedam
    (2) cum raedā   (4) raedā – (ablative of means)

16. Match the English words with their correct meaning on the right.

1. affiliate	(f)	(a) to inspire; to bring out feelings or memories
2. furtively	(g)	(b) everywhere present
3. benediction	(l)	(c) a position or job without anxiety
4. nautical	(j)	(d) a nine-sided polygon
5. novelty	(h)	(e) a measuring device on a plane to determine height
6. approximate	(k)	(f) to associate with someone as if your own child
7. pulchritude	(i)	(g) stealthily
8. verbose	(m)	(h) something new, a new idea
9. convocation	(n)	(i) beauty
10. ubiquitous	(b)	(j) having to do with sailing
11. altimeter	(e)	(k) nearly
12. sinecure	(c)	(l) a blessing, "speaking well"
13. nonagon	(d)	(m) wordy
14. evoke	(a)	(n) the act of calling together a group of people

Sentences

   adv. (abl. means)   nom.pl. dat.pl. (de + abl. pl.) 3/pl. imperf.
17. Non multis verbis discipuli viris de periculis narrabant.
    In not many words the disciples used to tell the men about the dangers. (or *were telling*)

  nom.pl. m. 3/pl. pres. acc.pl. n.
18. Boni amant   bona.
    Good men like good things.

  nom.pl.m.   acc.pl.n. 3/pl.pres.
19. Mali   mala   amant.
    Bad men like bad things.

20. Defessi ad villam esse amant.
The tired men like to be near the farmhouse. (or *at the house*)

Latin Composition
21. On the following lines write a story in Latin of two paragraphs. Each paragraph must have three sentences. Give your composition a Latin title.

Composition. Teacher, you will have to grade the composition according to your knowledge.

DRILL SHEET AFTER CHAPTER THIRTEEN.

1. Ambula, amice, quattuor horas. Friend, walk for four hours. (acc. duration of time)
2. Ambulate, viri, quattuor horas. Men, walk for four hours.
3. Ambula, mi fili, ad meam villam. Walk to my house, my son.
4. Ambulabisne ad meam villam quattuor horis? Will you walk to my house in four hours? (abl. time when)
5. Puta, mea filia, de Deo, et tum canta. My daughter, think about God and then sing.
6. Puto, mea filia, de te et meo filio. I think about you and my son, my daughter.
7. Putate de mandatis Dei nunc! Think about the commandments of God now!
8. Putate de mandatis Dei semper! Think about the commandments of God always!
9. Da dona amico tuo primum. First, give the gifts to your friend.
10. Dabamus dona nostris amicis saepe. We were giving gifts to our friends often.
11. Dabimus dona discipulis quod sunt boni. We shall give gifts to the disciples because they are good.
12. Date, servi, bona dona puellis puerisque. Servants, give good gifts to the girls and boys.
13. Ubi est firmamentum caeli? Where is the firmament of heaven?
14. Ubi erant inimici? Where were the unfriendly men?
15. Ubi est ludus? Where (or *when*) is the game? (or *school*?)
16. Ubi est liber legati? Where is the lieutenant's book?
17. Postea ambulabitis. Afterwards, you will walk.
18. Tantum ambulare amant. They only like to walk.
19. Equus diu ambulabat. The horse was walking for a long time.
20. Ubi es? Sum hic. Where are you? I am here.
21. Diu ibi habitabam. I was living there for a long time.
22. Tunc ambulabamus ad insulam. Then we were walking to the apartment. (They could not walk to the island, so use "apartment.")
23. Vocate pueros. Call the boys.
24. Voca pueros. Call the boys.
25. Specta puerum in villā. Look at the boy in the farmhouse.
26. Spectatisne puerum? Are you looking at the boy?
27. Specto puerum. I am looking at the boy.
28. Da, amabo, librum mihi. Please give the book to me.
29. Da, amabo, librum nobis. Please give the book to us.
30. Dabo vobis librum. I shall give the book to you.
31. Dabo tibi librum. I shall give the book to you.
32. Unā horā navigabimus. In one hour we shall sail.
33. Duo horas navigabimus. For two hours we shall sail.

34. Septem annos viri pugnabant. <u>For seven years the men were fighting.</u>
35. Septem annis viri navigabunt. <u>In seven years the men will sail.</u>
36. Quinque annos laborabamus. <u>For five years we were suffering (or working).</u>
37. Quinque annis in caelo erimus. <u>In five years we shall be in heaven.</u>

WORD SEARCH

Circle the Latin words for the English expressions listed below. The words may be read vertically, horizontally, or diagonally, in any direction.

1. war
2. hour
3. book
4. far
5. to
6. early in the day
7. teacher

8. pleasing
9. then, at that time
10. island
11. because
12. good
13. sword
14. with

15. God
16. in the middle of
17. I like
18. I live
19. eight

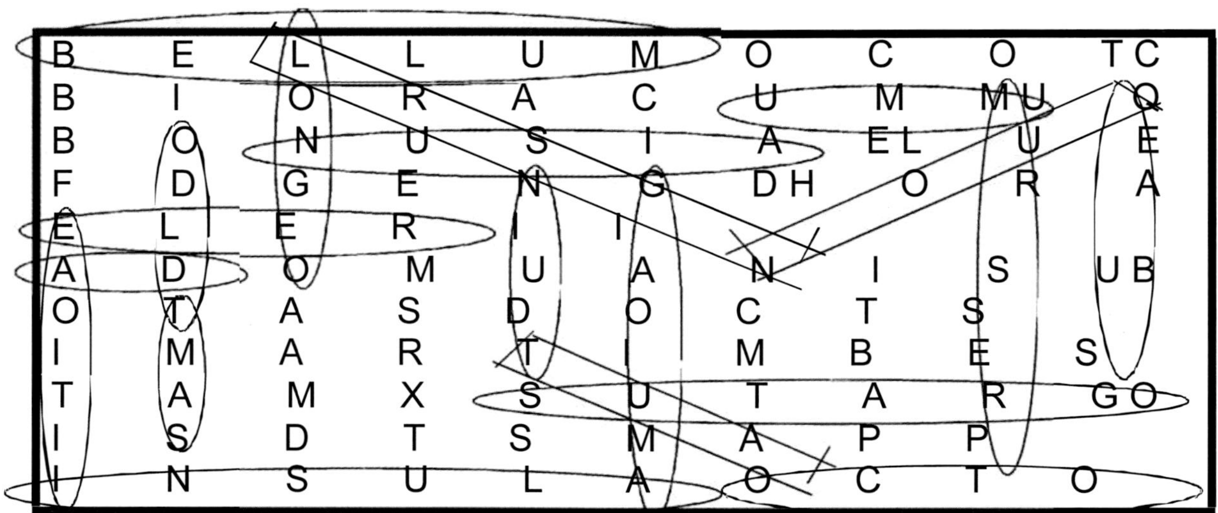

REVIEW ALL USES OF ACCUSATIVE AND ABLATIVE TO DATE

Contributed by Karen L. Koehler-Cesa, Hybrid Schoo l, New Jersey.

In addition to your Study Sheet of this week, you will need to review all the uses of the Accusative and Ablative cases ("case conventions"). For each one below, find an example. Write the English and the Latin of the example you find, and the page number from where you found it in your text.

ACCUSATIVE

Type of Use	Example (first in Latin, then in English)	Found on page:
Direct Object Latin-->		
English-->		
Place to Which, Latin-		
English-->		
Duration of Time, Latin--		
English-->		

ABLATIVE

Type of Use	Example (first in Latin, then in English)	Found on page:
Place Where Latin ->		
English ->		
Place from Which, Latin->		
English ->		
Ablative of Means, Latin->		
English->		
Time When Latin->		
English->		
Time Within Which, Latin->		
English ->		

- recite the endings for third declension nouns.
- use each derivative from the book in a sentence.

General Sequence of Instruction: Use each chapter's instructions for detailed plan, but a general plan is the following:
1.) Read the grammar.
2.) Learn the vocabulary.
3.) Do Study Sheet to reinforce.
4.) Do Drill Sheet for practice.
5.) Complete the Exercises in the chapter including the Reading Lesson
6.) Quiz orally or use bi-chapter tests to evaluate.

<u>**Chapter Fourteen**</u>

1. Enter the chapter phrase or one of those from the Teacher's Guide.
2. Read and discuss **I Grammar**. Third declension is a difficult one because it has nouns of all three genders. After a few lessons you will start to see a pattern regarding gender. Often, but not all the time, the nouns ending in -**c**, -**o**, -**n**, -**s**, -**u**, -**l** are masculine; the nouns ending in **-s**, **-o**, **-x** are feminine, and those ending in **-al** are neuter. At this time, it is very important to be sure your student learns the gender along with the meaning of nouns because the gender of any modifying adjective will have to agree with the gender of the noun and in many cases, the endings will not be the same. Remember: the most important thing to do in Latin is **DRILL, DRILL, DRILL**. This is particularly true when learning genders for third declension nouns, and this is why this first volume is so repetitious. Later volumes will be more diverse.
3. Copy the box with the paradigm for this chapter's declension.
4. Memorize the endings of the new declension listed in the box.
5. **II Vocabulary**. Commonly used derivatives (especially on SAT tests) are:
illuminate, cordially, mercenary.
6. **Study Sheet.**
7. **Exercise III** do **A, B**, and **C**.
8. **Drill Sheet**.
9. **IV Reading Lesson**
10.   Next do **Exercise D.** If possible, do this one along with the students.
11.   Review for the chapter test.
12.   Derivative test. Do not review for this test. Correct the test, and return but do not use this test grade in figuring a grade for your student.
13.   Extra: Some teachers like to have students make a card to learn the basic questions every journalist asks:

Who? What? When? Where? Why?

Quis? Quid ? Ubi? Ubi? Cur?

Chapter Fourteen

Dixitque Deus: Fiat Lux.
And God said, "Let there be Light"

Third Declension Nouns; <u>Report to Judea</u>

I. Grammar

The third declension nouns may be recognized by their ending **-is** in the genitive singular. One difficulty with this declension is that the nominative often does not show the stem. However, when you memorize both the nominative and genitive, you can easily see the stem in the genitive. The stem often resembles the English derivative, as in **iter, <u>itineris</u>**, *route, <u>itinerary</u>*.

They may be either masculine, feminine, or neuter in gender, so it is important to learn the gender as you learn the vocabulary. There are some general rules, which, of course, do have exceptions, to help you if you forget the gender.

GENDER	ENDINGS
Masculine	**-or, -tor, -l**
Feminine	**-tas, -tus, -tudo, -tio, -s,** or **-x** (unless a male person)
Neuter	**-us, -e, -al, -ar**

When using an adjective of the first and second declension with a noun of the third declension, endings will not be the same, but the case, number, and gender must still agree. Thus **magnus iudex** is *a great judge,* **magna mater***, a great mother,* and **magnum animal**, *a great animal.* Sometimes it helps to remember gender if you memorize a noun with the proper form of an adjective with the noun.

> A reminder: Notice that the neuter nominative and accusative cases are alike, and that in the plural, they end in **-a.**

NAVES LONGAE

This paradigm is of the third declension noun. It is to be copied and put into your notebook on the page titled <u>Third Declension</u> in the "Cases/Declensions" section of your notebook. Memorize each ending.

	frā′tĕr *brother*	lex *law*	nō′men *name*		
Cases		**Singular**		**M&F**	**, N.**
Nom.	fra′ter	lex	nomen	----,	---- -------
Gen.	fra′tris	le′gis	no′minis	-is	-is
Dat.	fra′tri	le′gi	no′mini	-i	-i
Acc.	fra′trem	le′gem	no′men	-em	-----
Abl.	fra′tre	le′ge	no′mine	-e	-e
		Plural			
Nom.	fra′tres	le′ges	no′mina	-es	-a
Gen.	fra′trum	le′gum	no′minum	-um	-um
Dat.	fra′tribus	le′gibus	nomin′ibus	-ibus	-ibus
Acc.	fra′tres	le′ges	no′mina	-es	-a
Abl.	fra′tribus	le′gibus	nomin′ibus	-ibus	-ibus

The nominative singular ending is left blank because it varies.

II. Vocabulary   English Derivatives

Put masculine nouns on blue cards (11), feminine on pink, (13), and neuter on yellow (3). (27 altogether) From now on, Roman numerals will tell you to which declension each noun belongs.

au′dītŏr, audītō′ris, III, m., *hearer, student*   (auditor, audit, auditory)

Clau′dīa, Clau′dīae, I, f., *Claudia*

cŏr, cŏr′dis, III, n., *heart, mind, judgment*   (cordially, cardiac)

cŏr′pūs, cōrpŏr′is, III, n., *body*   corporal, incorporate)

fāc′tŏr, fāctō′ris, III, m., *doer, maker*   (factory, manufacture, factor)

fōrtītū′dō, fōrtītū′dinis, III, f., *bravery, courage, strength*   (fortitude)

frā′ter, frā′tris, III, m., *brother*   (fraternity, fraternization)

fu′rŏr, fūrŏr′is, III, m., *madness, rage*

hō′mō, hō′minis, III, m., *man,* as in *mankind*

iū′dex, iū′dicis, III, m., *judge, juror*   (judiciary)

lex, lē′gis, III, f., *law*   (legal, legislature)

lūx, lū′cis, III, f., *light*   (lucid, illuminate, Lucifer)

mā′ter, mā′tris, III, f., *mother*   (maternal, maternity)

mer′cēs, mercē′dis, III, f., *wages, reward*   (mercenary, merchant)

mī′lēs, mīl′ītis, III, m., *soldier*   (military, militia)

mŭltītū′dō, mŭltītū′dinis, III, f., *great number*

nō′men, nō′minis, III, n., *name*   (nominal, nominate, synonym)

pā′ter, pā′tris, III, m., *father*   (paternity, paternal)
pāx, pā′cis, III, f., *peace*   (pacification, pacify, pacific)
plenītū′dō, plenītū′dinis, III, f., *fullness, plenty*
prin′ceps, prin′cipis, III, m., *ruler, prince*
rex, rē′gis, III, m., *king*   (regal)
sāl, sā′lis, III, m., *salt*
sōr′ōr, sōrō′ris, III, f., *sister*   (sorority)
ūx′ōr, ūxōr′is, III, f., *wife*
vīr′tūs, vīrtū′tis, III, f., *strength, power*   (virtue)
vōlūn′tās, vōlūntā′tis, III, f., *will,* e.g., *'good will'*   (voluntary)

III. Exercises

A. Decline the following.

altus puer	amic a mater	bonum nomen
alti pueri	amicae matris	boni nominis
alto puero	amicae matri	bono nomini
altum puerum	amicam matrem	bonum nomen
alto puero	amica matre	bono nomine
alti pueri	amicae matres	bona nomina
altorum puerorum	amicarum matrum	bonorum nominum
altis pueris	amicis matribus	bonis nominibus
altos pueros	amicas matres	bona nomina
altis pueris	amicis matribus	bonis nominibus

B. Forms. Translate from Latin to English.

1. Sanctus Deus
2. corpora alba
3. legem bonam
4. suis sororibus
5. multitudo feminarum
6. meum nomen
7. homines puri
8. cordi bono
9. uxoris virtus
10. lucem albam
11. multis regibus
12. cum rege malo
13. vestra mater
14. sal terrae
15. sanctas vitas

1. Holy God	6. my name	11. to/for many kings (by/with)
2. white bodies	7. pure men	12. with the evil king
3. a good law	8. to/for a good heart	13. your mother
4. to/for her sisters	9. a wife's strength	14. the salt of the earth
by/with her sisters	10. a white light	15. holy lives
5. a crowd of women		

C. Translate f rom Latin to English.

     adv. nom.s. f.   dat.s. 3/s. fut.
1. Mox mater mea mihi cantabit.
       Soon my mother will sing to me.

im pv. pl. voc.pl.   dat. pl. m.   acc.pl.
2. Date, poetae, vestris amicis epistulas.
       Give the letters to your friends, poets.

   nom .pl. m.   nom.pl.f.   abl.time when infinitive   3/pl. imperf.
3. Nostri patres matresque decimā horā   navigare   temptabant.
       Our fathers and mothers were trying to sail at the tenth hour.

   nom.s. abl.s.   nom.s. 3/s. pres. nom.s.f.
4. Puella nomine Claudia est   pulchra.
       The girl by the name of Claudia (literally: *Claudia by name*) is pretty.

   nom.s.f.   gen.pl.m.   adv. 3.s. pres. nom.s.f.
5. Natura hominum non est   *bona.
       The nature of man (*mankind* or *men*) is not good.

     nom.s.m.   3/s. pres. nom.s.m.   gen.s.f.
6. Noster princeps est   vir   fortudinis magnae.
       Our ruler is a man of great bravery.

   nom.s.f.   gen.pl.   (in + abl. sg.n.)   3/s. fut.
7. Multitudo militum in nostro oppido habitabit.
       A great number of soldiers will live in our town.

  3/s. im perf. nom.s.m. gen.s.
8. Erat septimus rex Romae.
       He was the seventh king of Rome.

   3/s.pres. nom.s.f.   (inter + acc.pl.)
9. Estne bona voluntas inter homines?
       Is there good will among men?

   nom.s. nom.s.f. acc.s.   3/pl. pres.
10. Vir et sua uxor Deum honorant.
       The man and his (own) wife honor God.

D. English to Latin   Mark each word.

  im pv.s.   acc.s. dat. pl.   idiom
1. <u>Give</u> the <u>light</u> (to the men), please.
       Da, amabo, hominibus (or *viris*) lucem. (or, *si tibi placet*, if you please)

  1/pl. pres. acc.s. conj.   acc.s.   conjunction
2. <u>We</u> <u>like</u> <u>peace</u> and <u>righteousness</u> also.
       Pacem et iustitiam etiam amamus.

---

*Meaning **not perfect**.

   adv.   3/s. im perf. abl.time when conj.   1/pl. imperf.   acc.pl. f.
3. <Soon> it was   evening   and we were looking at the beautiful lights.
       Mox erat vespere et luces pulchras spectabamus.

    nom .pl.   3/pl. pres. adv. nom.pl. m.
4. Brothers are   often good friends.
       Fratres saepe amici boni sunt.

    nom.s. f.   3/s. pres. (in + abl.s.) conj. adv. conj. (in + abl. s.)
5. Our reward is   (in heaven) and often also (on earth).   .
       Nostra merces in caelo etiam in terra saepe est.

     nom.pl.m. 3/pl. pres.   acc.s.   gen.s. m.
6. Small boys do not like the madness (of our ruler).
       Parvi pueri furorem principis nostri non amant.

   nom.s.n.   3/s. pres. nom.s.n. conj. gen.s. nom.s.n. 3/s. pres.
7. Your body is not large, but the farmer's body is.
       Corpus tuum non est magnum, sed agricolae *corpus est.*
       (You can eliminate the repetition of **corpus est** if you like.)

    3/s. fut.   nom.s.f.   adv.
8. There will be peace <for a long time>.
       Pax diu erit.

    3/s. pres. adv.   (in + abl.s.)
9. "It is <well> (with my soul)."
       "Bene in meo animo est." (Use "in" instead of "cum.")

    3/pl.pres. nom.pl.f.   nom.pl.m.   (in + abl.s. f.)
10. There are five sisters and six brothers (in our family).
       Sunt quinque sorores et sex fratres in nostra familia.

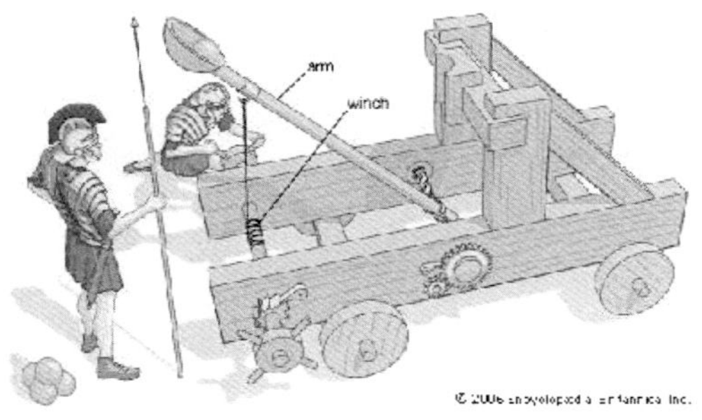

IV. Reading Lesson

From now on, if a word in Latin closely resembles its English meaning, the word may not be given in the Recognition Vocabulary.

Reporta ad
Iudeam

Unā die *(one day)* ubi Fidelius Ioannesque ad Praetoria Castra *(camp)* sunt, miles Fidelio epistulam dat. Est a Principe Tiberio. Tiberius Fidelio narrat, "Reporta ad Iudeam cum copiis tuis nunc!"

Ubi Fidelius erat puer parvus, habitabat in Iudeā, quoniam suus pater legatus in exercitū *(army)* Romano sub Caesare Augusto erat. Fidelius de terrā Iudeae et linguā et populo et moribus *(customs)* putat. Tiberius nunc familiam ad Iudeam mittit *(is sending)*.

Fidelius Ioannesque ad insulam properant. Sunt defessi. Fidelius familiae de epistulā a Tiberio narrare vult *(wants)*.

Ubi appropinquant *(they arrive)*, Fidelius familiae de epistulā narrat. Aquila et pueri beati non sunt. Puellae lacrimant. Diu fabulas de miserā vitā in Iudeā auscultaverunt *(have heard)*.

Iudea erat, et est, deserta, etiam terra est saxosa. Non sunt arbores ibi. Populus est molestus et Romanos non amant.

Fidelius familiae de Iudeā ubi puer erat narrat. Beatus erat ubi is (**is** = *he*) et sua pater et mater et fratres ibi habitabant. Eos *(them)* curabit et beati ibi etiam erunt. Itaque *(and so)* familia in Iudeā habitare parat.

Recognition Vocabulary

ār′bōr, ārbōr′is, f. *tree*
Cae'sārē Augū'stō, *Caesar Augustus*
dēsēr′ta, -ae, f., *desert*
mōles′tūs, -a, -ūm, *troublesome*
prō′pērō, - ā′re, -ā′vi, -ā′tūs, *hasten*
rēpōr′tō, - ā′re, -ā′vi, -ā′tūs, *report*
Rōma′nūs,-a, -ūm, *Roman*
sāxōs′us, -a, -ūm, *rocky*
Tībēr′īūs, *the emperor of Rome*

Reading Lesson

Report to Judea
One day when Fidelius and John are at the Praetorian Camp, a soldier gives Fidelius a letter. It is from the Emperor (Ruler) Tiberius. Tiberius tells Fidelius, "Report to Judea with your troops now! "

When Fidelius was a small boy he used to live in Judea, since his father was a lieutenant in the Roman army under Caesar Augustus. Fidelius is thinking about the land of Judea, the language, the people, and the customs. Now Tiberius is sending the family to Judea.

Fidelius and John hasten to the apartment. They are tired. Fidelius wants to tell the family about the letter from Tiberius.

When they arrive, Fidelius tells the family about the letter. Aquila and the boys are not happy. The girls cry. For a long time they have listened to stories about the unhappy life in Judea.

Judea was, and is, a desert, and also the land is rocky. There are not (*no*) trees there. The people are (Use "are" instead of "is" for the English translation.) troublesome and they do not like Romans.

Fidelius tells the family about Judea when he was a boy. He was happy when he and his father and mother and brothers lived there. He will take care of them, and they will also be happy there. So the family prepares to live in Judea.

Responde Latine. Answer in a complete sentence.
1. Quis est nuntius Fidelio a Tiberio?
2. Ubi *(When)* Fidelius in Iudeā habitabat?
3. Cur ibi habitabat?
4. Est familia beata de epistulā?
5. Qualis *(What kind of)* terra erat, et est, Iudea?

<u>Questions.</u> What is the message to Fidelius from Tiberius? Nuntius est, "Reporta ad Iudeam cum copiis tuis nunc." 2. When did Fidelius live in Judea? Fidelius erat parvus puer ubi in Iudea habitabat. 3. Why did he live there? Quoniam suus pater legatus in exercitu Romano erat. 4. Is the family happy about the letter? Minime. Aquila et pueri beati non sunt, et puellae lacrimant. 5. What sort of land was, and is, Judea? Iudea erat et est deserta et saxosa.

Name ____Date ____________________

Latin in the Christian Trivium
Study Sheet
Chapter Fourteen

Grammar

1. Does an adjective of the first and second declension always agree in case and number with the third declension noun it modifies? <u>yes</u>
2. What two cases of neuter nouns always have the same ending? <u>nominative and accusative</u>

Practice

3. Write the requested forms in Latin.

CASE   NUMBER LATIN WORD

		CASE	NUMBER	LATIN WORD
a.	judge	acc.	sg.	<u>iudicem</u>
b.	doer, maker	abl.	pl.	<u>factoribus</u>
c.	ruler	nom.	pl.	<u>principes</u>
d.	man	nom.	sg.	<u>homo</u>
e.	ruler	dat.	pl.	<u>principibus or regibus</u>
f.	father	acc.	pl.	<u>patres</u>
g.	madness	acc.	sg.	<u>furorem</u>
h.	wages	dat.	pl.	<u>mercedibus</u>
i.	soldier	abl.	pl.	<u>militibus</u>
j.	bravery	gen.	sg.	<u>fortitudinis</u>
k.	fullness	abl.	sg.	<u>plenitudine</u>
l.	king	nom.	pl.	<u>reges</u>
m.	salt	nom.	sg.	<u>sal</u>
n.	name	abl.	sg.	<u>nomine</u>
o.	brother	acc.	pl.	<u>fratres</u>
p.	peace	abl.	pl.	<u>pacibus</u>
q.	wife	nom.	pl.	<u>uxores</u>
r.	will	gen.	sg.	<u>voluntatis</u>
s.	sister	acc.	pl.	<u>sorores</u>
t.	strength	nom.	pl.	<u>fortitudines, virtutes</u>

4. Underline the correct translations of these sentences.

    a. **Homo puero mercedem dabat.**
1.) The boy gave the man his wage. 2.) The man will give wages to the boy.
3.) The man's son gave him rewards. <u>4.) The man was giving the boy a reward.</u>

    b. **Principis filius filiam iudicis amat.**
1.) The judge loves the son and daughter of the ruler. <u>2.) The son of the ruler loves the judge's daughter</u>. 3.) The daughter loves the ruler, the judge's son. 4.) The son chiefly loves the j udge's daughter.

    c. **Eratne tuum nomen Davus?**
1.) Why did he name you David? <u>2.) Was David your name?</u> 3.) Your name is David, isn't it? 4.) Did you know the man David?

5. Underline the Latin words which correctly translate only the italicized word.

    a. Rulers praise *laws*.
        legem <u>leges</u> legibus legum legi
    b. Mothers love *daughters*.
        filiae filiabus filiis <u>filias</u> filiis
    c. There [*]is a great *number of soldiers* in Gaul.
        numerum militum   numerus militibus   <u>numerus militum</u>
    d. Our ruler is a maker *of good laws*.
        <u>bonarum legum</u> boni leges bonas legas

---

[*]Since language changes over time, students may prefer to say, "there are a great number."

Latin in the Christian Trivium Volume I – Teacher's Guide

Sentence Work   Translate these after marking them properly.

    nom.s.   3/s. imperf.   (de + abl.s.)
6. The student was thinking (about the reward).
       Auditor de mercede putabat.

    nom.s.   3/s. im perf. nom.s. gen.s.   adv.
7. The judge was   a student (of the law) <for a long time>.
       Iudex auditor legis diu erat.

    nom.s.   gen.s. m.   3/s. im perf.   acc.s.f.
8. The bravery (of my brother) was saving our family.
       Fortitudo fratris mei familiam nostram servabat.

    nom.s.   (pro + abl. s.) 3/s. pres. (de + abl.s.)   conj. (de + abl.s.)   (sub + abl.)
9. A soldier (for Christ) thinks (about the law) and (about peace) (under God).
       Miles pro Christo de lege et pace sub Deo putat.

   nom.s. m. 3/s.pres. nom.s. m.   conj.   nom.s.f. 3/s. pres. nom.s.f.
10. A man is   happy,   because his wife is   a good woman.
       Homo est beatus quod sua uxor est femina bona. (or, *vir est beatus..*)

P ractice with vocabulary

11. About 70% of English words are derived from Latin words. You have probably
recognized many already. Circle the Latin root that you see in these words and then underline
the correct definition of each. You may use the dictionary if needed.

     a. pulchritude 1) obesity 2) daughter of a viscount 3) physical beauty 4) a mental
                  condition
     b. patriot 1) incompetent 2) martyr 3) hallucinogen 4) loyalist
     c. equestrian 1) dancer 2) pianist 3) horseman 4) acrobat
     d. verbiage 1) trickiness 2) wordiness 3) subtlety 4) codification
     e. convocation 1) an assembling by summons 2) meeting quite by chance
                3) a fortunate or providential coincidence 4) partnership

Latin Composition

12. On the following lines write a story in Latin of three paragraphs. Each paragraph must have
three sentences. Give your composition a Latin title. (Again, give student credit or no credit,
unless you feel that you want to grade this composition.)

1. corpus magnum <u>a large body</u>
2. corporis magni <u>of a large body, a large body's</u>
3. iudex altus <u>the tall judge</u>
4. iudicis alti <u>the tall judge's, of a tall judge</u>
5. iudicibus altis <u>to/for tall judges or by/with tall judges</u>
6. plenitudo pacis <u>plenty of peace, fullness of peace</u>
7. princeps nomine <u>ruler by name (meaning, a ruler in name only)</u>
8. miles albus <u>a white soldier</u>
9. militum nigrorum <u>of black soldiers, black soldiers'</u>
10. factor lucis <u>maker of light</u>
11. factor bonae legis <u>maker of a good law</u>
12. furor malus <u>evil madness, bad anger</u>
13. furori fero <u>to/f or a fierce rage, or by/with a fierce rage</u>
14. uxor pura et pulchra <u>a pure beautiful wife</u>
15. uxores bonae <u>good wives</u>
16. beata mater <u>happy mother, blessed mother</u>
17. beatis matribus <u>to/f or or happy mothers, or by/with happy mothers</u>
18. principes proximi <u>neighboring rulers/princes</u>
19. Princeps est paratus. <u>The ruler is prepared.</u>
20. Mater est mea. <u>The mother is mine. (or *She is my mother.*)</u>
21. Mater est defessa. <u>Mother is tired.</u>
22. Patria erat lata et longa. <u>The country was broad and long.</u>
23. Da militibus mercedes. <u>Give the soldiers the rewards. (*wages*)</u>
24. Da mihi mercedes. <u>Give me rewards.</u>
25. Date, viri, meae matri mercedes. <u>Men, give my mother the rewards.</u>
26. Rex est iudex, et est meus pater. <u>The king is a judge, and he is my father.</u>
27. Tuae leges sunt verae. <u>Your laws are true.</u>
28. Da, amabo, mihi salem. <u>Please give me the salt.</u>
29. Hominis virtus est magna. <u>The strength of the man is great.</u>
30. Bonus rex puram uxorem a mat. <u>A good king loves a pure wife.</u>
31. Erit pax hominibus bonae voluntatis. <u>There will be peace to men of good will.</u>
32. Erit mala merces hominibus malae voluntatis. <u>There will be a bad reward to men of bad will.</u>
33. Animi nostri sunt mali. <u>Our hearts are evil. (meaning less than perfectly good)</u>
34. Sed amamus esse filiae et filii Dei. <u>But we love to be daughters and sons of God.</u>
35. Et amamus esse fratres et sorores in Christo. <u>And we love to be brothers and sisters in Christ.</u>
36. Homines Galliae magni sunt. <u>The men of Gaul are large.</u>
37. Homines Italiae parvi sunt. <u>The men of Italy are small.</u>
38. in medio agro, in mediā silvā, in medio oppido <u>in the middle of the field, in the middle of the forest, in the middle of town.</u>
39. fortitudo hominum <u>the courage of men (or courage or strength)</u>
40. cum corporibus <u>with the bodies</u>
41. sine tuis fratribus, cum nostris sororibus <u>without your brothers, with our sisters</u>
42. corde magno <u>by (means of) a big heart</u>
43. In mediā insulā erat parva villa. <u>In the middle of the island there was a small farmhouse.</u>

44. In Galliā diu erimus. <u>We shall be in Gaul for a long time.</u>
45. sub villā, in viā <u>under the farmhouse, on the road</u>
46. pax per Christum <u>peace through Christ</u>

Test Seven to be taken after the completion of Chapter Fourteen

Grammar
1. The imperative singular mood of a verb is formed by removing the
       <u>–re ending</u> from the present infintive.
2. The <u>vocative</u> case is used for direct address.
3. Use the <u>ablative</u> case to express Time When.
4. Use the <u>accusative</u> case to express Duration of Time.

Practice *Give the vocative singular case for the following nouns.*
5. ancilla <u>ancilla</u>
6. Fidelius <u>Fideli</u>
7. meus <u>mi</u>
8. Marcus <u>Marce</u>

Give the present imperative singular for these verbs.
9. habito <u>habita</u>   12. lacrimo <u>lacrima</u>
10. laudo <u>lauda</u>   13. servo <u>serva</u>
11. porto <u>porta</u>   14. ambulo <u>ambula</u>

Translate into Latin and then give the present imperative plural for these verbs.
15. strengthen <u>confirmate</u>   18. defeat <u>superate</u>
16. love   <u>amate</u>   19. protect <u>servate</u>
17. honor   <u>honorate</u>   20. sing   <u>cantate</u>

21 – 25. **Declension**
Decline this third conjugation noun.

mi'les	milites
militis	militum
militi	militibus
militem	milites
milite	militibus

26-40. **Translation**
     Septem servi cum patre et matre ad parvum oppidum habitabant. Mater et pater erant boni, et vitam beatam servis dare temptabant. Pater servos liberabit ubi rex legem novam fecerit (*makes*). Quod pater erat agricola, servi pro patre in agris laborabant.
     Erant quattuor ancillae quae (*who*) matrem in villā adiuvabant (*used to help*). Parabant cenam (*dinner*) dum filiae familiae infantem (*baby*) curabant. Nonne familia erat beata familia? Ita vero!

Seven servants used to live with a father and a mother near (or *at*) a small town. The mother and father were good (people), and they were trying to give the servants a happy life. The father will free the servants when the king makes a new law. Because the father was a farmer, the servants used to work for father in the fields.

There were four handmaidens who used to help the mother in the house. They were preparing dinner while the daughters of the family were taking care of the baby. Wasn't the family a happy family? Yes!

Circle the MOST correct meaning for the following:

41. VERBIAGE (a) trickiness (b) wordiness (c) suability (d) codification
42. ITINERARY (a) book (b) program (c) trip plan (d) journal
43. FRAT ERNIT Y (a) animosity (b) brotherhood (c) buffet (d) sorority
44. MALEFACTOR (a) a manly multiplier (b) a juvenile (c) a criminal; evildoer (d) businessman
45. PULCHRITUDE (a) obesity in older people (b) daughter of a viscount in France (c) physical beauty (d) a mental condition in adolescent males
46. COPIOUS (a) exactly representing; identical (b) overflowing; abundant (c) voluminous manuscript (d) precise and exact
47. INSUPERABLE (a) insurmountable (b) not able to be super (c) the component in insulation which retains heat (d) easily overcome
48. UBIQUITOUS (a) everywhere (b) unconventional (c) limited (d) narrow
49. PATRIOT (a) incompetent (b) martyr (c) hallucinogen (d) loyalist
50. UNIT (a) addendum (b) masterpiece (c) composite (d) element
51. IGNITE (a) douse (b) saturate (c) kindle (d) squelch
52. MORTAL (a) life-giving (b) deadly (c) joyous (d) enduring
53. URBAN (a) rural (b) municipal (c) concealed (d) pastoral
54. NAVAL (a) hybrid (b) dark blue (c) umbilical (d) of sailors
55. DUAL (a) singular (b) unique (c) coupled (d) individual

- identify an i-stem noun.
- know all the irregular adjectives from the lesson and recite them.
- tell the history of the Bible.
- say who translated the Bible from Greek and Hebrew into Latin.
- give a brief report about Julius Caesar.

Chapter Fifteen

1. Chapter phrase or another from one in Teacher's Guide.
2. Read and discuss section **I-A Rules for -I stem nouns**.
3. Copy the boxes of the paradigm of i-stem nouns.
4. Memorize the paradigms that were just copied.
5. Look at section **I/C**. Irregular Adjectives. Make vocabulary cards. There are nine irregular adjectives of this type. The student has already learned one, **unus**, in Chapter Ten. An easy way to remember all of these is this acronym:

UNUS NAUTA

Ullus **N**ullus **U**nus **S**olus
Neuter **A**lius **U**ter **T**otus **A**lter

6. Make flash cards and learn **II Vocabulary**. Many teachers have their students decline all the feminine nouns on one day, and then the next day decline all the masculine nouns. The third day, they decline all the neuter nouns. That is another way of separating the genders in the student's mind. We emphasize: this is a very difficult concept for many students because genders are often not the same as they would be in English.

7. Read section **IV The Bible**, and discuss.
8. **Study Sheet**.
9. Translate **Drill Sheet**.
10. Read and translate **Exercise III**.
11. In section **VI**, look at the "Map of Judea
12. Translate **V. Bible Thoughts.**
13. Translate **VII. Selected Scriptures**. Ask the students to memorize one of them.
14. Read and discuss **VIII Julius Caesar**. Translate the Latin story from Caesar.
15. **IX**. Look at the "Map of the Country of Gallia". Be sure the students can identify the bodies of water and tribes in Gaul.

Chapter Fifteen

Qui Diligit Disciplinam Diligit Scientiam.
He who loves discipline loves knowledge.

Third Declension I-Stems; Irregular Adjectives; History of Bible; Translation of the Vulgate; <u>Caesar</u>

I. Grammar
A. Rules for i-stems

All the third declension nouns you learned in the previous chapter are called consonant stems because the stem ends in a consonant. However, some third declension nouns have an **-i** added to the stem in some of the cases. Usually the **-i** is included in the stem only in the genitive plural, for all three genders. Neuter nouns have an extra **–i** in ablative singular and nominative and accusative plurals.

You may recognize **-i** stems because they generally follow these patterns. Put this chart into your notebook in the "Cases and Declensions" section, on the page titled <u>Third Declension</u>.

<u>**General rules for i-stem nouns**</u>

Masculine and feminine nouns which

    1. end in **-is** and **-es** in the nominative singular and have the same number of syllables in both the nominative and genitive singular forms

        nav′is, nav′is, f., *ship*   **cae′des, cae′dis**, f., *murder*

    2. end in **-ns** or **-rs** in the nominative singular

        mens, men′tis, f., *mind*   **mors, mor′tis**, f., *death*

    3. have one syllable for the nominative singular and whose base ends in two consonants

        nox, noc′tis, f., *night*

Neuter nouns which

    4. end in **-al** or **-e** in the nominative singular

        a′nimal, anima′lis, n., *animal*   **ma′re, ma′ris**, n., *sea*

STILUS ET
ATRAMENTARIUM
ROMANUM

B. Paradigm for i-stem nouns

Put this chart on the page titled <u>Third Declension **i-stems**</u> in the section, "Cases/Declensions."

	cī′vis *citizen*	**urbs** *city*	**mā′rē** *sea*		
			Singular		
Cases	**M & F**		**Neuter**	**M & F**	**N.**
Nom.	ci′vis	urbs	ma′re	-------,	-------
Gen.	ci′vis	ur′bis	ma′ris	-is	-is
Dat.	ci′vi	ur′bi	ma′ri	-i	-i
Acc.	ci′vem	ur′bem	ma′re	-em	-------
Abl.	ci′ve	ur′be	ma′ri	-e	-i
			Plural		
Nom.	ci′ves	ur′bes	mari′a	-es	-ia
Gen.	ci′vium	ur′bium	mari′um	-ium	-ium
Dat.	ci′vibus	ur′bibus	ma′ribus	-ibus	-ibus
Acc.	ci′ves	ur′bes	mari′a	-es	-ia
Abl.	ci′vibus	ur′bibus	ma′ribus	-ibus	-ibus

Jerome

Tu auté cũ oraueris intra ĩ cubicłm tuũ: et clauso ostio ora patrẽ tuũ in abscõdito: et pat tuus qui videt ĩ absconoito reddet tibi. Orantes auté nolite multũ loqui: sicut ethnici faciunt. putant enĩ: q̃ in multiloquio suo exaudiatur. Nolite ergo assimilari eis. Scit enĩ pater vest quid opus sit vobis: antequam petitis eũ. Sic ergo vos orabitis. Pater noster qui es in celis sanctificeť nomen tuũ. Adueniat regnũ tuũ. Fiat volũtas tua: sicut ĩ celo et ĩ terra. Pane nr̃m supsubstãtialẽ da nobis hodie. Et dimitte nobis debita nostra: sicut & nos dimittimus debitoribꝫ nostris. Et ne nos inducas in teptatione: sed libera nos a malo. Si enĩ dimiseritis hoĩibꝫ peccã eou: dimittet et vobis pater vester celestis delicta vestra. Si auté nõ dimiseritis hoĩbꝫ: nec pater vester dimittet vobis peccata vr̃a. Cum auté ieiunatis: nolite fieri sicut ypocrite tristes. Exterminãt enĩ facies suas: ut pareant hoĩibꝫ ieiunãtes. Amen dico vobis: quia receperũt mercedẽ suã.

C. Irregular Adjectives

The following adjectives are declined like **unus** with **-ius** in the genitive, and **-i** in the dative singular. The plurals are regular j ust like **bonus**. Put these adjectives on green cards with black ink (8).

ālī′ūs, ālī′a, ālī′ūd, *another, other*

āl′ter, āl′tera, āl′terūm, *the other*
       (of two), second

neū′ter, neū′tra, neū′trūm, *neither*

nūl′lus, -a, -ūm, *no, not any*

so′ lūs, -a, -ūm, *only, alone*

to′tūs, -a, -ūm, *whole, entire*
       (sg., every)

ūl′lūs, -a, -ūm, *any*

ū′ter, ū′tra, ū′trum, *which (of two)?*

Following is a paradigm of **totus**. Notice that the plural forms are regular. You only need to learn the new gen., dat., acc., and abl. singular forms. Copy this chart into your notebook in the section labeled "Grammar" on the page titled <u>Adjectives.</u> Title this "Irregular Adjectives."

	MASCULINE	FEMININE	NEUTER
Singular			
Nom	**tō′tūs**	**tō′ta**	**tō′tūm**
Gen.	**tōtī′ūs**	**tōtī′us**	**tōtī′us**
Dat.	**tō′tī**	**tō′tī**	**tō′tī**
Acc.	**tō′tūm**	**tō′tām**	**tō′tūm**
Abl.	**tō′tō**	**tō′tā**	**tō′tō**
Plural			
Nom.	**tō′tī**	**tō′tae**	**tō′ta**
Gen.	**tōtō′rūm**	**tōta′rūm**	**tōtō′rūm**
Dat.	**tō′tīs**	**tō′tīs**	**tō′tīs**
Acc.	**tō′tōs**	**tō′tās**	**tō′ta**
Abl.	**tō′tīs**	**tō′tīs**	**tō′tīs**

II. Vocabulary   English Derivatives

Vocabulary from this lesson on will contain words from different declensions, and different parts of speech. You will recognize to which family the nouns belong by observing the genitive singular endings. The Roman numeral after the Latin word tells you to which declension the noun belongs. You will recognize verbs because the four principal parts are given. For this lesson, the **i-stem** nouns will be marked with an asterisk. There are verbs mixed in this lesson with the nouns. From now on, you should be able to recognize them.

Put **canis** and **civis** on blue cards and note that they can be either masculine or feminine. You will need 7 pink cards, 5 blue cards, and 4 yellow cards.

> **TEACHER:** This is a difficult declension. Make sure your student memorizes <u>each gender</u> along with the meanings. There are very few remaining i-stem nouns in this course, which should comfort students. Alius is declined in the back of the book.

*ā′nĭmāl, ānīmā′lis, III, n. *animal*
*ā′vis, ā′vis, III, f., *bird*   (aviary)
*cā′nis, cā′nis, III, m. or f., *dog*   (canine)
*cī′vis, cī′vis, III, m. or f., *citizen*   (civic)
flū′men, flū′minis, III, n., *river*   (flume)
*mā′rē, mā′ris, III, n., *sea*   (maritime, marine)
*mens, men′tis, III, f. *mind*   (mental)
*mī′lĭa, mī′lĭūm, III, n. pl., *thousands*
*mōns, mon′tis, III, m. *mountain*
*mōrs, mort′is, III, m. *death*   (mortal)
*nā′vis, nā′vis, III, f., *ship*   (naval, navigate)
*nox, noc′tis, III, f., *night*   (nocturnal)
*pā′nis, pā′nis, III, m., *bread*
 pēccā′tūm, pēccātī, II, n., *sin, fault*   (peccadillo)
*tūr′ris, tūr′ris, III, f., *tower*   (turret)
*ūrbs, ūr′bis, III, f., *city*   (urban, urbane, suburb)
ver′ĭtās, verītā′tis, III, f., *truth*   (very, veritable)
obser′vō, -ā′rē, -ā′vī, -ā′tūs, *notice, observe*
sepa′rō, -ā′rē, -ā′vī, -ā′tūs, *separate, divide*
stō, stā′rē, ste′tī, stā′tūs, *stand*

III. Exercise

Translate.
1. mercedes peccati 2. albae naves 3. altae turres 4. niger canis 5. nigrorum canium 6. duo
milia civium 7. aves in caelo 8. alius canis 9. solus campus 10. navis nocte 11. neuter civis
12. veritas sola 13. flumina lata 14. tota flumina 15. albus panis 16. panis niger 17. bonis
mentibus 18. animalia maris nigri 19. panis angelorum 20. nullus mors 21. Separabat a terrā
maria. 22. Stabant in montibus. 23. Veritas te liberabit. 24. Stamus in sanctā terrā. 25. Canis
turres urbis spectabat.

---

1. the wages (*payments*) of sin 2. white ships 3. tall towers 4. black dog 5. of black dogs
6. two thousand citizens (literally, *two thousands of citizens*) 7. birds in the sky 8. another
dog 9. only a field 10. a ship at night 11. neither citizen 12. truth alone (or *only the truth*)
13. broad (*wide*) rivers 14. all the rivers 15. white bread 16. black bread 17. by/with or
to/for good minds 18. animals of the black sea 19. bread of angels 20. no death
21. He separated the seas from the land. 22. They were standing on the mountains.
23. The truth will free you (or *set you free*). 24. We are standing on holy ground.
25. A dog was looking at the towers of the city.

IV. The Bible

A. Inspiration

The Bible is a most unusual book. One of the greatest early enemies of Christianity was Saul of Tarsus. After his life-changing confrontation with the resurrected Jesus Christ he was later to declare what became a central text for the Christian Church in its understanding of what the Bible is. Paul the Apostle wrote, (2 Tim 3:16) "All scripture *is* given by inspiration of God, and *is* profitable for doctrine, for reproof, for correction, for instruction in righteousness . . . ." T he word translated "inspiration" is important in that it asserts that the Bible is, literally, "God-breathed." That means that when the human authors of the Bible wrote they were not writing on their own; they were superintended by God's Spirit in such a way that they accurately composed without error His revelation to man. The Apostle Peter explained that " . . holy men of God spake as they were moved [carried along] by the Holy Spirit" (2 Peter 1:21).

It was because of "inspiration" that Jesus could confound his enemies with the authority of the Bible. He even based the proof of the resurrection on the tense of a verb (Matthew 22:32). Christ taught that inspiration extended to the writing of letters and the smallest distinguishing marks of the Biblical text (Matthew 5:18). The truth of "inspiration" is God's way of saying to us that we have a reliable and authoritative Word from Him.

The living God of the Bible not only gave the Word, but He has also preserved it over the centuries by an overwhelming number of manuscripts copied in the original languages and in translations that have been used to spread God's revelation of Himself to the world. The Latin Vulgate is one of the important early translations of the Bible that brought many nations into Christendom.

B. Vulgate

The Vulgate translation of the Scriptures was finished in AD 405 by Jerome, who was a Roman Catholic priest. Jerome was a very conscientious man who had loved all the ancient writers, but he came to believe that his time should be spent working on the translation of God's Word from the best Hebrew and Greek manuscripts available to him.

V. Some Bible thoughts

1. Semper boni non sumus. Sed Deus nos amat.
2. Christus est Filius Dei et de caelo ad terram venit *(he came)*.
3. Maria erat mater Christi. Angelum salutabat et angelo narrabat, "Sum ancilla Domini."
4. Iesus est Deus etiam vir.
5. (Jesus said:) Sum via et veritas et vita.
6. Angeli milites Domini sunt.
7. Etiam Domini milites sumus.
8. Christus est factor (*maker*) caeli et terrae.
9. Est iudex hominum.
10. Causa peccati natura hominis est.

VI. Map of Judea

Locate Jerusalem, Jericho, Samaria and the Dead Sea on this map.

VII. Selected Scriptures

Remember to try to figure out the words when they are similar to English ones.

1. Est firmamentum in mediis aquis et id *(it)* separat aquas ab aquis.
2. Et vocabat Deus firmamentum Caelum; et vespere et mane erant.
3. Erat in principio cum Deo.
4. Erat lux vera.
5. In mundo erat et mundus Eum *(Him)* ignorabat.
6. Ego sum Dominus tuus Deus.
7. Sabbatizate sabbata; est sacra.
8. In toto loco oculi Domini sunt, et observant bonos et malos.
9. Ego enim Dominus sum; non muto *(change)*.
10. Ausculta Dominum Deum nostrum: Dominus Deus est.
11. Amabis Dominum Deum tuum ex toto corde tuo, et ex totā animā tuā, et ex totā fortitudine tuā.
12. Id *(This)* est primum et magnum mandatum.
13. Eum *(Him)* amamus quod nos primum amabat.
14. Magna est merces tua in caelo.
15. Vos estis sal terrae.
16. Vos estis lux mundi.
17. Et ecce, angelus Domini stabat, et gloria Domini praestabat *(showed forth)*.
18. Mercedes enim peccatorum est mors; sed liberum donum Dei est vita aeterna *(eternal)*.

Recognition Vocabulary

ec′cē, interjection, *look! behold!*

ignō′rō, -ā′rē, -ā′vī, -ā′tūs, *is ignorant of, does not know*

sābbatī′zō, -ā′rē, -ā′vī, -ā′tūs, *keep holy*

Selected Scriptures

1. There is a firmament (*atmosphere*, or *support*) in the middle of the waters, and it separates waters from the waters.
2. And God called the firmament the *sky*; and it was evening and morning (early in the day).
3. He was in the beginning with God.
4. He was the true light.
5. He was in the world and the world knew Him not. (or, *did not know Him*.)
6. I am the Lord your God.
7. Keep holy the Sabbath; it is set apart.
8. The eyes of the Lord are in every place, and they notice (or *he observes*) good and evil (*men*).
9. For I am the Lord; I do not change.
10. Listen to the Lord our God; the Lord is God.
11. You will love the Lord your God from (*out of, with*) your entire (or, *whole*) heart, your entire soul, and your entire strength.
12. This is the first and great commandment.
13. We love Him because He first loved us.
14. Great is your reward in heaven.
15. You are the salt of the earth.
16. You are the light of the world.
17. And behold, an angel of the Lord stood (or *was standing*), and the glory of the Lord showed (or *was showing*) forth.
18. For the wages of sin is death; but the free gift of God is eternal life.

VIII. Julius Caesar

When Julius Caesar traveled throughout Europe conquering tribes and nations, he wrote about his exploits in a book titled *Commentaries on the Gallic Wars*. This book showed the precise literary style which was surpassed only by his colleague (and political foe) Marcus Tullius Cicero. We still have copies of this book today and it is interesting for historical studies as a second or third year Latin student, or you may prefer to read an English translation.

Here is a simplified version of the beginning of Book One. You may be able to translate some of this, and your teacher will do the rest for you.

Omnis Gallia est divisa in tres partes. Belgae unam partem incolunt; Aquitani aliam, Celtae tertiam. Belgae fortissimi Gallorum sunt, quod a provincia Romana longe sunt. Etiam sunt proximi Germanis, qui trans Rhenum habitant, cum quibus saepe pugnant.

Rhenus terras Belgarum a Germanis dividit; etiam terras Helvetiorum. Garumna Celtas ab Aquitanis dividit. Et Matrona et Sequana (**eos**, *them*) a Belgis dividunt.

Recognition Vocabulary

fōrtis′simūs, -a, -um, *bravest*

in′cōlūnt, *(they) inhabit*

om′nis, adjective, *all, as a whole, entire*

quī′būs, *whom (ablative case)*

Julius Caesar
All Gaul is divided into three parts. (More commonly translated: *Gaul as a whole is divided...*)
The Belgians inhabit the first part, the Aquitani another, and the Celts the third. The Belgians are
the bravest of the Gauls because they are far away from the Roman province. Also they are
nearest to the Germans, who live across the Rhine, with whom they often fight. The Rhine River
divides the lands of the Belgians from the Germans; also the lands of the Swiss (*Helvetii*).
Garonne River divides the Celts from the Aquitani. Both the Marne and the Seine divide (*them*)
from the Belgians.

IX. Map of Gallia

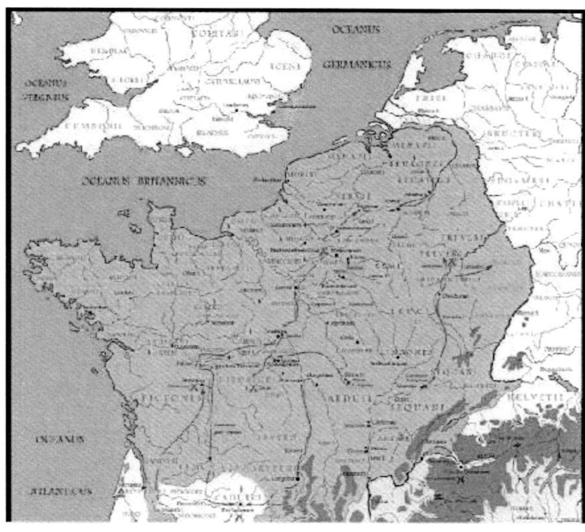

Map of Roma

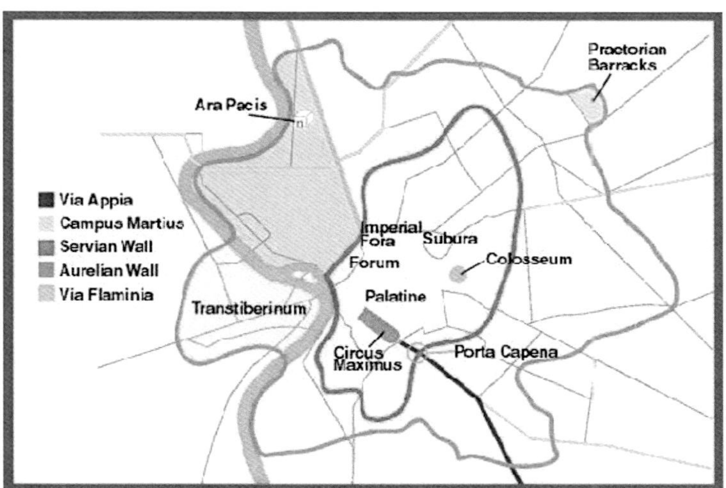

Name _______________________________________Date __________________

Latin in the Christian Trivium
Study Sheet
Chapter Fifteen

Grammar

1. In what case do **-i** stem nouns which are masculine or feminine show the **-i** in the stem?
   <u>in the genitive (plural)</u>
2. In what cases do **-i** stem nouns which are neuter show the **-i** of the stem?
   <u>ablative (singular), nominative and accusative (plural) and genitive plural</u>
3. Name the eight irregular adj ectives described in the lesson. <u>alius, alter, neuter, nullus,</u>
   <u>solus, totus, ullus, uter</u>

Vocabulary Work

4. Fill in the missing information.

NOM.	GENITIVES	GENDER	MEANING
animal	<u>animalis</u>	<u>n.</u>	<u>animal</u>
<u>avis</u>	avis	<u>f.</u>	<u>bird</u>
canis	<u>canis</u>	<u>m. or f.</u>	<u>dog</u>
<u>flumen</u>	<u>fluminis</u>	<u>n.</u>	river
<u>civis</u>	<u>civis</u>	<u>m. or f.</u>	citizen
lux	<u>lucis</u>	<u>f.</u>	<u>light</u>
<u>mare</u>	maris	<u>n.</u>	<u>sea</u>
<u>mens</u>	mentis	<u>f.</u>	<u>mind</u>
milia	<u>milium</u>	<u>n.</u>	<u>thousands</u>
mons	<u>montis</u>	<u>m.</u>	<u>mountain</u>
<u>mors</u>	<u>mortis</u>	<u>m.</u>	death
<u>navis</u>	navis	<u>f.</u>	<u>ship</u>
nox	<u>noctis</u>	<u>f.</u>	night
<u>panis</u>	<u>panis</u>	<u>m.</u>	bread
<u>turris</u>	turris	<u>f.</u>	<u>tower</u>
urbs	urbis	<u>f.</u>	<u>city</u>

5. Write the declension of:

mors	avis	flumen
mortis	avis	fluminis
morti	avi	flumini
mortem	avem	flumen
morte	ave	flumine

mortes	aves	flumina
mortium	avium	fluminum
mortibus	avibus	fluminibus
mortes	aves	flumina
mortibus	avibus	fluminibus

6. Decline the following adjective.

MASCULINE	FEMININE	NEUTER
neuter	neutra	neutrum
neutrius	neutrius	neutrius
neutri	neutri	neutri
neutrum	neutram	neutrum
neutro	neutra	neutro
neutri	neutrae	neutra
neutrorum	neutrarum	neutrorum
neutris	neutris	neutris
neutros	neutras	neutra
neutris	neutris	neutris

7. Give the ablative singular and genitive plural of these nouns.

	ABLATIVE SINGULAR	GENITIVE PLURAL
animal	animali	animalium
canis	cane	canium
flumen	flumine	fluminum
lux	luce	lucum
nox	nocte	noctium
panis	pane	panium

Word Study

8. Circle the root word (the Latin part you recognize) in each of the following, and then write a definition for each. You may use your dictionary if needed.

(Use definitions from the dictionary. The roots are:
mar-, noct-, lu-, flum-, avi-, soror-, merce-, luci-, milit-, cor-)

maritime	sorority
nocturnal	mercenary
illuminate	lucid
flume	militia
aviary	cordially

9. Use three of the words from the previous exercise in original Latin sentences of your own.
<u>Answer to this problem varies.</u>

1. totus mundus   <u>the whole world</u>
2. rex mundi totius <u>king of the whole world</u>
3. mater hominum omnium <u>mother of all the men (or *of all mankind*)</u>
4. Est pater noster. <u>He is our father.</u>
5. lux sola   <u>the light alone (*only the light*)</u>
6. bonum nomen   <u>a good name</u>
7. neuter puer   <u>neither boy</u>
8. neutra puella   <u>neither girl</u>
9. copia aquae   <u>a supply of water (*plenty of water*)</u>
10. Eramus sine aquā. <u>We were without water.</u>
11. Alter puer est Ioannes. <u>A second boy is John. (*the other boy...*)</u>
12. Sunt duo flumina in oppido. <u>There are two rivers in town.</u>
13. Date gloriam Deo soli. <u>Give glory to God alone.</u>
14. Neuter vir erat liber. <u>Neither man was free.</u>
15. Neuter apostolus est ferus. <u>Neither apostle is fierce.</u>
16. Uter apostolus erit defessus? <u>Which apostle will be tired?</u>
17. Canium cura erat magna. <u>The anxiety of the dogs was great.</u>
18. Est avis sola. <u>It is only a bird.</u>
19. Suntne ulla animalia in tuā villā? <u>Are there any animals in your house (or *villa* or *farmhouse*)?</u>
20. Suntne ulla flumina in Galliā? <u>Are there any rivers in Gaul?</u>
21. Sunt nulla flumina in nostrā patriā. <u>There are no rivers in our country.</u>
22. Neque canes neque aves in nostrā villā habitabant. <u>Neither dogs nor birds were living in our house (or *villa* or *farmhouse*).</u>
23. Est turris alta in nostrā urbe. <u>There is a tall tower in our city.</u>
24. Separabant viros puerosque. <u>They were dividing (or *separating*) the men and the boys.</u>
25. Da, amabo, servo panem. <u>Please give bread to the servant. (*Please give the servant bread.*)</u>
26. Non amo album panem.   <u>I do not like white bread.</u>
27. Est panis vitae. <u>He is the bread of life.</u>
28. Uter est meus amicus? <u>Which (one) is my friend?</u>
29. Uter puer est altus? <u>Which boy is tall?</u>
30. Utra puella est bona? <u>Which girl is good?</u>
31. Utrum animal est album? <u>Which animal is white?</u>
32. Nocte navis navigabat. <u>At night the ship was sailing.</u>
33. Tua mens est pura.   <u>Your mind is pure.</u>
34. Navigabatis in mari alto. <u>You were sailing in the deep sea.</u>
35. In turre statne? <u>Is he standing on the tower?</u>
36. In turre nigrā statis. <u>You are standing on a black tower.</u>
37. In turre albā stamus. <u>We are standing on a white tower.</u>
38. Est nullus mors nobis in Christo. <u>There is no death for us in Christ.</u>
39. Pax vobiscum. <u>Peace (be) with you. (a commonly used greeting, even at the Naval Academy in Annapolis!)</u>
40. Angelus vocabat, "Pax hominibus bonae voluntatis." <u>The angel was calling, "Peace to men of good will."</u>

- be introduced to the Second Conjugation verbs.
- have additional practice with i-stem nouns.
- identify Coriolanus.

Chapter Sixteen, a Supplementary Chapter

Teacher, this is an "extra" chapter, which is given to allow your students to have more practice with i-stem nouns, as well as introducing them to the Second Conjugation of verbs. These verbs will also be introduced in Volume II, Chapter Seven, but this preview may help them at that time when they are also going to learn three other conjugations of verbs.

An important point for you, the teacher, is to realize that second conjugation verbs are quite similar to first conjugation verbs. Then the other three, 3rd, 4th, and 3rd IO, are similar to one another too, but not to the first and second.

So, there are "families":
1st and 2nd.......................3rd, 4th, and 3rd IO.

1. Enter the phrase at the top of first chapter page into the notebook section titled "Phrases."
2. Read and discuss **I. Conversation.** Have students use these in conversation.
3. Practice "Conversation" at the beginning of class until finished with Chapter Sixteen.
4. Read and discuss **II. Grammar.**
5. Practice saying "mane'o" aloud in the indicative mood, active voice, present, imperfect, future tenses, and in the imperative mood, present tense, active voice.
6. Read and discuss **III. Vocabulary**. Make flash cards.
7. Practice saying new vocabulary words. Be sure to place the accent in the right place.
8. Look up English derivatives in dictionary and write the meanings in the student notebook section titled "English Derivatives."
9. Discuss English derivatives and relation to the Latin words with which they go.
10. Write and recite Exercise **IV. A**. and **B.**
11. Do the **Drill Sheet** and **Study Sheet** for this lesson.
12. Do **Ex. IV. C** and **D** orally with student(s).
13. Copy and mark sentences in **Exercise IV. E.**
14. Discuss the marking and make corrections.
15. Translate sentences in **Exercise IV. F.** and also **G.**
16. Translate **Coriolanus** and the **Reading Lesson.**

DRILL! DRILL! DRILL!

Chapter Sixteen

> Quaecumque sunt vera, quaecumque pudica, quaecumque iusta, quaecumque sancta, ...si qua virtus si qua laus haec cogitate.
>
> *Whatever is true, whatever is honorable, whatever is right, whatever is pure, ..., if there is any excellence and if anything worthy of praise, dwell on these things.*

Second Conjugation Verbs
More Practice with I-Stem Nouns

I. Conversation

Hello!	*Salve!
How are you today?	Quomodo es hodie?
Well, thank you.	Bene, gratias tibi ago.
What are you doing?	Quid facis?
I'm playing a game.	Ludum ludo.
What is the name of the game?	Quid est nomen ludis?
Play Station 2.	"Ludus Statio II" **
I am leaving now.	Discedo nunc.
I see you're having fun! Bye!	Video te esse ludibundum! Vale!

II. Grammar

The second conjugation verb is almost just like the first one. You still find the present stem by removing the **–re** from the second principal part.   Here is an example verb, **maneo**, which means *remain*.

The four principal parts are **mānē′o, mān′erē, mān′sī, mān′sūs**. Remove the **–rē** from **mānērē**, and what is left? Yes, **mā′nē-**.

---

*This form is singular and the plural is Sālvē′tē!

** Yes, we know. Play Station is no longer a popular game! What other games should be included?

Please put this paradigm into your notebook on a page titled Second Conjugation in the "Conjugations" section right after **āmo**.

Second Conjugation, Present Tense, Indicative Mood, Active Voice.

mānē′ō, mānē′rē, mān′sī, mān′sūs, *remain, stay*
present stem: **mānē-**

SINGULAR   PLURAL

mānē′ō, *I remain, stay*   **mānē′mus**, *we remain, stay*
mā′nēs, *you remain, stay*   **mānē′tis**, *you (all) remain, stay*
mān′et, *he, she, it remains, stays*   **mān′ent**, *they remain, stay*

Imperative Mood, Present Tense, Active Voice

mā′nē, *stay!*   **mānē′tē**, *stay!*

The imperfect and future tenses are very similar to first conjugation verbs.

Imperfect Tense		*Future Tense*	
mānē′bām	mānēbā′mus	mānē′bō	mānē′bīmus
mānē′bās	mānēbā′tis	mānē′bis	mānē′bītis
mānē′bāt	mānē′bānt	mānē′bit	mānē′būnt

III. Vocabulary   English Derivatives

Put the verbs on white cards with blue ink (8). Nouns go on blue for masculine (7), pink for feminine (3), yellow for neuter (1), all with black ink. The conjugation or declension number is the Roman numeral that follows the Latin word. (19 cards)

Nouns
***cae′dēs, cae′dis**, III, f., *slaughter, murder*
***cō′hōrs, cōhōr′tis**, III, f., *cohort*
duc′tor, ducto′ris, III, m. *leader*
dux, du′cis, III, m., *leader*
***fā′mēs, fā′mis**, III, f., *famine*
fes′tūm, fes′tī, II, n., *festival*
***hos′tis, hos′tis**, III, m. *an enemy, in pl.,* *the enemy* (military enemy)   (hostile)
***ig′nis, ig′nis**, m., *fire*
***in′fans, inf an′tis**, m. or f., *baby, infant*
***pons, pon′tis**, III, m., *bridge*   (pontoon)
 sōcī′ūs, sō′cī, II, m., *ally, friend*   (associate)

Verbs

āpprōpin′quō, āpprōpinqua′re, apprōpinquā′vī, āpprōpinquā′tūs, I, *approach, reach,*
come (*here*)   (approximate)
ārdē′ō, ārdē′rē, ār′sī, ār′sūs, II, *blaze, glow* (*with heat*)
censē′ō, cen′sē′rē, cen′suī, cen′ sūs, II, *think, suppose, judge; recommend;*
decree, vote, determine
flē′ō, flē′rē, flē′vī, flē′tūs, II, *weep, lament*
mānē′ō, mānē′rē, mān′sī, mān′sūs, II, *remain, stay*   (remain)
miscē′ō, miscē′rē, misc′uī, mix′tūs, II, *mix confuse, mingle*
possidē′ō, possidē′rē, posse′dī, posses′sūs, II, *own, occupy*   (possession)
sustinē′ō, sustinē′rē, sustin′uī, susten′tūs, II, *hold up, maintain, endure, withstand*

IV. Exercises

A. Tell the tense, mood, person and number of each verb. Then translate.
1. flebam, flebis, flet 2. appropinquant, appropinquate! appropinquas 3. censebatis,
censebunt, censent 4. flebat, manebam, mane! 5. miscebit, possidebit, sustinebit
6. ardebamus, ardebimus, ardemus 7. sustinet, sustinent, sustinete! 8. manebunt,
manent, miscent 9. ardent, ardebis, flebo 10. possidebas, censebant, appropinquat

Verb	Tense	Mood	Person	Number	Translation
1. flebam	imperfect	indicative	1	singular	I was weeping, lamenting
flebis	future	indicative	2	singular	you will weep, lament
flet	present	indicative	3	singular	he/she/it weeps, laments
2. appropinquant	present	indicative	3	plural	they are approaching, reaching
appropinquate	present	im perative	2	plural	approach!
appropinquas	present	indicative	2	singular	you are approaching
3. censebatis	imperfect	indicative	2	plural	you were thinking (etc.)
censebunt	future	indicative	3	plural	they will think
censent	present	indicative	3	plural	they are thinking
4. flebat	imperfect	indicative	3	singular	he/she/it was weeping
manebam	imperfect	indicative	1	singular	I was remaining, staying
mane	present	imperative	2	singular	Stay!
5. miscebit	future	indicative	3	singular	he/she/it will confuse, mix (etc.)
possidebit	future	indicative	3	singular	he/she/it will own, occupy
sustinebit	future	indicative	3	singular	he/she/it will endure (etc.)
6. ardebamus	imperfect	indicative	1	plural	we were blazing, glowing
ardebimus	future	indicative	1	plural	we will blaze, glow
ardemus	present	indicative	1	plural	we are glowing, blazing (hot)
7. sustinet	present	indicative	3	singular	he/she/it endures
sustinent	present	indicative	3	plural	they endure, maintain

					(etc.)
sustinete	present	imperative	2	plural	endure! withstand!
8. manebunt	future	indicative	3	plural	they will remain
manent	present	indicative	3	plural	they are staying, remaining
miscent	present	indicative	3	plural	they are mixing, confusing
9. ardent	present	indicative	3	plural	they glow, blaze
ardebis	future	indicative	2	singular	you will glow, blaze
flebo	future	indicative	1	singular	I will weep, lament
10. possidebas	imperfect	indicative	2	singular	you were owning, occupying
censebant	imperfect	indicative	3	plural	they were thinking, supposing
appropinquat	present	indicative	3	singular	he/she/it approaches, reaches

B. Translate. Use words from this vocabulary if possible.

1. we were staying, they were staying, he will remain 2. I shall approach, you were staying, they will own 3. we will lament, they were confusing, he recommends 4. he was supposing, he was enduring, we will approach 5. the fire was blazing, the judge is judging, the cohort is approaching 6. he is mixing salt with water, an enemy is weeping, she owns the bridge. 7. we will not mix fire and water, they were our allies   8. the enemy is approaching (use plural), the enemy occupied the country

> 1. manebamus, manebant, manebit 2. appropinquabo, manebas, possidebunt
> 3. flebimus, miscebant, censet 4. censebat, sustinebat, appropinquabimus
> 5. ignis ardebat, iudex censet, cohors appropinquat 6. salem cum aqua miscet, hostis flet, pontem possidet   7. ignem et aquam non miscebimus, nostri socii erant 8. hostes appropinquant, hostes patriam possidebant

C. Write the genitive singular, gender, ablative singular, nominative plural, and genitive plural of each noun.

1. caedes	6. animal	11. pons	16. civis
2. panis	7. mons	12. canis	17. mens
3. mors	8. cohors	13. flumen	18. navis
4. hostis	9. mare	14. avis	19. nox
5. socius	10. festum	15. turris	20. urbs

Nominative	Genitive	Gender	Abl. singular	Nom. plural	Genitive plural
1. caedes	caedis	f.	caede	caedes	caedium
2. panis	panis	m.	pane	panes	panium
3. mors	mortis	m.	morte	mortes	mortium
4. hostis	hostis	m.	hoste	hostes	hostium
5. socius	soci	m.	socio	socii	sociorum
6. animal	animalis	n.	animali	animalia	animalium
7. mons	montis	m.	monte	montes	montium
8. cohors	cohortis	f.	cohorte	cohortes	cohortium
9. mare	maris	n.	mari	maria	marium
10. festum	festi	n.	festo	festa	festorum
11. pons	pontis	m.	ponte (or ponti)	pontes	pontium
12. canis	canis	m. or f.	cane	canes	canium

13. flumen	fluminis	n.	flumine	flumina	fluminum
14. avis	avis	f.	ave	aves	avium
15. turris	turris	f.	turre	turres	turrium
16. civis	civis	m. or f.	cive	cives	civium
17. mens	mentis	f.	mente	mentes	mentium
18. navis	navis	f.	nave	naves	navium
19. nox	noctis	f.	nocte	noctes	noctium
20. urbs	urbis	f.	urbe	urbes	urbium

D. Translate, being careful to note whether the nouns are regular nouns, or i-stem nouns and do the endings accordingly. Use nominative case if no other case is obvious.

1. neither fire
2. with one ally
3. with the cohort
4. of only one night
5. a thousand animals
6. all the cities
7. many seas
8. the ships' animals
9. thousands of bridges
10. neither dog
11. the other allies
12. in every sea
13. the dogs' masters
14. thousands of rivers
15. many sins
16. of any ships
17. the enemy's friend (pl. enemy)
18. of the slaughters
19. number of citizens
20. which of the dogs

1. neuter ignis	6. totae urbes/omnes urbes	11. alteri socii	16. ullarum navium
2. cum uno socio	7. multa maria	12. in omni mari	17. hostium socius/amicus
3. cum cohorte	8. navium animalia	13. canium domini	18. caedium
4. solius unius noctis	9. milia pontium	14. milia fluminum	19. numerus civium
5. mille animalia	10. neuter canis or neutra canis	15. multa peccata	20. uter canium

E. Translate these short clauses or phrases.

1. The other dogs are standing. 2. The cohorts were observing the fires. 3. Which city is near to us? 4. He was separating the two dogs. 5. Neither friend (use *ally*) was staying with the animals. 6. The other (of two) ships were sailing. 7. Is there any bread for me? 8. The animals were standing near river. 9. The mind was still strong. 10. We will always think about truth.

1. Alterae* canes stant. (or *alii canes stant*) 2. Cohortes ignes observabant. 3. Utra urbs est ad nos? 4. Duos canes separabat. 5. Neuter socius cum animalibus manebat. 6. Alterae naves navigabant. 7. Estne ullus panis mihi? 8. Animalia ad flumen stabant. 9. Mens erat adhuc fortis. 10. De veritate semper putabimus.

F. Translate these sentences, after marking them.

nom. pl.m.   3/pl. imperf.   acc.s.   gen.pl. m.
1. The enemy was withstanding the strength (of our men).
Hostes fortitudinem (or *virtutem*) nostrorum virorum (or *hominum*) sustinebant.

---

*Since **canis** can be masculine or feminine, the adjective used may be either as well.

   3/pl. im perf.   acc.s.   adv.

2. <u>They</u> <u>were enduring</u> the <u>slaughter</u> sadly.
   Caedem misere sustinebant.

    nom. pl.   3/pl. imperf.   (ob + acc.s. or propter + acc.s.)

3. <u>The women</u> <u>were weeping</u> (on account of the slaughter).
    Feminae ob caedem flebant.

  nom. pl.m. 3/pl. pres.   (cum + abl.pl.)

 4. <u>Our allies</u> <u>remain</u> (with our friends).
    Nostri socii cum nostris amicis manent.

   3/s. imperf.   nom.s.   (in + abl.s.)

 5. <u>There was</u> a <u>festival</u> (on the bridge).
   Erat festum in ponti. (or *ponte*)

   3/s. im perf.   acc.s. (in + acc.s.)

 6. <u>He</u> <u>was mixing</u> <u>grain</u> (into the water).
   Frumentum in aquam miscebat.

    nom. s.m. 3/s. im perf.   (trans + acc.s.)

 7. <u>An enemy</u> <u>was walking</u> (across the bridge).
    Hostis trans pontem ambulabat. (or *inimicus ambulabat*)

   1/pl. imperf.   acc.pl.m. conj. 3/pl. imperf.

8. <u>We</u> <u>were listening to</u> <u>our allies</u> and <u>they</u> <u>were singing</u>.
   Nostros socios auscultabamus et cantabant.

   nom. pl. m.   3/pl. imperf.   acc.s.   conj. acc. pl. m.

9. <u>The enemy</u> <u>were attacking</u> <u>our town</u> and <u>our allies</u>.
   Hostes nostrum oppidum et nostros socios oppugnabant.

   nom.s.m. 3/s. im perf. acc.pl.   acc.s.

10. <u>Father</u> <u>was asking</u> the <u>allies for</u> a <u>horse</u>.
   Pater socios equum rogabat.

   G. Translate these more advanced sentences.
  1. Uter homo pulchram navem aedificabat?
  2. Princeps Romanus corpus Christi Iosepho, Pharisaeo, dabit.
  3. Iudices fabulam de morte hominis auscultabant.
  4. Iudex de caede hominis narrabit.
  5. Uxor agricolae panem sale parat.
  6. Multitudines ad festum totum noctem cantabant.
  7. Dei Verbi inquit, "Pax hominibus bonae voluntatis." Non inquit, "Pax et
     voluntas hominibus."
  8. Magnum amphitheatrum est in lato campo ad urbem.
  9. Mater discipulorum, Iacobi et Ioannis, erat soror quoque matris Iesūs. (gen. case)
  10. Ubi totus populus Israel erat in desertā, Deus eis panem de caelo dabat.
  11. Legatus et octo contubernia militum alium magnum pontem trans flumen in Galliā
     aedificabunt.
  12. Iacobus et Davidus et Petrus et Philippus sunt pauca nomina hominum in Dei Verbo.
  13. Est liber in Dei Verbo nomine Iacobo.
  14. Iesūs (gen. case) mater erat Maria et Iesūs pater erat Deus.
  15. Milia nautarum bonarum trans mare navigabunt.

16. Viginti novas naves aedificabamus et contra malos hostes pugnare (*to fight*) et
nostram patriam servare parabamus.
17. Sex canes et quattuor aves sunt animalia qui (*which* or *who*) cum discipulis ad
ludum habitant.
18. Dei Lex Veritatem et Lucem dat, si unus erit discipulus Verbi.
19. Sunt decem iusti reges, sed nullus est pater nostri principis.
20. Arbor in colle est sola; est sola quoniam est nulla alia circum eum (*it*).
21. Uter vestrum pro veritate stabit, etiam si vos ab amicis etiam tuā familiā separabit?
22. Dabant Romanis militibus salem mercedem.
23. Ubi erat fames in terrā, plenum frumentum feminis pani non erat.
24. Iesus est factor caelorum et terrae, etiam est Rex Regum et Princeps Principium.
25. Homo in Dei Verbo Cornelio nomine erat socius Fideli in fabulā in Latino libro.

1. Which man built (or *did build, was building*) the beautiful ship?
2. The Roman ruler will give the body of Christ to Joseph, the Pharisee.
3. The jurors (or *judges*) were listening to the story about the death of the man.
4. The judge (or *juror*) will tell about the murder of the man.
5. The wife of the farmer prepares the bread with (or *using*) salt.
6. The crowds at the festival were singing the whole night.
7. God's Word says, "Peace to men of good will." It does not say, "Peace and good will
to men."
8. The great amphitheatre is on a wide plain near the city.
9. The mother of the disciples, James and John, was also the sister of Jesus' mother.
10. When the entire nation of Israel was in the desert, God did give them bread from heaven.
11. The lieutenant and eight contubernium of soldiers will build another great bridge across
the river in Gaul.
12. James, David, Peter, and Phillip are a few (*of the*) names of men in God's Word.
13. There is a book in God's Word by the name of James.
14. Jesus' mother was Mary and Jesus' father was God.
15. Thousands of good sailors will sail across the sea.
16. We were building twenty new ships and we were preparing to fight against the evil
enemy and to guard our country.
17. Six dogs and four birds are animals who (or *which*) live with the students (*disciples*)
at the school.
18. God's Law gives Truth and Light, if one will be the disciple of the Word.
19. There are ten just (or *righteous*) kings, but none is the father of our prince.
20. The tree on the hill is alone; it is alone because there is none other around it.
21. Which of you will stand for truth, even if it will separate you from friends and even
your family?
22. They were giving the Roman soldiers salt as a wage.
23. When there was a famine on the earth, there was not plenty of grain for the women
for bread.
24. Jesus is the Maker of the heavens and the earth, and also the King of Kings and
Prince of Princes. (or *Ruler of Rulers*)
25. The man in God's Word named Cornelius (*by name of…*) was a friend (or *ally*) of Fidelius
in the story in the Latin book.

H. Word study

1. Name three words for *mind* in the Latin language.
2. Name two Latin words for *friend*.
3. What are the two words for *strength* in Latin?

1. animus, mens, cor
2. amicus, socius
3. fortitudo, virtus

V. Coriolanus

Erat magna fames (in) Romā, et cives frumentum rogabant. Rex Siciliae (*of Sicily*) frumentum pro civibus misit (*sent*), sed ductores Romae frumentum civibus non dabant. Coriolanus erat nomen ductoris tunc. Cives fiebant (*became*) iratissimi (*very angry*) et misit (*sent*) Coriolanum ex oppido.

Fiebat (*he became*) ductor *Volsciorum, et tunc Romam oppugnabat. Multis pugnis (*battles*) Romanos superabat, et cives timebant (*were afraid*).

Tum mater eum (*him*) rogabat, "Parce (*spare with dative*), amabo, Romae, Coriolane!"
Respondebat, "Mater, Romam servabas, sed tuum filium amisisti!"

Recognition Vocabulary (not in student book)
celeriter, *quickly*
diligenter, *hard, diligently*

There was a great famine in Rome, and the citizens were asking for grain. The king of Sicily sent grain for the citizens but the leaders of Rome did not give (lit., *were not giving*) the grain to the citizens. Coriolanus was the name of the leader at that time. The citizens became very angry and sent Coriolanus out of the town.

He became the leader of the Volscians, and he then attacked Rome. He defeated the Romans in many battles, and the citizens were afraid.

Then his mother asked him, "Please spare Rome, Coriolanus."

He responded, "Mother, you saved Rome but you have lost your son!"

---

*Volsicans, a tribe in Italy. You read about them earlier.

VI. Reading Lesson

Princeps Fidelium Vocat

Duobus diebus *(days)* Fidelius et familia et copiae naves transcendent *(will board)* et ad Iudeam navigabunt. Fidelius diligenter laborat et eos *(them)* *ut discedant *(to leave)* parent *(to prepare)*. Est arduum *(a hard task)* pro uno homine.

Diem dum Fidelius ad Campum Martium laborat, nuntius venit *(comes)* et aliud nuntium a Tiberio portat.

"Porto, Marce Fideli Centurio, nuntium tibi a Principe Tiberio."
Salutant.

Nuntium est: APPROPINQUA AD ROMAM STATIM!

"Veniam *(I will come)* statim, sed primum dabo iussum **signiferi," respondet Fidelius.

Fidelius vertit. "Quinte!" vocat.
Quintus appropinquat. "Me vocas-ne, *Optime Vir?" rogat.
"Visito principem statim. Do imperium tibi nunc. Nescio *(I do not know)* ubi hodie redibo *(I will return)*. Nunc, amabo, roga unum ex hominibus si feret *(he will bring)* equos pro me et Ioanne."

Quintus salutat et vocat, "Ita vero, Optime Vir!" Tum celeriter *(quickly)* discedit *(he leaves)*.

TEACHER: This is a good time to reintroduce the other two ways of saying *please* in Latin.

Si tibi placet, *if it is pleasing to you*…. and **quaeso**, I beg (of you). Although we have been using **amabo**, military men would likely use one of the other two forms. Encourage them to alternate words for *please*.

---

[1] corrected from **discedere**.

[2] A signifer carried the century's standard and organized the burial club for soldiers' funerals, and was like an XO today.

[3] **Optime Vir**, *Sir*.

The Emperor Summons Fidelius

Within two days Fidelius, the family, and the troops will board the ships and sail to Judea. Fidelius is working hard to get them ready. It is a hard task for one man.

During the day while Fidelius is working at the Field of Mars, a messenger comes and carries another message from Tiberius.

"Marcus Fidelius Centurion, I am carrying a message to you from Emperor Tiberius." They salute.

The message is: Come to Rome immediately!

"I will come immediately, but first I will give an order to my signifer," replies Fidelius.

Fidelius turns. "Quintus!" he calls.

Quintus arrives. "Are you calling me, Sir?" he asks.

"I am visiting the Emperor immediately. I am giving the command (*authority*) to you now. I do not know if (*when*) I will return today." "Now please ask one of the men if he will bring horses for John and me."

Quintus salutes and says, "Yes, Sir!" Then he quickly leaves.

Above is a signifer, carrying the standard.

Above right is a vexillifer.
Why do you suppose the man on the right as called an aquilifer? Think!

AQUILA

Name ____ Date ___________________________

Latin in the Christian Trivium
Study Sheet
Chapter Sixteen

Reminders:

Although the endings do not always match, nouns and their adjectives must be in the *same* case, gender and number as their nouns. Always check to see if the noun is an **i-stem noun** (it has an asterisk in front of it in the vocabulary) and follow the paradigm given in Chapter Fifteen.

Here are some examples:

1-32.

	case	number	gender		
big animals	nominative	plural	neuter	*animalia*	*magna*
to white bread	dative	singular	masculine	*pani*	*albo*
black ships	accusative	plural	feminine	*naves*	*nigras*
by/with evil enemy	ablative	plural	masculine	*hostibus*	*malis*

You see that the adjectives and nouns are in agreement but their endings are not always the same. You do these:

	case	number	gender	animals	big
to red fires	dative	plural	masculine	*ignibus*	*rubris*
tall citizens'	genitive	plural	masculine	*civium*	*altorum*

	case	number	gender		
neither brother's	genitive	singular	masculine	*fratris*	*neutrius*
all the men	nominative	plural	masculine	*viri (homines)*	*omnes*

	case	number	gender		
a large reward	nominative	singular	feminine	*merces*	*magna*
to a pleasing student	dative	singular	masculine	*auditori*	*grato*
with a good law	ablative	singular	feminine	*lege*	*bona*
by any name	ablative	singular	neuter	*nomine*	*ullo*

	case	number	gender		
all the murders	nominative	plural	feminine	*caedes*	*omnes*
entire bridges'	genitive	plural	masculine	*pontium*	*totorum*
unhappy cohorts'	genitive	plural	feminine	*cohortium*	*miserarum*
with a black light	ablative	singular	feminine	*luce*	*nigra*

	case	number	gender		
with a bad famine	ablative	singular	feminine	*fame*	*malo*
in the black sea	ablative	singular	neuter	*(in) mari*	*nigro*

of the black seas	genitive	plural	neuter	*marium*	*nigrarum*
a black night	accusative	singular	feminine	*noctem*	*nigram*

	case	number	gender		
all the murders	nominative	plural	feminine	*caedes*	*omnes*
only a festival	accusative	singular	neuter	*festum*	*solum*
with no famines	ablative	plural	feminine	*faminibus*	*nullis*
with the other name	ablative	singular	neuter	*nomine*	*altero*

Now you figure these out, with fewer clues. Decide which case is to be used.

	case	number	gender		
for new bridges	dative	plural	masculine	*pontibus*	*novos*
with a broad river	ablative	singular	neuter	*flumine*	*lato*
a fierce leader	ablative	singular	masculine	*duce (ductore)*	*fero*
which fires?	nominative	plural	masculine	*ignes*	*utri*

case	number	gender			
all the enemies	accusative	plural	masculine	*hostes*	*omnes*
only cohorts'	genitive	plural	feminine	*cohortium*	*solarum*
with no famines	ablative	plural	feminine	*faminibus*	*nullis*
with the other name	ablative	singular	neuter	*nomine*	*altero*

Translate these very short sentences.

33. The leaders were voting. <u>Duces (or *ductores*) censebant.</u>

34. The fire was white. <u>Ignis erat albus.</u>

35. Nulli hostes erant in nostro oppido. <u>None of the enemy were in our town.</u>

36. We were walking on the new bridges. <u>Ambulabamus in novis pontibus.</u>

37. Are all the animals in our town dogs? <u>Nonne omnia animalia in nostro oppido canes sunt?</u>

38. The sea is beautiful, isn't it?   <u>Nonne mare est pulchrum ?</u>

39. Your mind is prepared. <u>Tua mens est parata.</u>

40. Our allies are tired. <u>Nostri socii sunt defessi.</u>

Translate these Latin to English short sentences too.

41. Cohortes cum hostibus feris trans magnum pontem ambulant.

<u>The cohorts are walk ing with the fierce enemy across the large bridge.</u>

42. Mea mens est defessa. <u>My mind (*brain*) is tired.</u>

43. Animalium agri erant in Galliā. <u>The animals' fields were in Gaul.</u>

44. Manebatis in vestrā nave. <u>You (*all*) were staying on your ship.</u>

45. Villa parvae infantis est pulchra. <u>The little baby's house is pretty.</u>

46. Milia animalium erant in Romā. <u>Thousands of animals were in Rome. (or *there were....*)</u>

47. Auscultabasne milia animalium ubi eras in Galliā? <u>Did you listen to (*hear*) thousands of animals when you were in Gaul?</u>

48. Caedes milia animalium erat misera. <u>The slaughter of thousands of animals was sad.</u>

49. Caedes milia hominum est misera etiam! <u>The slaughter of thousands of men is sad too!</u>

50. Meus canis est bonus. <u>My dog is kind (or *good.*)</u>

DRILL SHEET AFTER CHAPTER SIXTEEN

TRANSLATE THESE PHRASES INTO ENGLISH. USE THIS CHAPTER'S VOCABULARY WHEN POSSIBLE.

1. voluntas Dei   the will of God
2. voluntatem Dei   the will of God
3. multitudo militum a crowd of soldiers
4. lux mundi the light of the world
5. alterius iudicis   of the other judge
6. mater omnium hominum   the mother of all mankind (or *men*)
7. nullus frater   no brother, not any brother
8. neutris fratribus to/for, or by/with neither of the brothers
9. ab utrā sorore?   by which sister? from which sister?
10. cum altero corpore   with the other body, with the second body
11. alterum corpus   the other body, the second body
12. nulli cives   no citizens, not any citizens
13. factor terrae   the maker of the earth
14. factor pontis   the maker of the bridge
15. ullus socius   any friend, any ally
16. ullae matres   any mothers
17. omnium fluminum in terrā of all the rivers on earth
18. meus hostis   my enemy
19. vester hostis   your enemy
20. vestri hostes   your enemy (as a plural enemy in English)
21. milia hostium thousands of enemy (plural)
22. milia ignium thousands of fires
23. milia canium thousands of dogs
24. milia turrium thousands of towers
25. milia noctium thousands of nights
26. milia montium thousands of mountains
27. mille montes   a thousand mountains
28. mille naves   a thousand ships
29. mille pontes   a thousand bridges
30. mille urbes   a thousand cities
31. centum sorores   one hundred sisters
32. viginti canes   twenty dogs
33. una pax   one peace
34. pax sub Deo peace under God
35. tres fames   three famines
36. tres reges   three kings
37. nullus sal   no salt, not any salt
38. cum nulli sale   with no salt, with not any salt
38. utrum animal?   which animal?

39. aliud animal   <u>the other animal, another animal</u>

40. bona mens   <u>a good mind</u>

Translate these phrases or short sentences into Latin:

41. The large animal is a dog.   <u>Magnum animal est canis.</u>
42. My father loves my mother. <u>Meus pater meam matrem amat.</u>
43. Dogs walk on the bridge with the soldiers. <u>Canes in ponte (or *ponti*) cum militibus ambulant.</u>
44. The entire bridge was blazing. <u>Totus pons ardebat.</u>
45. When will black birds reach the sea?   <u>Ubi nigrae aves ad mare appropinquabunt?</u>
46. When will the other birds approach the sea?   <u>Ubi aliae aves ad mare appropinquabunt?</u>
47. I love black dogs and white birds. <u>Nigros (or *nigras*) canes et albas aves amo.</u>
48. Is there any salt in the bread?   <u>Estne ullus sal in pane?</u>
49. The whole cohort is approaching the city. <u>Tota cohors ad urbem appropinquat.</u>
50. The night is black and there are many stars. <u>Nox est nigra et sunt multae stellae.</u>
51. He was standing on the bridge. <u>In ponte (or *ponti*) stabat.</u>
52. He will stand on the mountain.   <u>In monte stabit.</u>
53. The allies will stand near the tower. <u>Socii ad turrem stabunt.</u>
54. Fire is beautiful. <u>Ignis est pulcher.</u>
55. Will you stand on a tall tower?   <u>In alta turre stabisne?</u>
56. We notice your little dog. <u>Tuam parvam canem (or *tuum parvum…*) observamus.</u>
57. Were the students observing the judges?   <u>Auditoresne iudices observabant?</u>
58. All truth is from God's Word. <u>Tota veritas (or *omnis*) est a Verbum Dei.</u>
59. God is the maker of all things. <u>Deus est Factor omnium (or *totorum*).</u>
60. Which girls are prepared to be wives?   <u>Utrae puellae sunt paratae esse uxores?</u>
61. Which boys are prepared to be teachers?   <u>Utri pueri sunt parati esse magistri?</u>
62. Which boys are prepared to be sailors?   <u>Utri pueri sunt parati esse nautae?</u>
63. Is he the only judge? <u>Estne iudex solus?</u>
64. Was the famine bad?   <u>Eratne fames mala?</u>
65. Are any [of the] men soldiers?   <u>Suntne ulli homines (or *viri*) milites?</u>
66. Murder is bad. <u>Caedes est mala.</u>
67. A good judge judges sin. <u>Iudex bonus peccatum censet.</u>
68. The judge gives the soldiers rewards.   <u>Iudex militibus mercedes dat.</u>
69. Neither boy was staying.   <u>Neuter puer manebat.</u>
70. Neither animal will withstand the fires.   <u>Neutrum animal ignes sustinebit.</u>

Test Eight to be taken after the completion of Chapter Fifteen or Sixteen

Grammar Section

1. What is the mood for a declarative sentence? <u>indicative mood</u>
2. What is the mood used to give a command? <u>imperative mood</u>
3. What genders are nouns of the third declension? <u>masculine, feminine, and neuter</u>

Commands Translate the following commands, in the singular and also the plural.

ENGLISH WORD	SINGULAR COMMAND	PLURAL COMMAND
Example: *give*	**da**	**date**
4. *walk*	ambula	ambulate
5. *think*	puta	putate
6. *ask*	roga	rogate
7. *work*	labora	laborate
8. *praise*	lauda	laudate

Word Work
Circle (or underline) the MOST correct meaning for the following:

9.   **UNIT** a) addition b) masterpiece c) composite <u>d) single item</u>
10. **DUAL** a) singular b) unique <u>c) coupled</u> d) individual
11. **VIADUCT** <u>a) roadway</u> b) passage c) tunnel d) sidewalk
12. **MERCENARY** <u>a) merchant</u> b) musician c) one who shows mercy d) governor
13. **PATERNAL** a) ludicrous b) simple c) complicated <u>d) fatherly</u>
14. **CORDIALLY** <u>a) kindly</u> b) truthfully c) swiftly d) dangerously
15. **FORTITUDE** a) mathematical <u>b) strength</u> c) one-fourth d) love

Sentence Work

16. Translate this passage from Latin to English. If there are any words you do not know, they will be almost exactly the same in English as they are in Latin. Some are in the Recognition vocabulary at the end of the passage.

Philippus et Lucius erant amici boni.   Pueri erant discipuli ad villam magistri. Philippus in America habitabat sed Lucius in Romā (or, *Romae*). Amici per vias Romae ambulabant saepe. Olim Lucius cum Philippo in Viā Appiā ambulabat. Colloquium puerorum erat longum.

PHILIPPUS: Narrabisne mihi de vitā in Romā?
LUCIUS: Certe. In Romā (or, *Romae*) sumus discipuli ad ludum. Nostri magistri sunt boni viri et nobis multos libros dant. Puellae non sunt ad ludum discipulae sed ad villam cum matribus sunt.
PHILIPPUS: Amas ludum?
LUCIUS: Amo ludum quod sum beatus. Cantamus de Christo in nostro ludo. Is est ludus Christianus.
PHILIPPUS: Ille est gratus Deo. Laudamus Deum in meo ludo etiam.

Duo pueri beati erant quod erant Christiani.

Recognition Vocabulary
certe, adverb, *certainly*
Christiani, *Christians*
colloquium, colloqui, n., *conversation*

is, pronoun, *it*
ille, pronoun, *that*
Lucius, *a boy's name*
olim, adv, *once upon a time*

NOTE: If students get 90% correct, that is considered "A" work for this type of translating. Remember, that a correct translation may have slightly different words than are given here; it is the meaning which is important.

Also, if it is not obvious, Philip was visiting Rome, but he lives in America.

Philip and Lucius (or *Luke*) were good friends. The boys were students (*disciples*) at the house of the teacher (or *master*). Philip lived in America but Lucius lived in Rome. The friends often walked along (*through*) the roads of Rome. Once upon a time Lucius was walking with Philip on the Appian Way. The conversation of the boys was long.

PHILIP: Will you tell me about life in Rome?
LUKE: Certainly. In Rome we are students at school. Our teachers are good men and they give us many books. The girls are not students at school but they are at home (or *home or the farmhouse*) with (their) mothers.
PHILIP: Do you like school?
LUKE: I like school because I am happy. We sing about Christ in our school. It is a Christian school.
PHILIP: That is pleasing to God. We praise God in my school also.
The two boys were happy because they were Christians.

Name ____Date ______________________________

<u>Final Test</u> to be taken after the completion of Chapter Fifteen (or Sixteen). Please use notebook paper. You may make notes on this paper, but be sure your final answer is written on your notebook paper.

Section I.
Give the nominative, genitive, and gender in Latin for the follow ing nouns.
1. grain   frumentum, frumenti, n.
2. lieutenant   legatus, legati, m.
3. mother   mater, matris, f.
4. master, lord   dominus, domini, m.
5. heart (body part, not spirit)   cor, cordis, n.

Give the four principal parts for each verb.
6. walk, stroll   ambulo, ambulare, ambulavi, ambulatus
7. listen to, overhear   ausculto, auscultare, auscultavi, auscultatus
8. hasten   propero, properare, properavi, properatus
9. announce, report   nuntio, nuntiare, nuntia vi, nuntiatus
10. ask, ask for   rogo, rogare, rogavi, rogatus
11. attack, assault, besiege oppugno, oppugnare, oppugnavi, oppugnatus
12. give   do, dare, dedi, datus

Write the Latin adjectives for each English word.

13. pleasing, welcome   gratus (grata, gratum)
14. many   multus (multa, multum)
15. wide, broad   latus (lata, latum)
16. my   meus (mea, meum)
17. fourth   quartus (quarta, quartum)

Forms
18. Write the conjugation of the verb **servo** and its meanings. (Student may give any one of the three meanings for servo, *save, guard*, or *protect*.)

servo, I save	servamus, we save
servas, you save	servatis, you (pl.) save
servat, he/she/it saves	servant, they save

19. Decline the noun **nauta**.

nauta	nautae
nautae	nautarum
nautae	nautis
nautam	nautas
nauta	nautis

20. Decline the noun **pater** in Latin.

pater	patres
patris	patrum
patri	patribus
patrem	patres
patre	patribus

21. Decline the pronoun **ego** in Latin.
    ego, mei, mihi, me, me

Section II. Answer each question.

22. In what case is the subject of a verb?   nominative
23. In what case is the direct object of a verb?   accusative
24. What case is used to show possession?   genitive
25. What case is used for the indirect object?   dative
26. What case is used to show the means by which something is done?   ablative
27. What case is used to tell the duration of time?   accusative
28. What part of speech are numerals (numbers) in Latin?   adjectives
29. The imperative mood of a verb is used for what purpose?   to give a command
30. Give three examples of adj ectives in English.   (varies)

Section III. Phrases.
Tell what four of these Latin phrases mean in English. If you do them all, you will receive extra credit.

31. non sequitur   <u>not logical, or does not follow</u>   34. ex post facto   <u>done after the fact</u>
32. cave canem   <u>beware of the dog</u>   35. pax vobiscum <u>peace (be) with you</u>
33. semper fidelis <u>always faithful</u>   36. pro bono publico <u>for the public good</u>

Section IV. Identify the follow ing please.
37. translator of the Bible into Latin <u>Jerome</u>
38. nation who used hieroglyphics (picture writing) <u>Egypt</u>
39. name of mountain range bordering northern Italy and Helvetia (Switzerland) <u>Alps</u>
40. number of people in a century (not 100)   <u>80</u>
41. two of the three islands west and south of Italy in the Mediterranean Sea   <u>Corsica, Sicily, Sardinia</u>

Section V. Translate. If a word looks like an English word, then it probably is the same as the English; for example, Maria is Mary, and Iesus is Jesus.
42-45.

Maria, mater Iesūs in villam sororis Elisabethis ambulabat. Beata erat, quod mox erit mater novi infantis (*baby*). Elisabethis infans erat beatus etiam! Eius (*his*) nomen erat Ioannes; erit propheta.

> Mary, the mother of Jesus, was walking into the house of (her) sister Elizabeth. She was happy because soon she would be (*will be*) the mother of a new baby. Elizabeth's baby was happy also! His name was John; he will be a prophet.

Section VI. Essay Question Write a short paragraph of at least three sentences on either of these topics: <u>The Difference between a Republic and a Democracy</u> or <u>Things I remember about Various Kings of Rome</u>.
46-50.

> Teacher, be sure they mention that a republic is based on law, while a democracy is majority rule. For the second essay, consult the textbook for accuracy.

Paradigms

VERBS
First Conjugation

Principal Parts: **amo, amare, amavi, amatus**
Active Voice, Indicative Mood

I love, I do love, I am loving

Present Tense		*Imperfect Tense*		*Future Tense*	
amo	amamus	amabam	amabamus	amabo	amabimus
amas	amatis	amabas	amabatis	amabis	amabitis
amat	amant	amabat	amabant	amabit	amabunt

Imperative Mood, Present Tense

Active Voice	**Passive Voice**
Singular: ama, *love!*	amare, *be loved*!

IRREGULAR VERBS

Principal Parts: **sum, esse, fui, futurus**

Active Voice, Indicative Mood

I am		*I was, I used to be*		*I shall be*	
Present Tense		*Imperfect Tense*		*Future Tense*	
sum	sumus	eram	eramus	ero	erimus
es	estis	eras	eratis	eris	eritis
est	sunt	erat	erant	erit	erunt

NOUNS First
Declension
patria, patriae, f., *homeland, country*

Singular	Plural
patria, *a country*	patriae, *countries*
patriae, *of a country*	patriarum, *of countries*
patriae, *to/for a country*	patriis, *to/for countries*
patriam, *a country*	patrias, *countries*
patriā, *by/with a country*	patriis, *by/with countries*

Second Declension, Masculine

angelus, *angel*	**filius**, *son*	**puer**, *boy*	**vir**, *man*	**liber**, *book*
Singular				
angelus	filius	puer	vir	liber
angeli	fili	pueri	viri	libri
angelo	filio	puero	viro	libro
angelum	filium	puerum	virum	librum
angelo	filio	puero	viro	libro
Plural				
angeli	filii	pueri	viri	libri
angelorum	filiorum	puerorum	virorum	librorum
angelis	filiis	pueris	viris	libris
angelos	filios	pueros	viros	libros
angelis	filiis	pueris	viris	libris

Second Declension, Neuter

mandatum, n., *commandment*

Singular	*Plural*
mandatum	mandata
mandati	mandatorum
mandato	mandatis
mandatum	mandata
mandato	mandatis

Third Declension, All Genders

frater, m., *brother*		**lux**, f., *light*		**nomen**, n., *name*	
Singular	*Plural*	*Singular*	*Plural*	*Singular*	*Plural*
frater	fratres	lux	luces	nomen	nomina
fratris	fratrum	lucis	lucum	nominis	nominum
fratri	fratribus	luci	lucibus	nomini	nominibus
fratrem	fratres	lucem	luces	nomen	nomina
fratre	fratres	luce	lucibus	nomine	nominibus

Third Declension I-Stems

civis, m. or f., *citizen*		**urbs**, f., *city*		**mare**, n., *sea*	
Singular	*Plural*	*Singular*	*Plural*	*Singular*	*Plural*
civis	cives	urbs	urbes	mare	maria
civis	civium	urbis	urbium	maris	marium
civi	civibus	urbi	urbibus	mari	maribus
civem	cives	urbem	urbes	mare	maria
cive	civibus	urbe	urbibus	mari	maribus

Declension of alius from Chapter Fifteen.

alius	alia	aliud		alii	aliae	alia
aliuus	alius	alius		aliorum	aliarum	aliorum
alii	alii	alii		aliis	aliis	aliis
alium	aliam	aliud		alios	alias	alia
alio	aliā	alio		aliis	aliis	aliis

Cardinals / Ordinals

Cardinals	Ordinals
1. unus, -a, -um	primus, -a, -um
2. duo, duae, duo	secundus, -a, -um
3. tres, tria	tertius, -a, -um
4. quattuor	quartus, -a, -um
5. quinque	quintus, -a, -um
6. sex	sextus, -a, -um
7. septem	septimus, -a, -um
8. octo	octavus, -a, -um
9. novem	nonus, -a, -um
10. decem	decimus, -a, -um
11. undecim	undecimus, -a, -um
12. duodecim	duodecimus, -a, -um
13. tredecim	tertius decimus, -a, -um
14. quattuordecim	quartus decimus, -a, -um
15. quindecim	quintus decimus, -a, -um
16. sedecim	sextus decimus, -a, -um
17. septendecim	septimus decimus, -a, -um
18. duodeviginti	duodevicesimus, -a, -um
19. undeviginti	undevicesimus, -a, -um
20. viginti	vicesimus, -a, -um
50. quinquaginta	quinquagesimus, -a, -um
100. centum	centesimus, -a, -um
500. quingenti	quingentesimus, -a, -um
1000. mille	millesimus, -a, -um

Latin to English Vocabulary

We have made every effort to include all words in this volume, but if we have overlooked any, you can go online and google *Words by Whitaker*, a free Latin dictionary. Chapter numbers where the words first occur follow the definition. For example, 7 means Chapter Seven. I-stem nouns are marked with an asterisk (*).

A

a, ab, prep., with abl., *from, away from, by.* 7

appropin′quo, -a′ re, -a′vi, -a′tus, *approach, reach, come (here).* 16

ad, prep., w/acc., *to, toward, near, beside, at.* 7

ad′huc, adv., *still.*

aedi′fico, -a′re, -a′vi, -a′tus, *build.* 9

a′ger, a′gri, m., *field, land.* 6

agric′ola, -ae, m., *farmer.* 5

al′bus, al′ba, al′bum, *white.* 9

a′lius, a′lia, a′liud, *another, other.* 15

al′te, adv., *on high, deeply.* 12

al′ter, alter′a, alter′um, *the other (of two), second.* 15

al′tus, al′ta, al′tum, *high, deep, tall.* 9

ama′bo, idiom meaning *please.* 13

am′bulo, -a′re, -a′vi, -a′tus, *walk, stroll.* 3

amici′tia, -ae, f., *friendship.* 5

ami′cus, ami′ca, ami′cum, *friendly.* 9

a′mo, - a′re, -a′vi, -a′tus, *love, like.* 3

amphithea′trum, -i, n, *amphitheatre.* 10

an′cilla, -ae, f., *handmaiden, maidservant.* 4

an′gelus, -i, m., *angel, messenger from God.* 6

***a′nimal, -is,** n., *animal.* 15

a′nimus, -i, m., *soul, mind, spirit;* in plural, *courage.* 6

an′nus, -i, m., *year.* 6

an′te, prep., w/ acc., *before, in front of.* 7

apos′tolus, -i, m., *apostle.* 6

appel′lo, -a′re, -a′vi, -a′tus, *address, name, call.* 3

a′qua, -ae, f., *water.* 4

aquaeduc′tum, -i, n., *aqueduct.* 9

Aquitan′us, -i, m., *an Aquitanian.* 15

ar′bor, arbo′ris, f., *tree.* 14

arde′o, arde′re, ar′si, ar′sus, *blaze, glow with heat.* 16

auda′cia, -ae, f., *boldness, audacity.* 10

au′ditor, -or′is, m., *hearer, student.* 14

au′riga, auri′gae, m. *driver.* 11

auscul′to, -a′re, -a′vi, -a′tus, *listen to, overhear.* 3

au′tem, conjunction, *moreover, but.* 8

***a′vis, a′vis,** f., *bird.* 15

B

balae′na, -ae, f., *whale.* 4

bea′tus, bea′ta, bea′ tum, *happy, blessed.* 9

bel′lum, -i, n., *war.* 8

be′ne, adverb, *well.* 12

bo′nus, bo′na, bo′num, *good.* 9

C

***cae′des, cae′ dis,** f., *murder.* 16

cae′lum, -i, n., *sky, heaven.* 8

cam′pus, -i, m., *field, plain.* 10

***ca′n is, ca′nis,** m. or f., *dog.* 15

can′to, -a′re, -a′ vi, -a′tus, *sing.* 3

Capitoli′nus, *the Capitoline Hill.* 10

capti′vus, -i, m., *captive.*

car′rus, -i, m., *cart, wagon.* 6

cau′sa, -ae, f., *reason, cause.* 10

cele′riter, adv., *quickly.*

Cel′tae, -ar′um, m., *Celts.* 4 (map)

cense′o, cense′re, cen′sui, cen′sus, *think, suppose, recommend, decree, vote, determine.* 16

cen′ tum, *one hundred, a hundred* (C). 10

centur′ia, -ae, f., *century (originally a group of 100 men, later 80 men).* 13

cer′tamen, (singular) **certami′na** (pl.) *race.* 11

Chris′tus, Chris′ti, m., *Christ.* 6

cir′cum, prep., with acc., *around.* 7

cir′cus, cir′ci, m., *racetrack.* 11

***ci′vis, ci′vis**, m., or f., *citizen.*
15

cla′mo, -a′ re, -a′vi, -a′tus, *shout.* 11

Clau′dia, -ae, f., *Claudia.* 14

claus′trum, claus′tri, n., *barrier.* 11

cli′vus, -i, m., *hill.* 10

***co′hors, cohor′tis,** *cohort.* 16

***col′lis, collis,** n., *hill.* 16

confir′mo, -a′re, -a′vi, -a′tus,
strengthen, declare. 3

conse′cro, -a′re, -a′vi, -a′tus,
bless. 3

con′tra, prep., w/ acc., *against.* 7

contuber′nium, -a, n., *contubernium.* 13

co′pia, -ae, f., *abundance, supply,*
plenty. 10

copiae, -a′rum, f., *forces, troops.* 10

cor, cor′dis, n., *heart, mind, judgment.* 14

cor′pus, -oris, n., *body.* 14

cras, adverb, *tomorrow.* 12

cum, prep., w/ abl., *with.* 7

cur, adverb, *why.* 12

cu′ra, -ae, f., *care, anxiety.* 10

cu′ro, -a′re, -a′vi, -a′ tus, *care for, take*
care of. 3

cur′rus, *chariot.* 11

D

Da′vus, -i, m., *David.* 6

de, prep., w/abl., *from, down from,*
about, concerning. 7

de′cem, *ten* (X). 10

de′cimus, -a, -um, *tenth.* 10

defes′sus, -a, -um, *tired.* 9

deser′ta, -ae, f., *desert.* 14

De′us, De′i, m., *God.* 6

disci′pulus, -i, m., *disciple.* 6

diu, adverb, *for a long time.* 12

do, da′re, de′di, da′tus, *give.* 3

do′minus, -i, m., *lord, master, ruler.* 6

do′num, -i, n., *gift.* 8

du′ctor, ducto′ris, m., *leader.*

dum, adverb, *while.* 12

du′o, du′ae, du′o, *two* (II). 10

duo′de cim, *twelve* (XII). 10

dux, du′cis, m., *leader.*

E

e, ex, prep., w/ abl., *from, out of.* 7

ec′ce, interj., *look, behold!* 15

e′go, me′i, pronoun, *I, me.* 9

e′nim, conjunction, *for.* 8

epis′tula, -ae, f., *letter.* 5

equ′us, -i, m., *horse.* 6

es′se, infinitive, *to be.* 5

et, conjunction, *and.* 4

et′iam, conjunction or adverb, *and also,*
even. 5

Euro′pa , -ae, f., *Europe.* 4

exer′citus, *army.*

exspec′to, -a′re, -a′ vi, -a′tus, *wait for.* 7

F

fa′bula, -ae, f., *story, fable.* 5

fac′tor, factor′is, m., *doer, maker.* 14

fa′ma, -ae, f., *rumor, report.* 10

***fa′mes, fa′mis,** f. *famine.* 16

fami′lia, -ae, f., *family.* 4

fe′mina, -ae, f., *woman, wife.* 5

fe′rus, fe′ra, fe′rum, *fierce, wild,*
savage. 9

fes′tum, fes′ti, n. *festival.* 16

fi′lia, fi′liae, f., *daughter.* 5
(**Filia** is irregular in two forms:
the dative and ablative plural are
filia′bus.)

fi′lius, fi′li, m., *son.* 6

firmamen′tum, -i, n., *prop, support,*
firmament, atmosphere. 8

fle′o, fle′re, fle′vi, fle′tus, *weep, lament.* 16

flum′en, flu′minis, n., *river.* 10

fortis′simus, -a, -um, adj., *bravest,*
strongest. 15

fortitu′do, fortitu′dinis, f., *bravery,*
courage, strength. 14

fortu′na, -ae, f., *fortune, luck, chance.* 5

fra′ter, fra′tris, m., *brother.* 14

frumen′ tum, -i, n., *grain.* 8

fur′or, furo′ ris, m., *madness, rage.* 14

fur′tim, adverb, *stealthily.* 12

G

Gal′lia, Gal′liae, f., *Gaul.* 4

Garum′na, -ae, f., *the Garonne (river).* 15

Gena′va, -ae, f., *Geneva, a city in*
Switzerland. 4 (map)

German′ia, -ae, f., *Germany.* 15

gla′dius, gla′di, m., *sword.* 6

glo′ria, -ae, f., *glory.* 5

gra′ tus, gra′ta, gra′tum, *pleasing,*

welcome. 9

H

ha′bito, -a′re, -a′vi, -a′tus, *live, dwell.* 3
Helve′tia, -ae, f., *Helvetia (Switzerland).*
   15 (map)
hē′ri, adverb, *yesterday.* 12
hic, adverb, *here.* 12
Hispa′nia, -ae, f., *Spain.* 4 (map)

ho′die, adv., *today.* 12
ho′mo, hom′inis, m., *man.* 14
hon′ oro, -a′re, -a′vi, -a′tus, *honor.* 3
ho′ra, -ae, f., *hour.* 10
***hos′tis, hos′tis,** m., *enemy (military).* 16

I

Ia′cobus, Ia′cobi, m., *James, Jacob.* 6
iam, adverb, *now, already.* 12
i′bi, adverb, *there, in that place.* 12
Iesus, Iesūs, m., *Jesus.* 9
***ig′nis, ig′ nis,** m., *fire.* 16
igno′ro, -a′re, -a′vi, -a′tus, *is ignorant*
   of, does not know. 15
impe′rium, -i, n., *power,*
   command, empire. 13
in, prep., with abl., *in* or *on;*
   with acc., *into, against.* 4
in′colunt, *(they) inhabit.* 15
inimi′cus, inimi′ca, inimi′cum,
   unfriendly.
in′sula, -ae, f., *island, apartment.* 5
in′ter, prep., with acc.,
   between, among. 7
in′terim, adverb, *meanwhile.* 12
Iose′phus, -i, m. *Joseph.* 16
ita′que, *and so.*
i′ta ver′o, idiom, *so true, yes.* 8
Ital′ia, Ital′iae, f., *Italy.* 4
i′ter, itin′eris, n., *route, journey.* 14
Iude′a, -ae, *Judea.* 13
iu′dex, iu′dicis, m., *judge, juror.* 14
iusti′tia, -ae, f., *justice, righteousness.* 4

L

labo′ro, -a′re, -a′ vi, -a′tus,
   work, suffer, am hard pressed. 3
lac′rimo, -a′re, -a′vi, -a′tus, *cry, weep.* 3

La′tium, La′ti, *Latium, the district in*
   west central Italy where Rome is
   located. 10
la′tus, la′ta, la′tum, *wide, broad.* 9
lau′do, -a′re, -a′vi, -a′tus, *praise.* 3
lega′tus, -i, m., *lieutenant, ambassador.* 6
lex, le′gis, f., *law.* 14
li′ber, li′bera, li′berum, adj., *free.* 9
li′ber, li′bri, m., *book.* 6
li′bero, -a′re, -a′vi, -a′tus, *set*
   free, free. 3
lin′gua, -ae, f., *language, tongue.* 5
lit′tera, -ae, f., *letter* (of the alphabet);
   pl. *letter, epistle, or letters.* 5
lo′cus, -i, m., *place, location.*
   n., in plural. 9
lon′ge, adverb, *far, far away.* 12
lon′gu s, lon′ga, lon′gum, *long.* 9
lu′dus, -i, m., *game, school, sport.* 6
lux, lu′cis, f., *light.* 14

M

magis′ter, magis′tri, m., *master,*
   teacher. 6
mag′nus, mag′na, mag′num, *large,*
   great, big. 9
ma′le, adverb, *badly.* 12
ma′lus, ma′la, ma′lum, *bad, evil.* 9
manda′tum, manda′ti, n.,
   commandment, mandate. 8
ma′ne, adverb, *early in the day.* 12
manē′o, mane′re, man′si,
   man′sus, *remain, stay* 16.
***ma′re, ma′ris,** n., *sea.* 15
ma′ ter, mat′ris, f., *mother.* 14
Matro′na, -ae, f., *the Marne (river).* 15
me′dius, me′dia, me′dium, *middle of.* 9
memo′ ria, -ae, f., *memory.* 5
***mens, men′tis,** f., *mind, intellect.* 15
mer′ces, merce′dis, f., *wages, reward.* 14
me′us, me′a, me′um, *my, mine, my*
   own. 9
mi′les, mil′itis, m., *soldier.* 14
***mi′lia, mi′lium,** n. pl., *thousands.* 15
mil′le, indeclinable adjective, *one*
   thousand, a thousand (M). 10
min′ime, idiom, *at the very least, no.* 8
mi′rus, -a, -um, *amazing, spectacular.* 11
miscē′o, mis′cere, mis′cui, mix′tus, *mix,*

confuse, mingle. 16
mi′ser, mi′sera, mi′serum,
    unhappy, sad. 9
moles′tus, -a, -um, *troublesome.* 14
***mons, mon′tis,** m., *mountain.* 15
***mors, mor′tis,** f., *death.* 15
mox, adverb, *soon, in a short while.* 12
multitu′do, multitu′ dinis,
    f., *great number, crowd.* 14
mul′tus, mul′ta, mul′tum, *much,* pl.,
    many. 9
mun′dus, mund′i, m., *world.* 6

N

nar′ro, -a′re, -a′vi, -a′tus, *tell, relate.* 3
natu′ra, -ae, f., *nature.* 5
nau′ ta, -ae, m., *sailor.* 10
na′vigo, -a′re, -a′vi, -a′ tus, *sail.* 3
***na′vis, na′vis,** f., *ship.* 15
-ne, enclitic, expecting a *yes* or *no* answer.
    8
ne′que…ne′que, conjunction,
    neither…nor. 5
neu′ter, neu′tra, neu′trum, *neither.* 15
ni′ger, ni′gra, ni′grum, *black.* 9
noc′te, *at night.* 15
no′men, no′minis, n., *name.* 14
non, adverb, *not.* 5
non′ne, interrog. particle expecting a *yes*
    answer. 8
nonnul′lus, -a, -um, *some.* 9
no′nus, -a, -um, *ninth.* 10
nos, nos′trum, pronoun, *we, us.* 9
nos′ter, nos′tra, nos′trum, *our.* 9
no′ tus, -a, -um, *famous.* 9
no′vem, *nine* (IX). 10
no′vus, no′va, no′vum, *new.* 9
***nox, noctis,** f., *night.* 15
nul′lus, -a, -um, adj., *not any, no.* 15
num, interrog. particle, expecting a *no*
    answer. 8
nu′merus, -i, m., *number, group.* 6
nunc, adverb, *now.* 12
nun′tio, -a′re, -a′vi, - a′tus,
    announce, report. 3
nun′tius, -i, m., *messenger, message.* 6

O

ob, prep., with acc., *because of, on*
    account of. 7
obser′vo, -a′re, -a′ vi, -a′tus,
    notice, observe. 15
occidenta′lis, occidenta′le, *east.* 9
oc′cupo, -a′re, -a′vi, -a′tus, *seize, occupy.*
    13
octa′vus, -a, -um, *eighth.* 10
oc′to, *eight* (VIII). 10
o′culus, -i, m., *eye.* 6
om′nis, om′ne, *all, every.* 15
op′pidum, -i, n., *town.* 8
oppug′no, -a′re, -a′vi, -a′tus, *attack*
    assault, besiege. 3

P

Pala′tium, Pala′ti, *the Palatine Hill,*
    where wealthy Romans lived. 10
***pa′nis, pa′ nis,** m., *bread.* 15
para′tus,-a, -um, *prepared, ready.* 9
pa′ro, -a′ re, -a′vi, -a′tus, *prepare.* 3
par′vus, par′va, par′vum, *small, little.*
    9
pa′ter, pa′tris, m., *father.* 14
pa′tria, -ae, f., *homeland, home,*
    country, fatherland. 4
pau′ci, -ae, -a, (pl.) *few.* 16
pax, pa′cis, f., *peace.* 14
pecca′tum, -i, n., *sin.* 15
per w/ acc., *through, along.* 7
periculo′sus, -a, -um, adj., *dangerous,*
    risky. 11
peri′culum, -i, n., *danger, risk.* 8
Pet′rus, Pet′ri, m., *Peter.* 6
Pharisae′ius, Pharisae′i, m., *Pharisee.* 6
Philip′pus, Philip′pi, m., *Philip.* 6
plenitu′do, plenitu′dinis, f., *fullness,*
    plenty. 14
poe′ta, -ae, m., *poet.* 4
***pons, pon′tis,** m., *bridge.* 16
po′pulus, -i, m., *nation, people* (*not*
    persons). 6
por′ta, -ae, f., *gate.* 10
Por′ta Cape′na, *the gate in the Servian*
    Wall marking the beginning of the
    Via Appia. 10
por′to, -a′re, -a′ vi, -a′tus, *carry.* 3
possidē′o, possid′ere, posse′di, posses′sus,
    own, occupy. 16
post, prep., w/ acc., *after, behind.* 7

pos'tea, adverb, *afterwards.* 12
Praeto'ria Cas'tra, *Praetorian Camp.* 12
pri'mā lu'ce, *at dawn.* 12
pri'mum, adverb, *first.* 12
pri'mus, -a, -um, *first.* 10
prin'ceps, prin'cipis, m., *ruler.* 14
princip'ium, prin'cipi, n.,
    beginning. 8
pro, prep., w/ abl., *in front of, on*
    behalf of, for. 7
pro'pe, prep. w/ acc., *near.* 7
pro'pero, -a're, -a'vi, -a'tus, *hasten.* 14
prophe'ta, -ae, m., *prophet.* 4
prop'ter, prep., w/ acc., *because of,*
    on account of. 7
provin'cia, -ae, f., *province.* 4
prox'imus, prox'ima, prox'imum,
    neighboring, nearest. 9
puel'la, -ae, f., *girl.* 4
pu'er, -i, m., *boy,* plural, *boys, children.*
    6
pug'no, -a're, -a' vi, -a' tus, *fight.* 3
pul'cher, pul'chra, pul'chrum,
    beautiful, pretty. 9
pu'rus, pu'ra, pu'rum, *pure.* 9
pu'to, -a're, -a'vi, -a'tus, *think.* 3

Q

quae, *who,* 6, *which,* 9, *that.*
quar'tus, -a, -um, *fourth.* 10
quat'tuor, *four* (IV). 10
quem, *whom, what.* 8
-que, conjunction, *and.* 4
qui'bus, abl. form, *whom.* 15
quin'que, *five* (V). 10
quin'tus, -a, -um, *fifth.* 10
quis, *who.* 5
quod, conjunction, *because.* 8
quo'niam, conjunction, *because, since.*
    8
quo'que, *also.* 9
quot, *how many.* 8

R

rae'da, -ae, f., *carriage, coach.* 4
reg'num, -i, n., *kingdom, royal power.*
    8
repor'tat, *(he) reports.* 12
rex, re'gis, m., *king.* 14

ro'go, -a're, -a'vi, -a'tus, *ask, ask for.* 3
Ro'ma, -ae, f., *Rome.* 4
Roma'nus, -a, -um, *Roman.* 14
Ro'mulus Fide' lius Centu'rio, m.,
    Romulus Fidelius the Centurion. 6
ru'ber, ru'bra, ru'brum, *red.* 16

S

Sabba'ta, -o'rum, n. pl., *The Sabbath.* 8
Sabba'tum, -i, n., *The Sabbath.* 8
sabba'tizo, -a're, -a' vi, -a'tus, *keep the*
    Sabbath; set apart for God's
    purposes. 15
sa'cer, sa'cra, sa'crum, *sacred, holy,*
    consecrated, accursed. 9
sacer'dos, -o'tis, m., *priest.* 11
sae'pe, adverb, *often.* 12
sal, sa'lis, n., *salt.* 14
salu'to, -a' re, -a'vi, -a'tus, *greet.* 3
sancti'fico, -a're, -a' vi, -a'tus, *keep*
    the Sabbath, set apart for God's
    purpose. 3
sanc'tus, sanc'ta, sanc'tum, *pure,*
    holy, virtuous. 9
sa'no, -a're, -a'vi, -a'tus, *cure, heal.* 3
sapien'tia, -ae, f., *wisdom.* 4
saxos'us, -a, -um, *rocky.* 14
secun'dus, -a, -um, *second.* 10
sed, conjunction, *but.* 4
sed'ere, *to sit,* 9.
sem'per, adverb, *always.* 12
sepa'ro, -a're, -a'vi, -a' tus,
    separate, divide. 15
sep'tem, *seven* (VII). 10
sep'ties, adverb, *seven times* 11
sep'timus, -a, -um, *seventh.* 10
Sequa'na, -ae, f., *the Seine (river).* 15
ser'vo, -a're, -a'vi, -a'tus, *save,*
    guard, protect. 3
ser'vus, -i, m., *servant.* 6
sex, *six* (VI). 10
sex'tus, -a, -um, *sixth.* 10
sil'va, -ae, f., *forest, woods.* 4
si'ne, prep., w/ abl., *without.* 7
soci'us, so'ci, m., *ally, friend.* 16
so' lus, -a, -um, *alone, only.* 15
so'ror, soro'ris, f., *sister.* 14
spec'to, -a're, -a'vi, -a'tus, *look at,*
    watch. 3
stel'la, -ae, f., *star.* 4

stipen′dium, -i, n., *payment, wage.* 8
sto, sta′re, stet′i, stat′us, *stand.* 15
structu′ra, -ae, f., *organization,
    structure.* 13
sub, prep., w/ acc., *up to, close to;*
    prep., w/ abl., *under, at the foot of.*
        7
sum, es′se, fu′i, futur′us, *be.* 5
super, prep. w/ acc., *above.* 7
su′pero, -a′re, -a′vi, -a′tus,
    defeat, overcome. 3
**sustin′eo, sustin′ere, sustin′ui,
    susten′tus**, *hold up,
    maintain, endure, withstand.*
        16
su′us, su′a, su′um, *his own, their own.* 9

T

tan′dem, adverb, *at last.*
tan′tum, adverb, *so much, so greatly,
    only.* 12
tem′plum, -i, n., *temple.* 10
temp′to, -a′re, -a′vi, -a′tus, *try,
    attempt.* 3
ter′ra, -ae, f., *earth, land.* 4
ter′tius, -a, - um, adj., *third.* 10
testimon′ium, -i, n., *testimony, witness.* 8
Ti′ber, Tiber′is, m., *Tiber River.* 10
Tibe′rius, *an emperor of Rome.* 14
Ti′tus, Ti′ti, m., *Titus.* 6
to′tus, -a, -um, *whole, entire,
    all.* 15
trans, prep., w/ acc., *across, over.* 7
trēs, tri′um, *three* (III). 10
tu, tu′i, pronoun, *you (singular).* 9
tu′ba , -ae, f., *trumpet.* 5
tūm, adverb, *then, at that time.* 12
tunc, adverb, *then, at that time.* 12
tu′nica, -ae, f., *tunic.* 4
tur′ba, -ae, f., *common crowd, crowd,
    turmoil.* 4
***tur′ris, tur′ris**, f., *tower.* 15
tu′us, tu′a, tu′um, *your, yours, your own*
    (singular). 9

U

u′bi, adverb and conjunction, *where,
    when.* 12
ul′lus, -a, -um, *any.* 15
un′decim, *eleven* (XI). 10
u′nus, u′na, u′num, *one* (I). 10
***urbs, ur′bis**, f., *city.* 15
u′ter, u′tra, u′trum, *which (of two?)* 15
ux′or, uxor′is, f., *wife.* 14

V

ver′bum, -i, n., *word.* 8
ver′itas, verita′ tis, f., *truth.* 15
ve′rus, vera, ve′rum, *true.*
        9
ves′pere, *in the evening.* 12
ves′ter, ves′tra, ves′trum, *your, yours,
    your own (plural only).* 9
vi′a, vi′ae, f., *way, road, street.* 4
vigin′ti, *twenty* (XX). 10
vil′la, -ae, f., *farmhouse, house.* 4
vir, vi′ri, m., *man, husband.* 6
vir′tus, virtu′tis, f., *strength, power.* 14
vi′ta, vi′tae, f., *life, mode of life.* 5
vo′co, -a′re, -a′vi, -a′tus, *call.* 3
vos, ves′trum, pronoun, *you (plural).* 9
volun′tas, volunta′tis, f., *will,
    (as in 'good will').* 14

English to Latin Vocabulary

A

about, *de,* with abl.
above, *super,* with acc.
abundance, *copia, -ae,* f.
account, *numerus, -i,* m.
account, on account of, *ob* or *propter,* with acc.
accursed, *sacer, -cra, -crum.*
across, *trans,* with acc.
after, adv., *post.*
after, prep. *post,* with acc.
afterward, afterwards, *postea.*
against, *contra* with acc., *in* with acc.
all, *omnis, omne.*
ally, *socius, -i,* m.
alone, *solus, -a, -um.*
along, *per,* with acc.
already, *iam.*
also, and also, even (with verbs) *etiam;* with nouns and pronouns, *quoque.*
always, *semper.* **am,** ("I am") *sum.*
ambassador, *legatus,-i,* m.
among, *inter,* with acc.
and, *et, -que, atque.*
angel, *angelus, -i,* m.
animal, *animal, -is,* n.
announce, *nuntio, -are, -avi, -atus.*
another, *alius, -a, -um.*
anxiety, *cura, -ae,* f.
any, *ullus, -a, -um.*
apartment, *insula, -ae.,* f.
apostle, *apostolus, -i,* m.
aqueduct, *aquaeductum, -i,* n.
around, *circum,* with acc.
ask, ask for, *rogo, -are, -avi, -atus.*
at, abl. of time or place.
at, *ad,* with acc.
at dawn, *prima luce.*
at last, *tandem*
atmosphere, *firmamentum, -i,* n.
attack, assault, *oppugno, -are, -avi, -atus*
attempt, *tempto, -are, -avi, -atus.*
audacity, *audacia, -ae,* f.

B

bad, *malus, -a, -um.*

badly, *male.*
be, *sum, esse, fui, futurus.*
beautiful, *pulcher, -chra, -chrum.*
because, *quod, quoniam.*
because of, on account of, *ob* or *propter* with acc.
before, prep. *ante,* with acc.
beginning, *principium, -i,* n.
behalf, on behalf of, *pro,* with abl.
behind, *post,* with acc.
Belgians, *Belgae, -arum,* m.
besiege, *oppugno, -are, -avi, -atus.*
between, *inter,* with acc.
big, *magnus, -a, -um.*
bird, *avis, avis,* m. or f.
black, *niger, -gra, -grum.*
blaze, *ardeo, ardere, arsi, arsus.*
blessed, *beatus, -a, -um.*
body, *corpus, -oris,* n.
boldness, *audacia, -ae.,* f.
book, *liber, libri,* m.
both...and, *et...et.*
boy, *puer, -i.,* m.
bravery, *virtus, -utis,* f.; *fortitudo, -inis,* f.
bread, *panis, -is,* m.
bridge, *pons, pontis,* m.
broad, *latus, -a, -um.*
brother, *frater, -tris,* m.
build, *aedifico, -are, -avi, -atus.*
but, *sed, autem.*
by, *a, ab,* with abl.

C

Caesar, *Caesar, -aris,* m.
call, *voco, -are, -avi, -atus.*
call by name, *appello, -are, -avi, -atus.*
call together, *convoco, -are, -avi, -atus.*
captive, *captivus, -i,* m.
capture, *occupo, -are, -avi, -atus.*
care, noun, *cura, -ae,* f.
care for, *curo, -are, -avi, -atus.*
carriage, *raeda, -ae,* f.
carry, *porto, -are, -avi, -atus.*
carry up, *supporto, -are, -avi, -atus.*
cart, *carrus, -i,* m.; *raeda, -ae,* f.
cause, *causa, -ae,* f.
centurion, *centurio, -onis,* m.
chance, *fortuna, -ae,* f.
chief, *princeps, -cipis,* m.
children, *liberi, -orum,* m.;

pueri, -orum, m.

Christ, *Christus, -i,* m.
citizen, *civis, civis,* m. or f.
city, *urbs, urbis,* f.
coach, *raeda, -ae,* f.
cohort, *cohors, cohortis,* m.
command, *imperium, -i,* n.
commandment, *mandatum, -i.* n.
common crowd, *turba, -ae,* f.
concerning, *de,* with abl.
conquer, *supero, -are, -avi, -atus.*
consecrated, *sacer, -cra, -crum.*
control, *imperium, -i, n.*
courage, pl. *animi, -orum,* m.; *fortitudo, -inis,* f.
crowd, *multitudo, -dinis,* f.
cry, *lacrimo, -are, -avi, -atus.*
cry (cry out) *clamo, -are, -avi, -atus.*
cure, verb, *sano, -are, -avi, -atus.*

D

danger, *periculum, -i,* n.
daughter, *filia, -ae,* f.
dear, *carus, -a, -um.*
death, *mors, mortis,* f.
declare, *confirmo, -are, -avi, -atus.*
decree, *censeo, censere, censui, census.*
deed, *factum, -i,* n.
deep, *altus, -a, -um.*
defeat, *supero, -are, -avi, -atus.*
dinner, *cena, -ae,* f.
disciple, *discipulus, -i,* m.
doer, *factor, factoris,* m.
dog, *canis, -is,* m. or f.
down from, *de,* with abl.
dwell, *habito, -are, -avi, -atus.*

E

early, *primus, -a, -um* (with a noun),
    at dawn, *prima luce.*
early in the day, *mane.*
earth, *terra, -ae,* f.
eight, *octo.*
eighth, *octavus -a, -um.*
eleven, *undecim.*
empire, *imperium, -i,* n.
encourage, *confirmo, -are, -avi, -atus.*
end, noun, *finis, finis,* m.

endure, *sustineo, -ere, -ui, -tentus.*
enemy (military), *hostis, hostis, m.*
enemy (personal) *inimicus, -i,* m.
entire, *totus, -a, -um.*
epistle, *epistula, -ae,* f.
Europe, *Europa, -ae,* f.
even, *etiam.*
evening, in the, *vespere*
evil, *malus, -a, -um.*
eye, *oculus, -i,* m.

F

fame, *fama, -ae,* f.
family, *familia, -ae,* f.
famine, *fames, famis,* f.
famous, *notus, -a, -um.*
far, far away, *longe.*
farmer, *agricola, -ae,* m.
farmhouse, *villa, -ae,* f.
father, *pater, -tris,* m.
fatherland, *patria, -ae,* f.
festival, *festum, -i, n.*
field, *ager, agri,* m.; *campus, -i.,* m.
fierce, *ferus, -a, -um,*
fifteen, *quindecim.*
fifth, *quintus, -a, -um.*
fight, *pugno, -are, -avi, -atus.*
finally, *tandem,* adv.
fire, *ignis, -is,* m.
first, adj., *primus, -a, -um.*
first, adv., *primum.*
five, *quinque.*
foot, at foot of, *sub,* with abl.
for (on behalf of) *pro,* with abl.;
    (because) *quod;*
    conj., *enim.*
forces, *copiae, -arum,* f.
forest, *silva, -ae,* f.
fortune, *fortuna, -ae,* f.
four, *quattuor.*
fourteen, *quattuordecim.*
fourth, *quartus, -a, -um.*
free, adj, *liber, -era, -erum.*
free, set free, verb, *libero, -are, -avi, -atus.*
friend, *amicus, -i,* m.
friendly, *amicus, -a, -um.*
friendship, *amicitia, -ae,* f.
from, *a, ab, de, e, ex,* with abl.
fullness, *plenitudo, -tudinis,* f.

G

game, *ludus, -i.* m.
Garonne River, *Garumna, -ae,* f.
gate (of city or camp), *porta, -ae,* f.
Gaul, *Gallia, -ae,* f.
Gauls, *Galli, -orum,* m.
German, *Germanus, -i,* m.
Germany, *Germania, -ae,* f.
gift, *donum, -i.,* n.
girl, *puella, -ae,* f.
give, *do, dare, dedi, datus.*
glory, *gloria, -ae,* f.
God, *Deus, -i.,* m.
good, *bonus, -a, -um.*
grain, *frumentum, -i,* n.
great, *magnus, -a, -um.*
Greece, *Graecia, -ae,* f.
Greek, *Graecus, -a, -um.*
greet, *saluto, -are, -avi, -atus.*
group, *numerus, -i.*
guard, *servo, -are, -avi, -atus.*

H

handmaiden, *ancilla, -ae,* f.
happy, *laetus, -a, -um; beatus, -a, -um.*
hard pressed, be, *laboro, -are, -avi, -atus.*
hasten, *propero, -are, -avi, -atus.*
heal, *sano, -are, -avi, -atus.*
hear, overhear, *ausculto, -are, -avi*
  -atus.
hearer, *auditor, -oris,* m.
heart, *cor, cordis,* n.; *animus, -i.,* m.
heaven, *caelum, -i,* n.
help, *auxilium, -i,* n.
Helvetia, *Helvetia, -ae,* f.
Helvetians, *Helvetii, -orum,* m.
her, *sua, -ae,* (reflexive).
hero, *vir, viri,* m.
high, *altus, -a, -um.*
hill, *clivus, -i,* m.
his, *suus, -i,* (reflexive).
holy, *sacer, -cra, -crum; sanctus, -a, -um.*
homeland, *patria, -ae,* f.
honor, *honoro, -are, -avi, -atus.*
horse, *equus, equi,* m.
hour, *hora, -ae,* f.
house, *villa, -ae,* f.
human being, *homo, hominis,* m. or f.
hundred, *centum.*

hurry, *propero, -are, -avi, -atus.*
husband, *vir, viri,* m.

I

if, *si.*
ignorant, be ignorant of, *ignoro, -are,*
  -avi,-atus.
immediately, *statim.*
in, *in,* with abl.
in front of, *pro,* with abl.
intellect, *mens, mentis,* f.
into, *in,* with acc.
island, *insula, -ae,* f.
Italy, *Italia, -ae,* f.

J

James, *Iacobus, Iacobi,* m.
Jesus, *Iesus, Iesus.* m.
John, *Ioannes, -i,* m.
Joseph, *Iosephus, -i,* m.
journey, *iter, itineris,* n.
judge, *censeo, censere, censui, census.*
judge, juror, noun, *iudex, -icis,* m.
judgment, *cor, cordis,* n.
justice, *iustitia, -ae,* f.

K

kind, kindly, *bonus, -a, -um.*
king, *rex, regis,* m.
kingdom, *regnum, -i,* n.

L

labor, verb, *laboro, -are, -avi, -atus.*
land, *terra, -ae,* f.
language, *lingua, -ae,* f.
large, *magnus, -a, -um.*
later, adv., *postea.*
law, *lex, legis,* f.
legion, *legio, -onis,* f.
letter, of alphabet, *littera, -ae,* f.;
  (an epistle), *litterae, -arum,* f. pl.
  epistula, -ae, f.
lieutenant, *legatus, -i,* m.
life, *vita, -ae,* f.
light, noun, *lux, lucis,* f.
like, verb, *amo, -are, -avi, -atus.*
listen to, *ausculto, -are, -avi, -atus.*

little, *parvus, -a, -um.*
live, *habito, -are, -avi, -atus.*
location, *locus, -i,* m.;
          irreg. in pl. *loca, -orum,* n.
long, adj, *longus, -a, -um.*
long, for a long time, adv. *diu.*
look, look at, *specto, -are, -avi, -atus.*
lord, *dominus, -i,* m.
love, verb, *amo, -are, -avi, -atus.*
luck, *fortuna, -ae,* f.

M

madness, *furor, furoris,* m.
maintain, *sustineo, -ere, -ui, -tentus.*
maker, *factor, -oris,* m.
man, *vir, -i,* m.; *homo, -inis,* m.
mandate, *mandatum, -i.* n.
many, *multi, -ae, -a.*
Marcus, *Marcus, -i,* m.
Marne (river), *Matrona, -ae,* f.
master, *dominus, -i,* m.;
(teacher) *magister, magistri,* m.
me, use appropriate form of *ego.*
meantime, meanwhile, *interim.*
memory, *memoria, -ae,* f.
message, *nuntius, nunti,* m.
messenger, *nuntius, nunti,* m.
middle, middle (part) of, *medius, -a, -um.*
mind, *mens, mentis,* f.; *animus, -i,* m.;
       cor, cordis, n.
mix, *misceo, miscere, miscui, mixtus.*
money, *pecunia, -ae,* f.
moreover, *autem, tamen* (both
       postpositive).
mother, *mater, --tris,* f.
mountain, *mons, montis,* m.
much, *multus, -a, -um.*
multitude, *multitudo, -inis,* f.
murder, *caedes, caedis,* f.
my, *meus, -a, -um.*

N

name, noun, *nomen, -inis,* n.
name, verb, *appello, -are, -avi, -atus.*
nation, *populus, -i,* m.
native land, *patria, -ae,* f.
nature, *natura, -ae,* f.
near, *ad, prope,* with acc.

nearest, neighboring, *proximus, -a, -um.*
neither, adj., *neuter, neutra, neutrum.*
neither...nor, conj., *neque...neque*
       or *nec...nec.*
new, *novus, -a, -um.*
next, *proximus, -a, -um.*
night, at night, *nocte.*
nine, *novem.*
nineteen, *undeviginti.*
ninth, *nonus, -a, -um.*
no, not any, adj., *nullus, -a, -um.*
not, *non.*
now, *nunc, iam.*
number, *numerus, -i,* m.
number, a great, *multitudo, -dinis,* f.

O

occupy, *occupo, -are, -avi, -atus.*
of (concerning), *de,* with abl.
often, *saepe.*
on, *in,* with abl.
on account of, *ob* or *propter,* with acc.
one, *unus, -a, -um.*
only, *solus, -a, -um,* as adv., *only.*
organization, *structura, -ae.,* f.
other (of two), *alter, altera, alterum.*
our, *noster, -tra, -trum.*
our men, *nostri, -orum.,* m.pl.
out of, *e, ex,* with abl.
over, *trans,* with acc.
overcome, *supero, -are, -avi, -atus.*
overhear, *ausculto, -are, -avi, -atus.*
own, occupy, *possideo, -ere, -sedi, -essus.*

P

payment, *stipendium, -i,* n.
peace, *pax, pacis,* f.
people, *populus, -i.,* m.
peril, *periculum, -i,* n.
Peter, *Petrus, -i,* m.
Pharisee, *Pharisaeius, -i,* m.
Philip, *Philippus, -i,* m.
place, *locus, -i,* m.;
       irreg. in pl. *loca, -orum,* n.
plain, *campus, -i,* m.
pleasing, *gratus, -a, -um.*
plenty, *copia, -ae,* f.; *plenitudo, -inis,* f.
poet, *poeta, -ae,* m.

power, *imperium, -i,* n.;
    virtus, virtutis, f.
praise, *laudo, -are, -avi, -atus.*
prepare, *paro, -are, -avi,*
    -atus.
prepared, *paratus, -a, -um.*
pretty, *pulcher, -chra, -chrum.*
prop, *firmamentum, -i,* n.
prophet, *propheta, -ae,* m.
protect, *servo, -are, -avi, -atus.*
province, *provincia, -ae,* f.
pupil, *discipulus, -i,* m.
pure, *purus, -a, -um; sanctus, -a, -um.*

R

race, *certamen* (s.), *certamina* (pl.)
rage, *furor, furoris,* m.
ready, *paratus, -a, -um.*
reason, *causa, -ae,* f.
recommend, *censeo, censere, censui,*
    census.
relate, *narro, -are, -avi, -atus.*
remain, *maneo, -ere, -si, -sus.*
report, noun, *fama, -ae,* f.
report, verb, *nuntio, -are, -avi, -atus.*
reputation, *fama, -ae,* f.
reward, *merces, mercedis,* f.
Rhine (river), *Rhenus, -i,* m.
Rhone (river), *Rhodanus, -i,* m.
righteousness, *iustitia, -ae,* f.
risk, *periculum, -i,* n.
river, *flumen, -inis,* n.
road, *via, -ae,* f.
rocky, *saxosus, -a, -um.*
Roman, adj., *Romanus, -a, -um.*
Roman, noun, *Romanus, -i,* m.
Rome, *Roma, -ae,* f.
rose, *rosa, -ae,* f.
route, *iter, itineris,* n.
royal power, *regnum,-i.,* n.
ruler, *princeps, principis,* m.
rumor, *fama, -ae,* f.

S

Sabbath, *Sabbata, -orum,* n.pl.
sacred, *sacer, -cra, -crum.*
sad, *miser, misera, miserum.*
sail, *navigo, -are, -avi, -atus.*
sailor, *nauta, -ae,* m.

salt, *sal, salis,* n.
salute, *saluto, -are, -avi, -atus.*
savage, *ferus, -a, -um,*
save, *servo, -are, -avi, -atus.*
school, *ludus, -i,* m.
sea, *mare, maris,* n.
second, *secundus, -a, -um;*
    alter, altera, alterum.
Seine (river), *Sequana, -ae,* f.
seize, *occupo, -are, -avi, -atus.*
servant, *servus, -i,* m.
set apart for God's purpose, *sanctifico,*
    -are, -avi, -atus.
set apart for God's Sabbath, *sabbatizo,*
    -are, -avi, -atus.
set free, *libero, -are, -avi, -atus.*
seven, *septem.*
seventeen, *septendecim.*
seventh, *septimus, -a, -um.*
ship, *navis, navis,* f.
shout, verb, *clamo, -are, -avi, -atus.*
sin, *peccatum, -i,* n.
since, *quoniam.*
sing, *canto, -are, -avi, -atus.*
sir, *optime vir.*
sister, *soror, -oris,* f.
six, *sex.*
sixteen, *sedecim.*
sixth, *sextus, -a, -um.*
size, great, *magnitudo, -inis,* f.
sky, *caelum, -i,* n.
slaughter, *caedes, caedis,* f.
small, *parvus, -a, -um.*
so greatly, so much, *tantum.*
soldier, *miles, militis,* m.
son, *filius, fili,* m.
soon, *mox.*
soul, spirit, *animus, -i,* m.
Spain, *Hispania, -ae.,* f.
Spanish, *Hispanus, -a, -um.*
sport, *ludus, -i,* m.
star, *stella, -ae,* f.
stay, remain, *maneo, -ere, -si, -sus.*
stealthily, *furtim.*
still, *adhuc.*
story, *fabula, -ae,* f.
street, *via, -ae.,* f.
strength, *fortitudo, -inis,* f.;
    virtus, virtutis, f.
strengthen, *confirmo, -are, -avi, -atus.*
stroll, *ambulo, -are, avi, atus*

structure, *structura, -ae.,* f.
student, *auditor, -oris,* m.
suffer, *laboro, -are, -avi, -atus.*
supply, *copia, -ae,*
support, *firmamentum, -i,* n.
suppose, *censeo, censere, censui,*
    census.
sword, *gladius, -i,* m.

T

take care of, *curo, -are, -avi, -atus.*
tall, *altus, -a, -um.*
teacher, *magister, -i,* m.
tell, *narro,-are, -avi, -atus.*
tempt, *tempto, -are, -avi, -atus.*
ten, *decem.*
tenth, *decimus, -a, -um.*
test, *tempto, -are, -avi, -atus.*
testimony, *testimonium, -i,* n.
then, *tum, tunc.*
there, *ibi.*
there is/there are, *est, sunt.*
think, *puto, -are, -avi, -atus.*
think, *censeo, censere, censui, census.*
third, *tertius, -a, -um.*
thirteen, *tredecim.*
thousand, *mille*; in pl.; *milia, milium.* n.
three, *tres, tria.*
through, *per,* with acc.
Tiber (river), *Tiber, Tiberi,* m.
tired, *defessus, -a, -um.*
Titus, *Titus, Titi,* m.
to, *ad,* with acc.
today, adv., *hodie.*
tomorrow, *cras.*
tongue, *lingua, -ae,* f.
toward, *ad,* with acc.
tower, *turris, turris,* f.
town, *oppidum, -i,* n.
tree, *arbor, arboris,* f.
troops, *copiae, -arum,* f.
troublesome, *molestus, -a, -um.*
true, *verus, -a, -um.*
trumpet, *tuba, -ae,* f.
truth, *veritas, -atis,* f.
try, *tempto, -are, -avi, -atus.*
tunic, *tunica, -ae,* f.
turmoil, *turba, -ae,* f.
twelve, *duodecim.*
twenty, *viginti.*

twenty-one, *viginti unus.*
twenty-five, *viginti quinque.*
two, *duo, duae, duo.*

U

under, with verb that expresses motion, *sub,*
    with acc.; with verb that does not
    express motion, *sub,* with abl.
unfriendly, *inimicus, -a, -um.*
unhappy, *miser, misera, miserum.*
up to, *ad,* or *sub,* with acc.
us, use appropriate form of *nos.*

V

valor, *virtus, -utis,* f.
virtuous, *sanctus, -a, -um.*
vote, *censeo, censere, censui, census.*

W

wage, *stipendium, -i,* n.
wage, *merces, mercedis,* f.
walk, *ambulo, -are, -avi, -atus.*
war, noun, *bellum, -i,* n.
watch, *specto, -are, -avi, -atus.*
water, *aqua, -ae,* f.
way, *via, -ae,* f.
we, *nos.*
weep, *lacrimo, -are, -avi, -atus.*
well, *bene.*
whale, *balaena, -ae,* f.
when, *ubi.*
where, *ubi.*
which, *quae.*
which (of two), *uter, utra, utrum.*
while, *dum.*
white, *albus, -a, -um.*
who, *quis.*
whole, *totus, -a, -um.*
why, *cur.*
wicked, *malus, -a, -um.*
wide, *latus, -a, -um.*
wife, *uxor, -oris,* f.
wild, *ferus, -a, -um,*
will, *voluntas, voluntatis,* f.
wisdom, *sapientia, -ae,* f.

wish, *voluntas, voluntatis*, f.
with, *cum,* with abl.
without, *sine*, with abl.
witness, *testimonium, -i,* n.
woman, wife, *femina, -ae,* f.
woods, *silva, -ae,* f.
word, *verbum, -i*, n.
work, verb, *laboro, -are, -avi, -atus.*
world, *mundus, -i.,* m.
worn out, *defessus, -a, -um.*
wound, *vulnero, -are, -avi, -atus.*
wretched, *miser, -era, -erum.*

Y

year, *annus, -i*, m.
yesterday, *heri.*
yet, *tamen.*
you, *tu, tui*; pl. *vos.*
your, **yours,** *tuus, -a, -um*; pl., *vester, -tra,*
    -tru

Grammatical and Topical Index
Volume number and chapter numbers are given after the reference, i.e., 1.12 means Volume I, Chapter 12.

A

ablative case, means, 1.9; place from which, 1.7; place where 1.4; time when, 1.13; time within which, 1.13
accusative case, direct object, 1.5; duration of time, 1.13; place to which, 1.7
adjectives, description of, 1.9; agreement of, 1.9; first and second declension, 1.9; irregular adjectives, 1.15
adverbs, forming, 1. 12
alphabet, 1.2
appositives, definition, 1. 6

B

Bible (Vulgate), 1.15
bibliography, 1;page 127

C

Caesar, Julius, 1.15
calendar, 1.10
character of Romans, 1.12
complementary infinitive, definition and usage, 1.5
conjunction, 1.5

D

dative case, indirect object, 1.10

E

enclitics, 1.8

F

family life, 1.2
future tense,
1.11

G

genitive case, possession, 1.6
glossary, after paradigms
grammar review, 1.2

H

history of Italy, 1.3

I

imperative mood, 1.13
imperfect tense, 1.11

indicative mood, defined, 1.13
infinitives, complementary. 1.5

K

kings of Rome, 1.11

L

Latin phrases, see Teacher's Guide
locative case, 1.13

M

maps, Italy, 1.2; Gaul, 1.4 and 1.15. Roman Empire, 1.5; route through Italy, 1.8; seven hills of Rome, 1.8; city of Rome, 1.10

N

nouns, first declension, 1.4; second declension, 1.6 and 1.8; third declension, 1.14, third declension i-stems 1.15
numerals, 1.10

O

order of words, 1.2

P

parts of speech review, 1.1
Pater Noster, 1; page117-118
Pledge of Allegiance, 1; page 119
predicate nominative, 1.4
prefixes, 1.7
prepositions, 1.7
principal parts, 1.3
pronouns, (personal) 1.9
pronunciation guide, 1.2

Q

questions, 1.8

R

religion of Romans, 1.13

Bibliography

Durant, Will and Ariel, *Caesar and Christ, A History of Roman Civilization and of Christianity to A.D. 325*, New York: Simon and Schuster, 1954.

Gildersleeve, B.L. *A Latin Grammar*, New York: University Publishing Co.,1882.

Lawall, Gilbert and David Tafe, *Ecce Romani: A Latin Reading Course*, New York:
Longman Inc., 1988.

Maier, Paul. *Pontius Pilate*, Grand Rapids: Kregel Publications, 1968.

Maier, Paul. *The Flames of Rome,* Grand Rapids: Kregel Publications, 1968.

Rose, James B., *A Guide To American Christian Education*, Camarillo, California: American Christian History Institute, 1987.

Rushdoony, R. J., *The "Atheism" of the Early Church,* Blackheath, New South Wales, Australia: Logos Foundation, 1983.

Sayers, Dorothy. "The Lost Tools of Learning", ca. 1850.

Smith and Thompson, *First Year Latin*, Boston: Allyn and Bacon, Inc., 1967.

Spalding, Romalda*, The Writing Road to Reading*, New York: Morrow Quill Paperbacks, 1969.

Chisholm, Jane, *Living in Roman Times*, London: Usborne Publishing Ltd., 1982.

Webster, Noah. *American Dictionary of the English Language*. Permission to Reprint granted by G. & C. Merriam Company. San Francisco: Foundation for Christian Education, 1967. Welch, Robert. "Republics and Democracies", Appleton, WI: The New American Magazine, 1962.

Resources:

American Classical League, Miami Universit y, Oxford, Ohio

Illustrations: Every effort has been made to contact artists to obtain permission for all photos.

Original photos taken in Rome by Stefanie Harrington Wyatt, on pages 4, 14, 32, 38, 47, 56,

71. Alinari-Anderson photo
Bettman Archive
Bob Jones University Press
Boston Public Library
Collar, William, *First Latin Book,* Ginn and Co., 1901.
Collar, William, *First Year Latin*, Ginn and Co., 1901.
Dictionary of Roman and Greek Antiquities.
Lateran Museum, Rome
Longmans, Green, and Co., London, New York, and Bomba y.
  1901. pp. 756.
Pompeii Radio Times Hulton Picture Library
Roman Forum 19th Century Drawing, ruins of Forum; Epstein Archive, Chicago; Scott, Harry Fletcher, *First Latin Lessons*, Scott, Foresman and Co., 1922.
Fred Wight, *Manners and Customs of Bible Lands*; Moody Publishers, 820 N. LaSalle
  Blvd., Chicago, IL 60610

Pa′tĕr No′stĕr, qui ĕs ĭn cae′lis:

Sanctifice′tur no′mĕn tu′um.

Adve′niat rĕg′num tu′um.

Fi′at volun′tas tu′a, si′cut ĭn cae′lo, ĕt ĭn tĕr′ra.

Pa′nĕm no′strum quotĭd′ianum da no′bis

ho′die. Ĕt dĭmĭt′te no′bis dĕb′ita no′stra, si′cut

ĕt nos Dĭmĭt′timus dĕbito′ribus no′stris.

Ĕt ne nos ĭndu′cas ĭn tĕnta′tionĕm.

Sĕd li′bĕra nos a ma′lo. Amĕn.

Pater Noster, qui es in caelis:

Sanctificetur nomen tuum.

Adveniat regnum tuum.

Fiat voluntas tua, sicut in caelo, et in terra.

Panem nostrum quotidianum da nobis hodie.

Et dimitte nobis debita nostra, sicut et nos

Dimittimus debitoribus nostris.

Et ne nos inducas in tentationem.

Sed libera nos a malo. Amen.

The Pledge to the American Flag

**Fidem meam obligo
Vexillo civitatium Americae Foederatarum
Et rei publicae, pro qua stat, uni natione
Deo ducente, non dividendae,
cum libertate iustitiaque
Omnibus.**

**I pledge allegiance to the flag
Of the United States of America, And
to the republic for which it stands, One
nation, under God, indivisible, With
liberty and justice for all.**

Chart

Objective Genitive

-fear of us – timor nostri
-fear of you – timor vestri

Partitive Genitive

-a thousand of us – mille nostrum
-part of us – pars nostrum
-some of you – nonnulli vestrum
-four of you – quattuor vestrum

Other Forms

-four of the boys – quattuor e pueris
-seven of the soldiers – septem e militibus
- five of the handmaidens – quinque ex ancillis

-the rest of the men – reliqui viri
-a few of the men – pauci viri

Helps for Translation from Latin to English

1. Underline all endings of words so you can see what case they are in.

2. Notice any prepositional phrases. Circle them; now they are out of the way of the main sentence structure.

3. Look for verb(s). Underline the endings. Notice the tense, person, and number.

4. Look for words which may be in the nominative case, and may function as the subject of the verb.

5. Note any words in the accusative case which have no prepositions preceding them. They might be the direct objects of verbs.

6. Translate the sentence literally at first, and then say the same thought in good English. The goal of translating is to translate the thought, not necessarily the exact words.

Review of Translation from English to Latin

1. Circle or put parentheses around all prepositional phrases if there are any. Write above each circle the preposition needed plus the case which follows it. Example: **cum + abl.**

2. Find the subject next. About *whom* or *what* is the sentence (or clause)? Underline it once and write "no m." (for nominative) above it. Be sure to underline once the adjective which modifies it also.

3. Next, what does the subject *do*? Or what word *links* the subject to a predicate nominative? That will help you identify the verb. Underline the verb with two lines. Notice what person, number and tense it is, and abbreviate that above the word also.

4. For any nouns which show possession or which should be in the genitive case, write "gen." above them.

5. If there is a direct object, the subject does something to someone or so mething. If there is one, underline it with a wavy line, and write "acc." above it.

6. If the subject "equals" something, then there is a predicate nominative after the linking verb. Write "nom." above any predicate nominatives.

7. Notice any nouns of direct address, adverbs, or conjunctions.

8. Go back through and mark "s." or "pl." for singular or plural; "m., f.," or "n." for masculine, feminine or neuter nouns, pronouns, or adjectives.

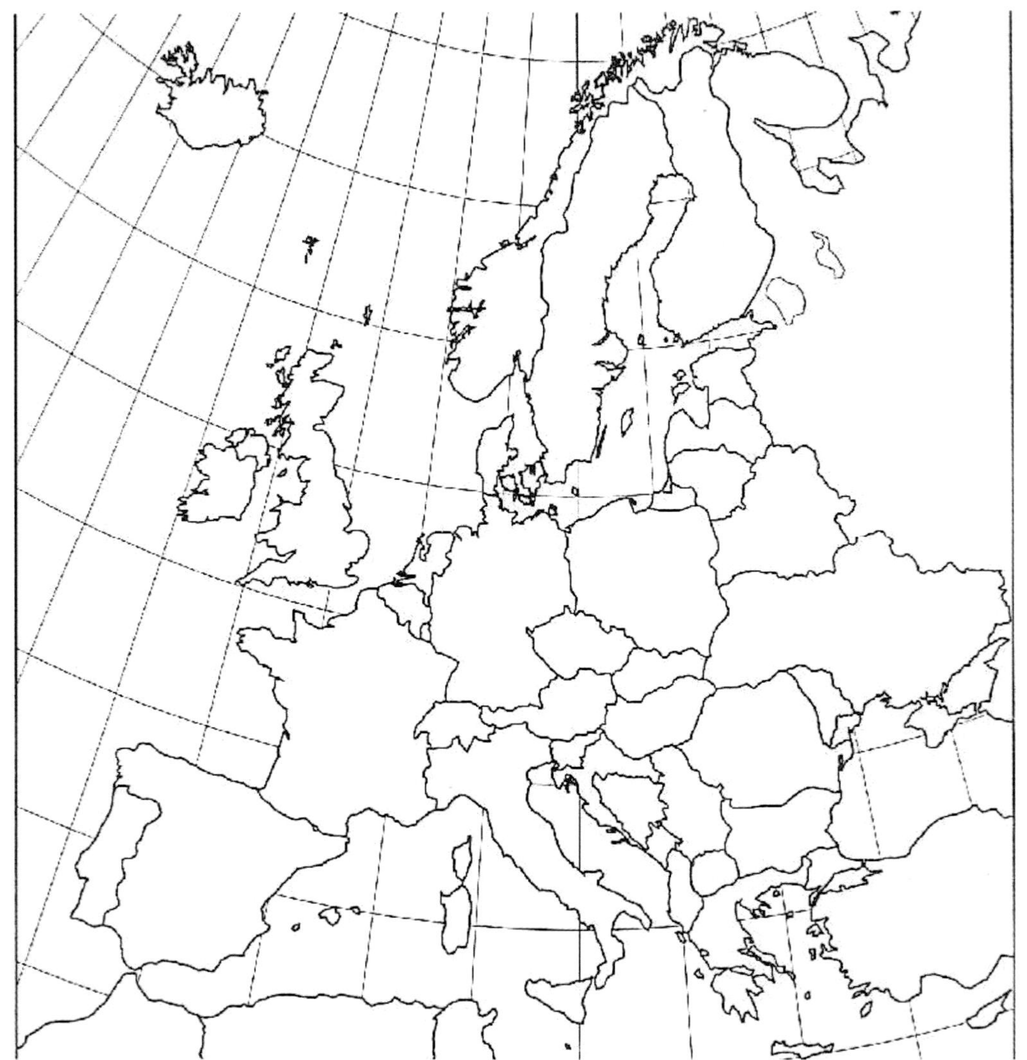

Map of Europe

World